Broken Hearts and New Creations

Also by James Alison

Faith Beyond Resentment
On Being Liked
Knowing Jesus
Raising Abel
The Joy of Being Wrong
Undergoing God

Broken Hearts
and
New Creations

Intimations of a Great Reversal

James Alison

DARTON·LONGMAN + TODD

For the purposes of conversation regarding *Broken Hearts and New Creations* James Alison can be reached at
cgfragments@btinternet.com

First published in 2010 by
Darton, Longman and Todd Ltd
1 Spencer Court
140-142 Wandsworth High Street
London SW18 4JJ

ISBN 978-0-232-52796-4

A catalogue record for this book is available from
the British Library.

Phototypeset by Kerrypress Ltd, Luton, Bedfordshire
Printed and bound in Great Britain by Page Bros, Norwich

Table of Contents

Introduction

Doing theology is a slow business.

If God were an object, theology would be a high-octane discipline. Analytical reason, so good at distinctions, would be able to zip around making deductions and diagnoses. Or it might engage in fencing matches with those who deny the existence of the object in question. The trouble is that our reason, as has become clearer and clearer to us the more we discover about how our brains work and how interconnected we all are, is, in fact, dependent on, a product of, our navigation of our inter-relatedness. And God we only know at all not as an object in, or on the edge of, our mental horizon, but as an act of communication having incidence in our human inter-relatedness. Which is to say, an act of communication opening up possibilities of reasonableness and truthfulness as our ways of being together shift. This is what it means to say 'And the Word was made flesh'.

In classical terms, the discipline which the Catholic Church understands as theology (as opposed to theodicy, philosophy of religion or religious studies) is strictly only possible as a response to *Deus Revelans*. That is to say, it is the rigorous and ordered study both of *what has been revealed* and thereafter of *everything that is* strictly in the light of God who reveals. In this classical perspective then, one to which I endeavour to be faithful, theology is not a discipline in which humans try to discover something about a relatively inert distant object concerning which it is difficult to know anything – i.e. 'God'. The presupposition of theology is that it is itself, as a discipline, a small but important subsection of God's continuing self-communication to all people. Furthermore, it presupposes that

the One who is 'pushing' this discipline, the discipline's protagonist as it were, is God, not the humans who become theologians. It
is God who wishes to share a certain *scientia* about God's self and
about everything that is with humans. We are, as it were, the relatively inert distant objects which are, as it happens, being invited
into this form of knowing, thus becoming subjects. And we tend to
be resistant to the invitation. We are not so much searchers as ones
who are being found.

So, theology is a slow business. As slow as the time it takes for us
who are its practitioners to be found. As unhurried as the patience
of a protagonist for whom time is not an enemy. Any value it has
is not so much in its deliverance of intellectual excellence, vital
though that be. Its real value is in the communicable shifts of lens,
of perspective, undergone by its practitioners as we become aware
how the enfleshed Word is having incidence on us while we work
through the patterns of relationality which bring us into being. This
working through then enables us to communicate glimpses of fresh
vision, of newness of life and of abundance to those with different
gifts and charges who are sharing with us in the ecclesial outpour-
ing of the Spirit. '*Contemplata aliis tradere*' – passing on the fruit of
contemplation to others – is St Thomas Aquinas' way of referring
to this.

The chapters of the book you are embarking on are culled from
my thinking, praying and teaching over the last four years. Years in
which it has been my privilege to find myself one among a growing
number whose endeavour as theologians has been and is to work
out ever more fully the fecundity for our discipline of what René
Girard describes as his two ideas: the mimetic nature of desire,
and the discovery of the implications for hominisation and cultural
foundations of the scapegoat mechanism – the creation of peace out
of frenzy by the random designation and expulsion of one against
whom all can unite.

Three different emphases run through these chapters. All three
of them are theological workings out of different facets of Girard's
thought – or Mimetic Theory, as it is sometimes called. The first
of these three emphases flows from Girard's insight that we desire
according to the desire of the other. And thus that the other, the

social other, always precedes us, moves us and gives us to be. In other words, while I may think I have made an independent rational choice to act on my own impulse in buying this or that object, there is in fact a huge social powerhouse, a weight of gravity, moving me from within to develop that desire, follow that impulse and 'find' myself within the experience of being the chooser and owner of the object in question. Now of course the social, human, other which brings us into being, moves us and gives us to be, is much more nurturing than we often think, but it is also a violent and contradictory other, and so we are brought into being formed by and in rivalry with each other.[1]

Theology is concerned not, in the first instance, with the social other, but with the Other other, one who is not part of the social other at all, but who has brought the social other into being and maintains it in being. So the self-disclosure of this Other other in our midst is not in the first place some sort of imparting of information about an object, but is rather to be sensed as a communication of a desire which is not in rivalry with us. What interests me, fascinates me, as a theologian is a dawning awareness of the incomparable richness, power, weight and solidity of this Other other. Talking about God as if we were talking about an object does nothing at all to bring out what I am more and more convinced is the word's necessary hinterland: a huge psychological reversal.

Allow me to try to bring out something of this reversal by the image of a child's seesaw.[2] Having started by thinking of ourselves as stable, self-starting protagonists, we begin to sense instead that we are lightweight symptoms sitting on one end of a seesaw. The tiniest finger of something utterly colossal placed on the other end of the seesaw is enough to keep us riding up, and up. The pivot is the point where all that weight has incidence in our world, the anthropological point of entry through which the colossal weight moves us. But often enough, so complete is the movement within which we find ourselves that we have long lost sense even of the fulcrum, the

---

1   I give fuller introductions to Girard's thought in this area in Chapter 4, 'Discipleship and the shape of belonging', and Chapter 10, 'Love your enemy: within a divided self'.

2   In Chapter 6, 'Like Children sitting in the marketplace', I attempt to use another image, that of crumbs in a paper bag, to bring out the same sense of reversal.

pivot, that provides the leverage. So sure is the ride that it escapes us that there is a colossal weight keeping us in movement.

So, for me, the richest theological fruit of Girard's purely anthropological insight (that we desire according to the desire of the other, that the desire of the other is prior to the constitution of the self), lies in the massive hint it gives, for those who want to take it that way, in the direction of the sheer grandeur, weight and power of the Other other who is not on the same level as anything that is, and is not in rivalry with anything that is. It is the psychological consequences of this – thinking of myself, and relaxing into thinking of myself, as a 'becoming-empowered symptom of something much bigger than myself', without being in any way in rivalry with it – that I refer to as 'the Great Reversal'. And it is intimations of this that I most hope you receive through these pages.

If the first emphasis that I want to bring out in this book is on the weight of the One pressing down on one end of the seesaw, the second emphasis is more on the fulcrum, the pivot, the anthropological point of incidence in our world by which that weight moves us. And it corresponds in Girard's thought to the discovery of the scapegoat mechanism, the way that mechanism structures human togetherness and the astounding consequences at a purely anthropological level of the way in which that mechanism was gradually, and then, finally and definitively, revealed for what it is in Christ's Passion. The Passion rendered the scapegoat mechanism forever suspect as the source for human togetherness. The scapegoat mechanism works well for as long as you don't know that the one against whom you are ganging up is innocent, for as long as you do not doubt the righteousness of your fury. However, it shrivels in effectiveness the moment you suspect that the 'guilty' one is innocent and your righteousness a terrible form of group possession or hallucination. Thus does the Passion throw down a challenge for us to find new ways to live together, by making us un-forget our lifelong complicity in violence where we least want to see it.

So you will find, in the chapters that follow, a fair amount of exploration of how that that pivot has incidence in our lives. If Girard's insight is correct, then a considerable part of the effect of the Christian revelation will be a shaking up of what is apparently 'right' and what is apparently 'wrong' as we get used to how falsified our 'reason' has been by our violence, how dangerous our 'goodness' is, and how long and slow is the path by which we enter into our right minds. More often than not the occasions I have been given for dealing with this matter have been those associated with trying to work out the implications as a human being, a Catholic and a priest, of our comparatively recent human discovery that being gay is a regularly occurring minority variant in the human condition rather than a vice or a pathology.

From my own perspective, my own discussions of matters gay would be of little value if they were not simply the small scale working out, in a particular case, of something which I take to be true on a much bigger, broader, anthropological level, something with application far beyond the immediate and urgent political and religious concerns which I share with my gay and lesbian brothers and sisters.

Whether I have applied the consequences of Jesus' life, death, resurrection and teaching to matters gay well or badly is, for me, secondary to a deeper conviction: when Jesus told his interlocutors 'If you had known what this meant "I want mercy and not sacrifice" you would not have condemned the guiltless' or 'you ... make void the word of God through the tradition that you have handed on', he was giving words to a revolution in anthropological understanding that he was himself instantiating and bringing in. In other words, he was opening up a dynamic of human self-critical learning which he was and is making available to us so that we can enter both painfully and joyfully into what is true, and live accordingly. When I refer in my title to 'broken hearts and new creations' it is to this anthropological dynamic that I am referring: we find ourselves being given the offer of having our hearts, formed as they are in ways of being together which are too small, narrow and violent, broken open by One who longs for us to have a bigger, richer heart. And as we find ourselves gifted with these broken hearts, undergoing the great reversal that I describe, we simultaneously find ourselves being pointed towards, and beginning to enjoy, a flourishing whose full shape is still beyond us.

The third emphasis is also something I have learned from Girard. It is from Girard as a master reader of texts that I have begun to sense what might be meant by Jesus fulfilling the Scriptures. The more I have 'sunk into' the fecundity of Girard's thought over time, the more it has made available for me some of the intellectual flexibility necessary to recover a way of handling the texts of Scripture that is, as far as I can tell, much closer to ancient or patristic styles than to ones we've become used to over the last couple of centuries. Girard's thought has taught me to read the Hebrew Scriptures for signs of the One who was coming into the world, in the light of the actual shape that that coming into the world took in the Passion. In short, he makes it possible to read this passage from the Epistle to the Hebrews[3], quoting the Septuagint, as a rigorous instantiation of a hermeneutical model:

> when he came into the world he said, 'Sacrifices and offerings thou hast not desired, but a body hast thou prepared for me; in burnt offerings and sin-offerings thou hast taken no pleasure. Then I said, "Lo I have come to do thy will, O God, as it is written of me in the roll of the book."'

So, in the chapters that follow, and despite the fact that I am by formation a systematic theologian, and not a Scripture scholar,[4] you will find various attempts of mine to read Scripture in the light of Mimetic Theory and to think through what it might mean to recover an ecclesial sense of Jesus fulfilling the Scriptures that seeks to avoid being supersessionist or anti-semitic.

I would like to conclude this introduction by offering you a reading of a passage of the Hebrew Scriptures which brings out all three of the emphases I have been describing: the gravitational power of the Other other; the anthropological pivot undoing the scapegoat mechanism, leading to a restructuring of human being together; and possible senses of 'scriptural fulfilment' which allow us to

---

3   Heb. 10:5-7.
4   Systematic theologians, a wag once pointed out, do indeed believe in the existence of the Scriptures, because there are references to them in the documents of the Council of Trent.

see the New and Old Testaments nestling in each other in quite unexpected ways.

Isaiah 66, the last chapter of that great book, opens with the prophet, often now called 'Third Isaiah', railing against the second Temple establishment, those who were rebuilding the Temple after the return from Babylon and creating the new rules of 'who's in and who's out' that we find in the later Second Temple period. The wonderful raw ends of the Hebrew prophetic tradition are rarely more alive than when engaged in fostering deep self-criticism of the Hebrew people. So, a century or more earlier, the prophet Jeremiah had formally denied[5] that God gave any instructions at all to the people of Israel on their way out of Egypt concerning burnt offerings and sacrifices – indicating that he would not have recognised the inspiration of God in a significant amount of what we now consider to be the Pentateuch.

In Chapter 66, Isaiah does something similar: the Temple is woefully inadequate as a pivot by which all the grandeur that is God can move the earth.

> Thus says the LORD: Heaven is my throne and the earth is my footstool; what is the house that you would build for me, and what is my resting place? All these things my hand has made, and so all these things are mine, says the LORD.

The prophet is clearly writing from within the Great Reversal which I have attempted to describe. He is not merely talking about God: he is talking from the inside, as it were, of a sense of God who has become for him a great weight which relativises all other possible sources of gravitational pull. And to match that great weight there is only one possible pivot, one possible dwelling place:

> But this is the one to whom I will look, to the humble and contrite in spirit, who trembles at my word.

---

5   Jer. 7:22-3 'For on the day that I brought your ancestors out of the land of Egypt, I did not speak to them or command them concerning burnt-offerings and sacrifice. But this command I gave them "Obey my voice, and I will be your God and you shall be my people…"' I would like here to express my debt to Michael and Lori Hardin, who first pointed out to me the importance of this verse, and in whose company I began to work out my reading of Isaiah 66.

Our word 'contrite' is too hygienically religious. It scarcely brings out the sense of brokenness, of being beaten down, crippled in spirit, which is in the Hebrew. This is where Isaiah shows how he has glimpsed the pivot from which the incidence, the full weight of the Other other, is to affect all of created reality. A sure dimension of the full appearance of the forgiving Victim of the Passion. The prophet then moves on to what is a clear anthropological critique of a pattern of desire. As opposed to that of one who 'trembles at my word', and who is vulnerable to God, the pattern of desire under critique is that of those who have created a secure, non-trembling identity for themselves, a form of goodness grasped through ritual sacrifice:

> Whoever slaughters an ox is like one who kills a human being;

It could scarcely be said more clearly that sacrifice and murder are the same thing, one is just an apparently 'religious' cover for the other.

> whoever sacrifices a lamb, like one who breaks a dog's neck;

How insultingly the prophet mixes the sacred with the utter banality and cruelty of snapping a dog's neck! And he is not merely suggesting that it is forms of sacrifice involving killing which are bad, while other, seemingly more peaceful, activities are just fine.

> whoever presents a grain offering, like one who offers swine's
> blood;

The repugnant idea of sacrificing a pig, the symbol of uncleanliness, and in particular its blood, the very life-form of uncleanliness, is as holy as presenting a grain offering. And even something as seemingly gentle as a memorial offering of frankincense is treated with contempt: there is quite simply no difference in the anthropological significance of offering incense to God and making a similar offering to an idol – the pattern of desire at work is the same regardless of the notional 'recipient' of the honour.

> whoever makes a memorial offering of frankincense, like one who
> blesses an idol.

Then comes the point:

> These have chosen their own ways, and in their abominations they
> take delight;

All these forms of sacrifice, from big bullocks all the way down to
grains of incense, are part of a pattern of desire by which people
form themselves in their own image, lock themselves into projections of themselves, and then proceed to call good, to delight in,
things which are not good at all. This projection of fake goodness is
linked to the creation of a form of security, but one that is utterly
fragile:

> I also will choose to mock them, and bring upon them what they
> fear;

The great reversal will show itself in collapsing their pattern of desire, for what they have 'chosen' and what the Other other 'chooses'
are the inverse of each other. The Other other has a huge desire and
longing to get through to his people but, by their opting for sacrificial 'goodness', they have in fact made themselves invulnerable to
God:

> because, when I called, no one answered, when I spoke, they did
> not listen; but they did what was evil in my sight, and chose what
> did not please me.

As part of the great reversal, God presents himself as if he were the
one doing the praying, calling out, begging for an answer, seeking a
listening ear, while those involved in sacrifice have become a pagan
god, a Baal, that has no ears to hear, and is unable to enter into, let
alone be moved by, the desire of the suppliant.

Just in case anyone should think that this critique of sacrifice is
simply a superior expression of distaste for the accoutrements of
religion, the prophet immediately goes on to link it to the relation between the righteously sacrificing crowd and their rejection
of ones they hate:

> Hear the word of the LORD, you who tremble at his word: Your
> own people who hate you and reject you for my name's sake have
> said, 'Let the LORD be glorified, so that we may see your joy';

Here is a familiar group dynamic! The group that has constructed their own righteousness by sacrifice is simultaneously the same group that hates, and throws out, those who tremble at the word of the Lord, and so do not join in the blasphemous unanimity. The very language by which the vulnerable before God are rejected, the injunction to 'Praise God as we do, enter into unanimity with us, so that we can see that you are on the same side as us' is at the same time the formula for the shunning, for the shaming. For the shadow side of exactly the same words is 'Not to enter into unanimity with us is to refuse praise to God, and so we are right utterly to cast you out'. The pattern of desire that leads to goodness through religious sacrifice and the pattern of desire that leads to violent rejection is the same.

And yet, the prophet can already see the ease with which the weighty Other other is going to be the real source of the glory of those who are vulnerable, and thus how those who have grasped onto false glory will end up judged by the shame that they have meted out:

> but it is they who shall be put to shame.

Now we come to a point where, I would like to suggest, the prophet Isaiah and the evangelist John meld together; where they seem to be singing from the same score, not, I suspect, because John was simply borrowing text from Isaiah, nor because Isaiah had had a magical vision of the events in Jerusalem several centuries after his death. Rather, Isaiah has already seen, with astounding clarity, as Chapter 66 bears witness, the link between the weight – the Other other – and the pivot – the beaten-up trembling one – such that the contours of the shape of the act of communication of the One coming into the world were luminescent to him. And John, in the light of Jesus' teaching and resurrection, knew that the full instantiation of that act of communication had taken exactly the shape that the prophet had glimpsed, the blurry edges of that vision gathered at last into the tight focus of a lived-out piece of history.

> Listen, an uproar from the city! A voice from the temple! The voice of the LORD, dealing retribution to his enemies![6]

---

6   Isaiah 66:6

In John 7, Jesus cries out loud, twice, in the Temple, producing a mini-uproar, a hint of what is to come. In John 12, at Jesus' last public appearance before the uproar in the city which leads to his Passion, a voice is heard from heaven,[7] and later on Jesus cries aloud[8]. Someone, Jesus, is about to be hated and rejected by the Temple authorities, and that rejection is going to be the source of judgment of those rejecting[9] – their shame. In between we get a number of quotes from other sections of Isaiah, and the wonderfully dense observation:

> Isaiah said this because he saw his glory and spoke about him.[10]

The possibility of a duet between our authors continues when, in John's Gospel, as part of Jesus' preparation of his disciples for his Passion, he used the image of the pains of travail, familiar from a number of prophets:

> Truly, truly, I say to you, you will weep and lament, but the world will rejoice; you will be sorrowful, but your sorrow will turn into joy. When a woman is in travail she has sorrow, because her hour has come; but when she is delivered of the child, she no longer remembers the anguish, for joy that a child is born into the world. So you have sorrow now, but I will see you again and your hearts will rejoice, and no one will take your joy from you.[11]

What Isaiah 66 enables us to see is the link between the imagery of travail, which he also uses, and the way in which John's description of the Crucifixion is that of an act of parturition, of giving birth, even before Jesus' final pains had come upon him.

> Before she was in labour she gave birth; before her pain came upon her she delivered a son. Who has heard of such a thing? Who has seen such things? Shall a land be born in one day? Shall a nation be delivered in one moment? Yet as soon as Zion was in labour she delivered her children. Shall I open the womb and not deliver?

---

7   Jn 12:28-9
8   Jn 12:44
9   Jn 12:47-8
10 Jn 16:2002
11 Jn 16:20-2

says the LORD; shall I, the one who delivers, shut the womb? says your God.[12]

Compare this with these 'moments' from John's account of the crucifixion:

> When Jesus saw his mother, and the disciple whom he loved standing near, he said to his mother, 'Woman, behold, your son!' Then he said to the disciple, 'Behold, your mother!' And from that hour the disciple took her to his own home.[13]

Or again:

> But one of the soldiers pierced his side with a spear, and at once there came out blood and water.[14]

The reference to Jesus' mother as 'woman', taking us back to the creation of Eve, and the piercing of Adam's side from which Eve was taken, as well as the flowing out of afterbirth, opens up a possible way to see what Isaiah might have been onto with the notion of birth and delivery coming before the pangs. A great reversal is going on: bizarrely, impossibly, in Jesus going to his death, the definitive Adam has already given birth to the new Eve, and his mother has become the mother of his sisters and brothers.[15] It is only after the resurrection – i.e. when his death has 'birthed' them – that Jesus, for the first time ever refers to 'my brothers' and talks about God as 'my Father and your Father'.[16]

Please notice what I am *not* saying. I am not claiming that John is quoting Isaiah 66 at these points – in fact he quotes quite other passages from Isaiah. I'm fumbling for something more difficult to set out clearly: that when John says 'Isaiah said this because he saw his glory and spoke about him' John was aware of being on the inside

---

12 Isaiah 66:7-8
13 Jn 19:26-7
14 Jn 19:34
15 I examine this inverted parturition in Chapter 2.
16 In many places in John's Gospel the evangelist refers to 'his mother' and 'his brothers'. However Jesus never refers to his mother as 'my mother', calling her 'woman' at Cana and the Cross. Only in the Garden after the Resurrection does he cease to distinguish between his own and his disciples' relation to the Father, calling them 'my brothers', and referring to 'My Father, my God and your God'.

of the same vision of the glory of the One coming into the world that Isaiah had had. The contours of this vision are quite regular, not capricious and subject to whim, and can be properly if distantly ·pointed to in the pattern of 'gravity of the Other other, improbable anthropological pivot related to a scapegoat mechanism, and great reversal leading to new Creation'. And that in the Passion narrative the fullness of this same vision, in as sharp a focus as we can manage, was instantiated as a fully human acting-out in our midst.

I hope this may serve as a highly tentative introduction to how Girard's thought enables us to approach the Hebrew Scriptures in a way that is both very free, and yet somewhat rigorous, as well as to hint at how well Girard's emphases correspond with those of the inner workings of the prophetic writings themselves.

With this, I would invite you to dabble in the chapters that follow. Rather than arranging them in blocks according to subject matter, I have left them in more or less the order in which they were written, in the hopes that you will detect for yourself the thematic unity which I've attempted to set out in this introduction.

I would like to thank here, from among all those who have made these chapters possible, my hosts at different venues over the last four years, who have with great generosity drawn the work out of me: Stephen Schloesser SJ, Revd Mark D. Chapman, Bishop David Stancliffe, Darlene Weaver, Catherine Pepinster, Christine M. Bochen, Mark Dowd, Carlos Mendoza OP, Richard R. Gaillardetz, Revd Richard Carter, Norbert Reck, Benoît Chantre, Dorothy Whiston, Peter Tyler, and Michael Kirwan SJ.

Once again I am enormously indebted to my friend and editor Brendan Walsh and his colleagues at DLT, as well as to my friend Robin Baird-Smith at Continuum, for their belief in the worthwhileness of this project. Not for the first time it has involved them in having to cope with the vagaries of an author who is too rarely stable to be tied down to proper production schedules. Their forbearance has been no small part of their generosity. I would also like to thank Andrew McKenna and Sebastian Moore, whose constant input over these last years has done so much to improve the quality of what you are embarking on. During the last two years, I have been able to survive, move to Brazil, get settled in, write, travel and teach, thanks entirely to the Board of the newly established foundation Imitatio[17], Peter Thiel, Robert Hamerton-Kelly and René Girard, who awarded me a generous fellowship for the years 2008 to 2010. To them, and to Lindy Fishburne, the Executive Director of Imitatio who has done so much to turn the idea of Imitatio into a reality, I dedicate these pages with my heartfelt thanks.

James Alison
São Paulo, Feast of the Baptism of the Lord 2010

17 For details, see www.imitatio.org

CHAPTER 1

Is it ethical to be Catholic? Queer perspectives

The question 'Is it ethical to be Catholic?' is, to my mind, a somewhat surprising one, even when asked from a queer perspective[1]. It
has had me scratching my head. You see, it would never have crossed
my mind to wonder whether it is ethical to be Catholic, and I am
not at all sure that I understand where the question is coming from.
I guess that the reason for my bafflement is that I have never met
anyone who became a Catholic for ethical reasons. Every Catholic I know is so either because they were baptised as an infant and
brought up that way, or because they converted to Catholicism later
in life. When I have heard conversion stories, not many of them are
to do with ethics, and mine is no exception. I became a Catholic
when I was eighteen, at a time when there was no Pope (Paul VI
had just died), and so, at my reception into the Church, I recited
a formula of obedience to 'Our Pope "N"'. He has been one of my
favourites ever since. Every now and then, over the last twenty-five
years or so, I have been tempted to want him to come back soon,
though at the moment I am very happy with his substitute.

However, what brought me into the Church was a mixture of two
graces. The first was having fallen in love with a Catholic classmate
at school some years earlier. He was and is straight, but I perceived
a certain warmth of personality in him which seemed untypical of
the world of Protestant schoolboys in which I lived, and I associated that warmth with his being Catholic. The second was a special

---

1   This chapter was born as my participation in a panel discussion for LGBT people in Most Holy
Redeemer Parish Church, San Francisco, in February 2006. The title 'Is it ethical to be Catholic?'
was given us by the hosting group based at the University of San Francisco, and I was invited to
represent a positive answer to the question in the face of other panellists who represented the
view that it is not ethical for a gay or lesbian person to continue to be a member of the Catholic
Church.

grace at a time when I was at a very low ebb, having just started to 'come out' as a gay man in a very hostile conservative evangelical environment, shortly before going to university. This grace I associate absolutely with the intercession of Padre Pio, since it came at a time when I glimpsed something of the link between his stigmata and the sacrifice of the Mass; I then knew, and have always since known, the Mass to be no mere memorial supper. This grace, which was accompanied by an astounding joy, literally blew me into the Church. It was the gift of the Catholic faith. Once it had fallen upon me, I knew myself to be involved on the inside of something which has been a love affair ever since; something which just seems to open out and get bigger and better all the time. I was aware even then that my often-tortuous journey of self-acceptance as a gay man and my becoming a Catholic were part of the same movement of joy. And God has been faithful, keeping the texture of those loves intertwined and slowly bringing them into one love and one blessing, nurturing the heart that it has been his idea to give me and keeping it safe from Lord alone knows how much erratic behaviour, slowness to trust and cowardice, on my part, as well as from the defamation of love and the hatred espoused by so many whose job it is to speak in God's name.

It certainly never crossed my mind back then to think that it was ethical to be Catholic. It seemed self-evident to me at the time, with my English middle-class prejudices, that Protestants were much more moral people than Catholics. Not far beneath the surface of the 1950s style evangelical Protestantism of my background was the suspicion that the Pope was Antichrist. I remember some weeks of what I can only call spiritual pain as I worked through the scar on my soul that had been left by my exposure to that lie and the fear which went with it, that by becoming a Catholic I might be handing over my life to the service of evil. A couple of years later, I read that John Henry Newman had experienced working through just such a pain as part of his own process of being brought by God into the life of the Church. And since then other converts from the same background have mentioned a similar passage of pain. But here we are talking not, I think, about a level-headed discussion concerning what is good, but a deep, existential terror that I might be being sucked into the service of evil, part of that terror being that I would not even know that evil was what I had become. Such moments of fear have assailed me every now and then since that time, compounded in my case by very deep fears of being evil which seem to be common to gay youths from religious backgrounds. But I have learned to sit back, look at these assaults, giggle, and be aware that God is much bigger, more powerful, more gentle and more trustworthy than my heart, and that I should not take myself so seriously as to think that I could really get in God's way very effectively or for very long.

Then again, one of the reliefs about coming into the Church was precisely that it was not ethics-obsessed. I remember realising, a year or so after becoming a Catholic, that one of the first things I had to learn about being a Catholic – bizarrely – was how to sin. In the world of my formation, being good was obligatory and boring. And sinning, being bad, was a terrible letting down of the side; a sort of failure of English gentlemanliness. This meant, in fact, a constant struggle to live up to 'being good', whatever that meant. Curiously, a strong belief in 'justification by faith alone' seemed to have as its psychological counterpart an extreme need to justify oneself. As a Catholic, I had to learn that sin is boringly normal, and that what is exciting is being pulled into learning new things, called virtues, which are ways in which a goodness, which is not ours, becomes connatural with us, and that this is something of an adventure. I had to learn how not to be so concerned with whether I was getting things right or wrong, but to learn instead to relax into the given-ness of things. I can scarcely tell you how strange it sounds in retrospect, but I was discovering that it is part of the mercy of the Catholic faith that those of us who are infected by spiritual haughtiness find ourselves being lowered slowly and gently into the mud, the slime, of being one of ordinary humanity, and learning that it is *this* ordinary humanity which is loved as it is. If there are to be any diamonds, they will be found amidst the clay, and as the outworkings of the pressures in the clay, not perched on high, on stalks, trying to avoid being infected by so much common carbon.

Part of this induction into being Catholic has been the discovery of the secret presence of Our Lady, permeating everything. For many of those of us brought up in Protestant backgrounds, it takes a long time to begin to make sense of what can come across as a psychological weirdness with which it is difficult to identify, which does not seem to strike chords in us. But I have come to rejoice in and love Our Lady and the difference she constitutes in the Church. For it is she who makes it impossible for the Church to turn itself successfully either into an ideology or into a moralistic enterprise. She can never quite be co-opted into standing for something other than what she is. And what I have come to associate her with being is the link, the non-opposition, between the old creation and the new, between nature and grace, between the Israel of the Prophets and Patriarchs and the new, universal Israel of God. Far too delicate to be clearly delineated, and far too present to be dismissed, she has underlined, seated, and made three-dimensional for me elements of the faith in what her Son is doing which can only be lived-into over time.

The feast of the Assumption, in particular, is one where my heart soars, and I have, over my twenty-seven years of being a Catholic, enjoyed two special moments of grace from Our Lady on the Solemnity of the Assumption. One, when out for a walk in Cochabamba, Bolivia, where a sense of the openness of heaven gave me the inspiration for the second half of my book *The Joy of Being Wrong*. And, more recently, and even more surprisingly, a grace came when I was desperate to think of a way to finish my book *Faith Beyond Resentment*. I was in Rio de Janeiro, running out of time before I had to hand in the manuscript, and was stuck, at the end of my tether, and on my way to sleep, having spent Sunday, 15 August failing to do anything on the computer other than play FreeCell and Solitaire. As I fell asleep, I was given the parable of Nicodemus, the Inquisitor and the boys in the square, which became the end of the last chapter of the book. I remember giggling, so preposterous did it seem as an ending for the book. I also remember thinking, as I wrote it out the next day, that Our Lady's love for her queer children, one of the best-kept but also best-known, secrets of the Church, is something which no amount of ecclesiastical homophobia can vanquish.

I recently came across what was, for me, an entirely new and wonderful avocation of Our Lady: Our Lady Un-doer of Knots. In Brazil, I stumbled upon a locally-carved statue of her, which I bought without knowing anything about the devotion. It turned out to come from Augsburg in Germany, from a painting by an unknown artist dating from 1700. What on earth, you may ask, was a devotion from a baroque part of Germany doing being sculpted in Salvador, the most African part of Brazil? But this is part of the uncanny wonder of the Catholic Church. The image is of Our Lady of the Immaculate Conception holding a cord with knots, which she is undoing. This avocation gives me great peace, since it is clear to me that the knots concerning the relationship between grace and desire, sin and concupiscence, which have been so tied-up into a *skandalon* for gay people in the life of our Church, are being gently and carefully undone by hands blessed with far more patience and delicacy than I could hope to muster.

Well, I hope you can see why I was surprised by the question 'Is it ethical to be Catholic?' Being Catholic for me has meant discovering myself on the inside of something where God and many wonderful people are doing things *for me* long before I can manage to do anything minimally presentable for others. The relationship between being Catholic and ethics is not a straightforward one, and I would like to give you a brief reminder of its strangeness before turning to look at how this impacts the queer perspectives which you have invited me to discuss.

A few years back, I attended the funeral of a well-known London parish priest, Father Michael Hollings, in Westminster Cathedral. The Requiem Mass was presided over by Cardinal Basil Hume, and there was a huge turnout. Father Michael had been a decorated military officer, well-known spiritual author, university chaplain and innovative parish priest. A complex man, widely but discretely known to be gay, he had, late in life, been suspended for some time following an allegation of molesting a youth. Although charges were not brought, Fr Michael had himself asked the police for two other accounts of inappropriate behaviour to be taken into account. I do not think anyone who knew him thought of him as flawless, but he was one of those people whose flaws were often transparent to grace, and people loved him, as was shown by the huge number of people of all ethnic backgrounds who came to his funeral. Cardinal Hume was on particularly fine form, directing his homily to Father Michael in his coffin, talking fondly, chidingly, infuriatedly, lovingly. What I, and others, came away with from this funeral Mass, and this is not something that any liturgist can just 'produce', was a palpable sense of the proximity, solidity and openness of eternal life. The Catholic faith is in the first place, and above all, to do with eternal life. And I suppose it is important just to remember that: why do any of us become Catholic and remain Catholic? Well, ultimately, because it is God's way of giving us eternal life, God's own life.

There is something special about this, something characteristic and odd. We find our hearts, minds and imaginations being opened up to perceive that YHWH, the God of Israel and Creator of all things, was present in the life, teaching and signs worked by Jesus of Nazareth in such a way that that very special rock-solidity of presence associated with YHWH was recognised in Jesus' own person. A group of not particularly distinguished people whom Jesus had chosen to be the witnesses to what he was about, found, after his death, that he was present to them in the way that was proper to YHWH, the Rock, the one who knows not death and who causes all things to be. These same undistinguished people began to understand that that Rock, the one who makes all things to be and keeps them in unfrustratable being, had been present in Jesus all along, such that his acting out of his life, living into the role of High Priest, victim, altar and sacrifice on the Cross, was a new and definitive glimpse at the 'inner' life of God, showing just how much God loves us as humans, and wants to empower us to come and share his life from within, so that we can be much, much more than we ever thought possible before.

This undistinguished group of people even became aware that when Jesus had nicknamed one of them, the notoriously volatile and unstable character Simon, 'Rock', this wasn't just an ironic joke, but was part of the way that the Rock of Israel was going to make itself present in the life of humans to their advantage. In other words, the rock-solidity of salvation opened up and made present by Jesus was not just going to float in the air as some sort of spiritual doctrine for *cognoscenti,* but was going to be made available to anybody at all through a witness given by a whole collection of highly implausible and improbable characters. In the midst of these characters, a certain derivative rock-quality, associated with the ministry of Peter, would also, always, be made available as part of the indestructible opening up of the gates of Heaven on Earth. This indestructible quality resists all our death-bound-ness, all our waves of desire, patterns of hatred, fear and refusal of life. This gift of a continuing rock-quality, a sheer, unsnuffable-out, 'having already happened and being open for us', quality is largely independent of the character and the highly mutable moral qualities of all of us, and certainly of the often undependable and mutable character of Simon Peter's successors.

From my perspective, John Paul as a character was high on bluster and sounding firm and certain about everything, and so the quality of divinely-given 'rockitude' was rather more difficult to glimpse beneath the showier elements of his own personality until his last weeks, when he gave a glorious witness to the palpable abundance of eternal life in the midst of his failing. But one of the things I especially like about Papa Ratzi is that he is evidently a much more modest, self-effacing and even timid man, and this enables the rock quality, the authentic Petrine touchstone quality, to shine through rather more perceptibly. He knows that it is not about him, and yet I think that ordinary Catholics in Italy sensed rather quickly that the Petrine charism, the surety, is alive and shining in him.

Now I'd like to suggest that this rock quality actually permeates the Catholic faith in a whole lot of different areas. I sometimes describe it as the 'just there' quality, and I suppose the area we tend to know it from most regularly is the liturgy – the 'just there' quality of the presence of Jesus in the Mass. There seems to me to be something quite wonderful about this, the quiet, serene, relaxedness, the lack of self-consciousness about Catholic worship, because we all know that Jesus is 'just there', giving himself for us and inviting us in, and that he's bigger than the flakiness of so many of our liturgies and the idiocy of so many of our homilies and he's obviously bigger and better than the flawed-ness of our priests and, of course, of ourselves.

Now, I know that this 'just there' quality, the *ex opere operato* nature of the sacraments, has often enough led us into a generalised attitude of the presumption of grace, and for that reason we typically spend far less time preparing our liturgies, give far less responsibility to proper musicians to organize real singing, spend far less time training preachers actually to know and love the Gospel text and preach from it, than we have any right to do. Yet this casual certainty of the complete dependability of the self-giving of God to us, the knowledge that however much we screw up, it is not our show but someone else's, seems to me to be a quite extraordinary gift, and one which I associate with real faith. It is also one I associate with our Church order.

You see, curiously, I think that this very 'given-ness', this very 'just there', quality actually enables us all to be far more relaxed about popes, bishops, theologians, doctrines and so on than would be the case if we had to take such people desperately seriously, as though the matter ultimately depended on them getting it right.

On the one hand, we can be relaxed about Jesus in the Eucharist, because we know that he is there, and that he will show himself to us as he will, in the way he will, in the way that is suitable for us to receive and that will guide us with love. And this means that we don't have to work ourselves up into knots of appropriate feeling, or self-consciousness, or liturgical perfection in order to 'get it right', because the real 'getting it right' is being done by someone else, and the most we can do is to be more or less appropriate in the respectfulness and gratitude of our response.

And, on the other hand, I think the same is true about our theological squabbles in the Church. We can relax about having to get it right, because we know that the one who is making things right, who is bringing us into a new creation, is doing so hugely, safely, spaciously, gently. And that in the face of this huge, unstoppable 'just ... having happened', this 'just ... being there', we are all tiny parts of a more or less chaotic response to the upheaval. And we – popes, bishops, priests, theologians and every conceivable other sort of faithful – are all on the same receiving side, part of this more or less chaotic response to the upheaval; all of us are undergoers of it and not its protagonist, some holding onto the remains of the termite hill which seems to have been completely uprooted, others dashing around looking for something new that looks as though it might be home.

And this, I think, is something huge and wonderful, and specifically Catholic. Because the upheaval is bigger than any of us, and all of us are undergoers of it, it means that over time we can learn to stand back from any and all of the things that we hold sacred, and see how the One who just is, who is happening in our midst, is beginning to reshape things. In other words, the real sacredness of what is coming about is not only in texts, or acts of worship, but in what is happening, in the signs of a new creation emerging in the midst of our collapsing termite hill. And these signs are, over time, detectable by us – we are after all not servants, but friends, daughters, sons and heirs, on the inside of this project, not people to whom the project just happens. It is not a building project by a foreign corporation which arrives and plants a huge factory on our street without any consultation or any legal guarantees and says in the face of our consternation: 'You say you mind? Do we look to you as though we're concerned? We aren't doing this for your benefit!' No, it is a project which is being done for us, and the signs of it happening are taking us by surprise. Nevertheless, the whole point of signs is that they are genuinely difficult to interpret – what looks like 'good news' for some people does look like 'the end of the world as I know it' for others.

This being shaken up as part of being saved means that we can be un-preoccupied about being wrong! Part of the joy of belief in the infallibility of the salvation with which God is gifting the Church is not having to hold too tightly to any notion of us getting it right, but rather being aware that we are being taken on the rollercoaster of it being got right by someone other than ourselves, with occasional contributions from us, and sometimes despite what seems to us to be our better judgement. This is because the One who is getting it right loves us, and is getting through to us in ways which we do not at first understand, ways which it takes time for us to be able to grasp as being for our benefit. But we have been *found*, and can trust that we will get to understand, and it will make sense – in fact, that we will be taken into all truth even in the midst of all our rows and disagreements.

This sense seems to me to be particularly important for us as gay and lesbian Catholics now. We are in the midst of a huge, and very highly-emotionally charged, row in our Church – one that often seethes in silence and breaks out in strange and awful ways. And yet what I find splendid is that, in the Catholic Church, over time, faith prevents this row from being about ideology. In the Catholic Church, this is ultimately a row about *what is*, which means our taking it for granted that *what is* is something which is bigger than us and which is opening itself up to us, and which we don't control. Ideology is what you have when you don't have faith. When you are *not* aware that there is Another, bigger than us, who is holding all of us in his hand through the upheaval, and that ultimately we are safe, there is room, we can be wrong and we can learn to get it right, then you are frightened of disagreement and what you need to do is to produce a unanimity of opinion, of ideology – you need to get everyone to agree, and have those who are in, in, and those who are out, out.

But this is the classic sign of people who have a compulsion for certainty, a compulsion for being right, and a compulsion for being considered to be good, and so who grasp onto a fake certainty, a re-solved righteousness, too small a togetherness. If we react like this, then it means that our anchor is not in the rock beyond the veil. If it were, then we would be happy to know that we can all be wrong together, all learn together and that our squabbling about what is right is a necessary part of the process of all of us learning. In fact, faith in the goodness and trustworthiness of the Creator, as revealed by Jesus being prepared to undergo a lynch death and so undo our lynching ways, has as its direct consequence the belief that we can be brought into knowing what is objectively true by the paths of human reason. Those paths involve the very great difficulty of our learning to be reasonable and to reason together by learning not to lynch, learning to detect when we are closing down our possibilities of growth by lying and murdering so as to grasp what we take to be our identities, whether as individuals or as groups. This means that

how we conduct our rows and arguments is inseparable from what
we discover to be true.

Something like this is going on at the moment for us as gay and
lesbian people in the Church. A certain sense of truth about who we
are is beginning to become available to us in the midst of frightening and violent struggles, shouting and name-calling. It has begun to
become available precisely in the degree in which we learn to stop
defining a particular group of people as evil so as to hold on to what
turns out to be a spuriously narrow sense of what is good. And this
is the only way anything about being human has ever been learned.
It is only as we learn to see and love our neighbours as ourselves
that we find out who *we* are, and find that we are much more than
we thought we were.

Recently, this dynamic of learning to see and love our neighbours
as ourselves has put into crisis a traditional way of looking at what
was assumed to be a weird and evil 'other'. It is beginning to become possible to make a huge new anthropological distinction, even
at the highest level in the life of the Church, between two things
which, before, we had not been able to distinguish properly as a
normal part of our race's way of living together. The distinction is
between forms of behaviour which are a distortion of what people
are, on the one hand, and forms of behaviour which can be a responsible part of what some people are, on the other[2]. We all know
and understand that there are some distorted forms of behaviour
into which males, particularly, but also sometimes females, get inducted, by force of circumstance, same-sex confinement, war, long
journeys, imprisonment or strange religious cults. These forms of
behaviour seem to have a sexual component, but the sexual elements are in fact symptoms of frenzied group behaviour run by fear,
power, desire for dominance, financial advantage and demarcation
of property. These, the Church has always and everywhere considered to be grave forms of depravity, never to be approved under any
circumstances.

---

2   I take it that the recent Roman distinction between 'transitory' and 'deep-seated' homosexual
    tendencies opens up the possibility of eventual development in this direction.

What is beginning to become apparent is that there is a more or less regular minority of people of both sexes who, entirely independently of circumstance, war, long journeys, imprisonment, cults and so on, simply are principally attracted to people of their own sex at an emotional and erotic level. It is furthermore becoming clear that this is in most cases a stable and lifelong feature of who these people are, is not in any sense a dysfunction and does not in any way diminish the viability of the people who just are this way. And it is even beginning to become clear that such people are able to develop and receive that full-heartedness of love for each other, that delicate birth of a being taken out of themselves for the other which is not just lust, nor a defect of some other sort of love which they really ought to have, but don't seem to be able to, but is quite simply the real thing, which, when present, is recognised as a gift from, and an access to, God.

It is also beginning to become apparent that the attempt to describe these people by using the same ethical and descriptive tools as were used to describe the wayward form of behaviour is simply a category mistake. If you want to know what I mean by a category mistake, take a look at the famous picture of poor Private Lynndie England and her dog on a leash and the pile of humiliated male prisoners in Abu Ghraib. Then look at a picture, taken almost the same week in 2004 that the Abu Ghraib photos became available, of two women walking down the steps of Boston City Hall waving a marriage certificate. Ask yourself: to which of these two images does the biblical category of 'Sodom' rightly apply? The category mistake is to say: 'Well, in some deep sense, they are both the same thing'. Holding onto a category mistake as it becomes clear that something *just is*, ultimately constitutes a failure of faith, a refusal to allow ourselves to trust being pulled into the bigger picture which is the new creation. And part of our trust in the Petrine gift that is a key element of the Church is that we know that ultimately, however much kicking and screaming goes on, God won't let such a failure of faith close down our access to that new creation.

Peter's job is to keep us together as we squabble over the extraordinary possibilities of truth and freedom which keep on being opened up for us, as God reveals to us who we are and how much we are loved. And, of course, keeping us together often means giving succour to brethren of weak conscience, those most frightened of change, those who most miss the apparent protection of the good old termite hill. As you would expect, it is such people who are most attracted to what they take to be the stability of the rock, and often enough they do quite a good job of hiding the fact that that stability of the Petrine rock derives from a Living Rock, one from which flows living water.

What I want to say at this point is: now is not the moment to be despairing of the Church! I was taught at school that there is a so-called 'J-curve' theory of revolutions, according to which, while people are really oppressed and downtrodden, right down at the bottom of the J, they don't rise up against the regime. It is only when their circumstances start to improve and the regime starts to lighten up that they finally rise up and throw off their shackles, at the beginning of the upward curve. And this, I suppose is what I make of the question you posed to me. From a queer perspective, why should we be wondering whether it is ethical to be Catholic now? We have just survived twenty-five years of John Paul, who, with all his qualities and virtues, seemed to me, at the distance from which I saw such things, a poor judge of character, and a man who gave succour to his sycophants. The result was that on his watch the Catholic faith did seem to become associated with a sort of totalising moral ideology in which we were simply a source of evil to be denounced and criticised.

It seems to me to be the height of perversity to get worried about whether it is ethical for us to be Catholic now, just as it is becoming clear that we are in a much bigger and better space! The harshness of tone has gone, the temperature is going down. The visitation of seminaries seems, from what I have heard, to have been in many cases a less unpleasant experience than was feared. The long-awaited Instruction on not admitting gay people to the seminary seems to have fallen flat on its nose, with no indication that anyone in Rome is anything other than rather embarrassed by it. Certainly, there seems to be no inclination to make public agreement with the Instruction into the litmus test for episcopal appointments which *Humanae Vitae* became under John Paul. The psychological backing for the Instruction met with well-nigh universal incredulity, and it seems that we are well on the way to the issue of whether or not being gay is really, as has been claimed, a psychological disorder, being taken out of the sphere of doctrine and left where it belongs, in the sphere of the human sciences, with all the consequences which will follow from that.

Around the world, various forms of same-sex partnership laws appear to be becoming normal, Catholic countries having shown a great deal of ease in getting their heads around this. The result has been bishops everywhere (with, of course, some loud-mouthed exceptions) having to learn rather fast to move from the vitriolic language and somewhat artificially dramatic displays of being shocked that such things could even be talked about, to something closer to adult discussion of the issues at stake. I rather think that Benedict is steering the very heavy John Paul emphasis on the 'family' in a more productive direction. He appears to be keen that governments support the family; but, rather more subtly than John Paul, he is keen that this be a search for *positive* initiatives favouring the family. In other words, he has showed that it is possible to shift on from an emphasis on the family which was conceived of as 'over and against' gay people and their best interests to one which need not necessarily be over and against gay and lesbian people, and indeed is far better interpreted by us as including us. His privileging of monogamous heterosexual marriage as an especially blessed form of love in his recent encyclical should not, I think, be read as a blow *against* same-sex love. It leaves room for us and I suggest that we read it as an invitation for us to work out what the rich elements and gifts of same-sex love can be, and how we are to set about creating a Catholic culture of same-sex love.

It is up to us! That is where I think the ethical bit comes in. Are we going to allow ourselves to be given new life? What will be the shape of our moving from Creation into New Creation? This means working out what the shape of holiness of life and of heart is for us as gay and lesbian Catholics. It means noting with joy that we are now closer than ever to being able to imagine that a rejoicing gay heart and a rejoicing Catholic heart can be the same heart, and a normal, healthy and holy thing. We can imagine a seminar reading *Brokeback*

Mountain in the light of *Deus Caritas Est*, or vice versa, and this would be something that could easily make sense to all those, straight or gay, who took part in such a session. And one of the things which, as the Pope rightly insists, we might find ourselves learning, is how the development of our love should feed into, and be fed by, our development of charitable practices, of practical Catholic outreach to the poor, the sick, the imprisoned and the marginalised. It seems presumptuous of me even to mention it here in this parish church, in this city of San Francisco, where the ethical response to the HIV-AIDS pandemic by so many Catholic groups and individuals has been such a beacon, but, even so, it is worth hammering home this point: Catholic faith without a love of the poor is not the real thing, and the Catholicity of gay love will be seen by the way in which it is part of our empowerment to love the dispossessed. And this is something no one will be able to take away from us.

My concern with the matter of ethics at the moment is this: let us be magnanimous victors. There are some people in our Church who have been seriously upset by the way that ordinary Catholicism in all its disputatiousness and diversity is breaking out again under Pope Benedict. They are going to be terribly sore as it becomes clear that the Church, in its stumbling, bumbling, chaotic way, is just learning how to deal with the new reality of honest, straight-forward lesbian and gay people, learning how to treat differences of opinion in this sphere as discussions concerning third-order truths which do not exclude from the life of the Church.

There are also a good number, maybe a majority, of priests and bishops who genuinely do not know what to do, who are them-selves to some degree implicated in all this and who have never been able to face for themselves the issues of conscience which go with the deep fear about just being gay; people who have been hop-ing against hope that Church structure would somehow save them from having to face the issue of their own truth squarely, and who are now genuinely at sea with coping with all this. For them, the gentle temperature-lowering way in which, as far as I can see, Pope Benedict wants to deal with this issue is, maybe for the first time in their lives, a permission not to have to be certain about this, not to have to get it right. It will take some time for people like this to be able to say 'I just don't know what's right here, but let's try and help each other out of the hole'. So, let us be gentle! Ethics is very much to do with how we extend mercy to the fearful, just as we have found ourselves the recipients of mercy at a time when we have been frightened, tortured, annihilated by voices telling us how evil we were.

For me, the real ethical challenge as a Catholic now is: I don't have an excuse any more. It is no good pretending that the Pope or the Church is really against me for the long haul, so that I have to fight him or them. Instead, I will have to grow up and learn to love, starting where I am, and being aware that the gift of a gay Catholic heart is a heavy responsibility, pregnant with love and opportunity.

CHAPTER 2

Living the Magnificat

I am going to be slightly naughty this evening. It is the first Vespers of the feast of the birthday of Our Lady, so I thought that I would take advantage of the fact that, although you are gathered principally to look at ethical matters, you have chosen to do so through the words of Our Lady[1]. Now, ethics without grace tends to moralism; and the shape, the pattern, of grace, which informs ethics, is a far subtler matter, and one much more difficult to pin down, than we usually attend to. So I am going to try to offer you something in the way of prefatory remarks about the shape of grace, as revealed to us through the presence of Our Lady.

Over the last few years I have been giving, in different places, an adult catechesis course – a sort of introduction to the Christian faith. As time has gone by, I have become increasingly aware of how much more important the presence of Our Lady is in the life of faith and the life of the Church than I had previously thought, and than seems to be current. I do not mean her presence as an add-on extra, a nice metaphor for talking about the Church corporately or an obligatory piece of fusty piety, but as a currently active player in the lived out drama of salvation in the midst of which we come to be Church. I mean her presence as a currently active player with a far larger and more sophisticated role than has been allowed in these isles for several hundred years[2]; one to whom we have direct access, to whom we can talk and from whom we can receive abundantly. In other words, I want to suggest as part of my introduction to the

---

1   This chapter was born as a presentation for the meeting of the Anglican "Affirming Catholicism" group held in Durham, England, in September 2006.

2   The cult of the Virgin Mary was suppressed fairly brutally in different parts of what later became the United Kingdom, starting in the mid-sixteenth century.

faith that if, in our enthusiasm and delight for having been invited into, and encouraged to play around within, this extraordinarily safe drama which is Christianity, we are *not* assumed to be idolaters when it comes to Our Lady, then there may well be something wrong with the way we are receiving and living the Catholic faith.

Let me spin out with you an analogy which, even in its inexactitude, will I hope make the point. My friends know to their cost that I am a member of that small, but completely mad, group of devotees known as 'Rossini nuts'. For some reason, the music of the Genius of Pesaro gets to us, fills our souls and cartwheels around with delight inside us in a way that no other music does. Well, for the sake of this analogy, please assume that Rossini is God, and that you are attending the opera '*The Barber of Seville*' (but only because performances of '*Matilde di Shabran*' are so hard to come by). It does not actually matter which opera: you are attending God's creation. In this performance of the *Barber*, the role of Rosina will be sung by a stunning soprano, whom we will call Maria. From the moment the music starts, Rossini is everywhere, permeating everything, his music filling out the spaces and the interstices with creative energy and beat. But Rossini is not visible. It is the music which gives him away, and the music which envelops you. As the opera develops, different characters come on, among them Rosina, sung by Maria. In a really good performance, it will seem as though the music that she sings is coming through her, that she really is incarnating the person whom the music conjures up. That is: the more herself she really is, the more irrepressible and bubbly and daring and fun and intelligent, the more Rossini's music will have done what it intended to do.

And when it gets to the end of the opera, the audience will likely go quite mad about her, whooping and cheering and stomping. Now imagine some dour commentator saying: "That's all wrong. They should have been whooping and cheering for Rossini, not for her. In fact, by adoring her in this way, they were undercutting the praise they owed to the composer." I hope that the excited public would have the good sense to reply: "But this is nonsense: what she did was what Rossini made, and every praise of her falls on him. Rossini's music wouldn't have been better if she had kept silent during all the bits when her character sings, so that we only heard Rossini. In fact, it was only because she was so exultantly performing Rossini that we heard what Rossini was really about at all. Her performance was Rossini made three-dimensional and fulfilling its creative possibilities'.'

This, as I understand it, is what is meant by the first line of the Magnificat: "My soul magnifies the Lord". It means exactly what it says: God is made bigger, magnified, by Our Lady's soul. The lived-out shape of her bodily life over time is actually going to make God be more God than before, in just the same way, I would suggest, as a really superlative operatic heroine will make Rossini be more Rossini than he was before her performance. And Rossini would have been delighted to be made more than he was before by the heroine: that was why he was busy providing the raw material from which the heroine created the role. So we can imagine God delighting in being made spontaneously great in the life of Our Lady. And we can, perhaps, also imagine the sadness of the angels at those people who feel that God's being more is somehow threatened by the really superlative performance of someone who is in no way at all in rivalry with God.

The second line of the Magnificat helps to fill out something about the shape of the role Our Lady is performing. Her spirit whoops for joy at God her saviour. And ἀγαλλιάω, a word which comes into Greek from biblical sources, really does have that unkempt, unbound quality of exultation which it is the peculiar genius of we northern peoples to have excluded from the serious adult business known as religion. But this is something I would like to emphasise: the presence of Our Lady in the household of faith is hugely tied up with joy, with rejoicing, with bubbling over. Just think how many of the anthems corresponding to Our Lady begin "*Gaude!*" – 'Rejoice!', how her feasts are all occasions of joy, how tawdry it is that in England we have just had an 'August bank holiday' rather than the holiday for the Assumption more common among our neighbours to the south and how impoverished is our understanding of what we have been given when Marian rejoicing is not allowed to pulsate as the constant backdrop to our faith.

What I would like to do with you now is begin to develop my operatic image in such a way as to make it more three-dimensional. There is something rather special about the particular performance of *The Barber of Seville* which we are discussing. For in this performance, Rossini, not content with providing the music, and thus being everywhere in the opera, is actually performing the very demanding tenor role of the Count of Almaviva himself. Thus, in addition to being everywhere he is also going to be present in a strictly limited sense. As an historical note, I should indicate that Rossini did have a tenor voice, and occasionally used it to sing in public performance. That he appears to have had a higher sense of its musical worth than did his contemporaries is something in which we unacknowledged heroes or heroines of the operatic shower cubicle can take delight.

So, Rossini is everywhere, as indicated by the music, and he is present in a quite particular sense in the role of the Count of Almaviva. Surely this will give comfort to our dour commentators! Now they can mutter that Maria, singing Rosina, shouldn't really be given more than tepid applause, while all the applause at the end should go to Rossini, both for his immediate presence in singing Almaviva and for his background presence in having written the whole opera. Again, I hope you would see that this is nonsense. For Rossini to have been a great Almaviva will have required a performance of the whole opera in which the role of Almaviva interacted with the other characters. Almaviva will have helped suggest the character of Rosina into being, by singing with her, or against her, as the scene determines, but producing a tension and that sense of artists sparking off from each other, and becoming more than themselves, which is the characteristic of a truly great performance. And, of course, it is not only Almaviva who will have sparked off Rosina, but it will have been the other way round as well: a Rosina who is on fire in her role will nudge a performing Almaviva into producing a yet more dazzling account of his role. And the public will go nuts at the end, in the degree of the affection they have for, and the enjoyment they have received from, each of the characters, but it will certainly not occur to them to think that they should dampen their enthusiasm for the other characters merely because Rossini was on stage rather than in the conductor's box, or behind the scenes

Well, so far, so obvious. There is, in principle, nothing about praising a creature, for her particular excellence in her living out her creatureliness, which diminishes the honour due to the creator. And when, as in the Incarnation of our Lord and Saviour, the Creator chooses to act out the role of principal protagonist in a drama set entirely within the bounds of creatureliness, the role of the inter-acting creatures is made not more opaque, but at least potentially, more magnificent. The presence of the composer as a character on stage does not upstage his fellow performers, but rather adds brilliance to them.

Now let me move even further into my bizarre Rossini heresy (not to be confused with the recently rehabilitated 'errors' of Rosmini). This is the moment when we finally move from the theatre into life, so where Rossini, instead of being merely a theatrical composer, becomes God, everywhere, and we, instead of being spectators at a theatrical performance, become people invited into becoming live participants in the definitive creation of the definitive masterwork called not Grand Opera but 'Opus Dei' (with apologies to those who seek to patent the whole performance for their group). What this means is that as we accept the invitation and take the show live, so we find ourselves increasingly interacting with the members of the original cast and engaging in a creative multiplying effect. Because of this, it is worthwhile thinking a little bit about our relationship to some of those original cast members.

Of course Rossini singing the role of the Count was unforgettable, and of course his performance is likely to be definitive, something that all subsequent lyric tenors who undertake the role should study to see how it should be done. But it was not definitive in the sense that no one else could ever sing the role again because they wouldn't be him. On the contrary, it was definitive in the sense that it set out the parameters which made it possible for many, many other people to be him. Or, as Someone Else said:

> Truly, truly, I say to you, he who believes in me will also do the
> works that I do; and greater works than these will he do, because

> I go to the Father. Whatever you ask in my name, I will do it, that
> the Father may be glorified in the Son; if you ask anything in my
> name, I will do it.[3]

Again, as an historical aside, Rossini was not a control freak in his
music: he used to listen to the singers he had to hand first and then
actually wrote the arias for them in order to show off their voices
at their best, and his music gives singers plenty of chances to run
around doing their own thing. Rossini would have been the first to
recognise that there are different qualities of tenor voice than the
one his physiognomy gifted him with, and that each should see what
he could make of the role starting with what he had. Empowering
others for flexible imitation is the underlying dynamic of this performance. Just as it is of the performance whose protagonist is the
Incarnate Word.

We are all familiar with the way in which we should learn to perform the role of Rosina in flexible imitation of the way that Maria
first sang it. In fact, we tend to get rather too many sententious
reminders that Maria's role is the same as ours, that we too should
give our consent to the angel, and bring forth the Word into the
world. On the one hand, we tend to insist on the unique and sacred
nature of the performance carried out for us by the composer when
he came onto the scene as protagonist, in a way which obscures the
sense of his performing the role so as to make it possible for us to
create more wonderful and freer performances. And on the other
hand, we have in recent years been taught to insist on the non-
unique and non-sacred nature of the leading lady's role, and how all
the really important bits about her role are ones which we do anyhow, so we don't really need to interact with her. Because of that we
tend to downplay the bits of her role which she was the first to do,
which she created under very specific circumstances, and which,
having been created by her, are marked by her forever.
Please note that these tendencies are just the flip sides of the same
quality of rivalistic thinking. It is as though making the one more
unique and the other more ordinary could really help us understand

---

3   John 14:12-14.

the completely non-rivalistic benevolence which went into the composer choosing to enter into the drama as a character in the first place. It was, after all, he who opted to be on the same level as all the other characters, making the choice not to be more unique and wonderful than they, but interacting with them so that they should all come to share in his unique wonderfulness in ways entirely proper to them. It was the entire performance that he wanted to infuse with his creative spirit.

At this point, to your relief, I would like to let Rossini go back to heaven, where he belongs, so that he can get on with astounding the angels with different ways of getting them to sing different things, at different rhythms, all at the same time. And I would like to step out of my operatic analogy into its primary analogate, which is of course the living performance known as 'Our Salvation'.

I want to start from the end, which is of course where we always start from. We can only start from the end because we can only tell stories whose end we already know. We recount them forwards, but we compose them backwards. If we don't know the end, then it is not clear what story we are starting to tell, and thus whether we have a story at all. The end of this story, the drama of our salvation, is the Assumption into heaven of Our Lady and her Coronation. This is, if you like, the maximum declaration of God's victory in Christ, and a sign of the shape of that victory. Of course, the victory was won, the battle was over, the moment that heaven became forever a human story when Christ ascended to the right hand of God, taking a human nature, meaning a lived-out human story, to be the paradigm of heaven. But the fullness of the shape of that victory only really becomes clear with the Assumption into heaven of Our Lady and her Coronation. That is when it becomes quite luminous not merely that we have been saved, but what it is that has been saved and what it looks like to be saved.

And what it looks like is: creation made new and utterly alive. There was somebody who was entirely part of creation, and she was able to participate in the birth of the new creation in such a way that there was no opposition from her to it, no resistance to the bringing about of the new creation, and, because of this, there is an uninterrupted continuity between creation and new creation. And this means that creation is good! Everything human is, in principle, good, and is to be brought to a good end. The whole of Mary's bodily life, from Immaculate Conception to Dormition and Assumption, was good. Which means that, in principle, our bodily life is as well. There was nothing intrinsically evil about any part of Mary's human life process, from the fully sexual reproduction by which her parents conceived her, to the moment when her biological finitude reached its proper end in her Dormition or death. And so there is nothing intrinsically evil about any part of our human life process. Even though, in our case, the normal strains and stresses of growth and learning get mixed up with our becoming frightened, and so grasping onto too small an identity and resisting being taken into the fullness of creation. In that alone, we are different from Mary.

The difference is between those for whom our involvement in our being created has to reach us first through our being forgiven, so there is a sense of rupture between who we thought we were, where we were trying to head, and who we now find ourselves coming to be, and the person for whom there was no such rupture. Her life was a – no doubt stretched and strained – continuous movement towards being created and coming to share in the life of the Creator, without any resistance or rupture. This does not mean that she did not make mistakes, it does not mean that she did not have to learn, that she did not find things difficult to understand, that she might have been impetuous, or any other number of character traits. But it means that she was, without any sense of comparing herself with anyone else, fully implicated in the adventure of being given to be who she was to become.

So, from the end of the story, the Assumption, we see not only that someone has done something for us, which of course they have – that is Jesus' role – but we also see the beginnings of the living, active shape of what it is like to have that something done for us. But there is more. That the story has come to an end does not mean that it is over and done with, its denizens quietly retired to some celestial Eastbourne[4]. On the contrary, it means that in just the same

---

4   A seaside town on the South Coast of England famous for its retiree population.

way as Jesus, the self-giving lamb, is alive on the altar in heaven, his victory having been forever sealed and his self-giving being made alive for us constantly and given to us, so the sharers in his risen life, the saints, and first among them, Our Lady, are not only part of a story that is now over, but share in all the living story-empowering creativity of the resurrection life being made available for us now.

It is not the case that these are lucky people who are just there on the other side of the great divide, and that we are here, stuck on this side, with, in every generation, the same tragic and heroic choices to make, decisions to stick to and so on, which might just get us allowed in to the other side, about which we can know nothing. The whole point of the resurrection life being already lived by real people with real names and real life histories, a resurrection life which is cast for us in the shape of the image of creation itself in the Assumed Virgin, is that it means that the great divide is not so great, the other side is even now bending towards us, and tends even to interpenetrate our own side, so the adventure is not one of tragic heroism, but is a much safer story than we normally dare to believe. After all, salvation that didn't come with an expansive sense of safety wouldn't be worth much.

Now lest you think that, in giving you this very highly condensed account of the doctrines of the Assumption and the Immaculate Conception, I am merely talking about nice doctrinal symbols, I would like to move back from the end of the story to that mid-point in real lived-out history where we can begin to tell it. And I say mid-point since this story is, as I have mentioned, told from the end. But it is a story that had many dress rehearsals before it was eventually, definitively and triumphantly, performed by Mary of Nazareth. St Luke gives us hints of these dress rehearsals in his use of Greek words reflecting previous attempts at the performance which became definitive in Mary. So the Spirit of God will over-shadow — ἐπισκιάσει — her[5]. The dress rehearsals for this include the Ark of the Covenant being overshadowed by the cherubim — συσκιάζοντες[6], and the Presence overshadowing the Tabernacle

---

5   Luke 1:35.
6   Exod. 25:20.

– ἐπεσκίαζεν[7], in the book of Exodus. But those were the dress rehearsals and, as all dress rehearsals, are in some need of fine-tuning.
For what we learn in Luke is that the Ark and the Tabernacle were
figures of Mary. And not in Luke alone: in the book of Revelation,
the Ark is associated with the woman who is to give birth[8]. This is
much more significant than it seems, because the whole point of
the Holy Place in the centre of the Temple, and indeed of the Tabernacle from earlier times, was that it was through the Holy Place
that God, with his angel hosts, made creation. The Holy Place was
deemed to be outside created matter and the veil surrounding it
was the beginning of material existence. Moving outwards from the
veil there were to be found, in the Temple, the symbols of the days
of creation: the lights, the waters, the animals and so on.

A key moment in the liturgical year would be on the Feast of
Atonement, when the High Priest, considered a temporary incarnation of the divinity, and thus able to worshipped as YHWH, would
come out through the veil, thus symbolising God coming into the
midst of his creation to perform sacrifice for his people. In coming
through the veil, he would vest himself with a seamless tunic made
of the same material as the veil, thus making the, in principle, Invisible One, materially visible. Luke is more than hinting that all these
rites were dress rehearsals for the Real Thing. And the Real Thing
took the form of the Great High Priest, YHWH himself, vesting
himself with flesh to come into materiality and then go up to Jerusalem to perform the real sacrifice. This is the background imagery,
if you like, to what is happening at the Annunciation. Mary is to be
the real Holy of Holies, the real Ark bearing the Covenant, the real
Tabernacle into which Moses could not go. And, because it is the
real High Priest, YHWH himself, the Creator, who is to emerge
from her, no man needs to go into her first in order to come out
again in different robes, as would have been the case with the high
priests of the Temple.

I stress this, since I think it very important in our post-Freud-
ian era to emphasise that conception by a virgin has nothing to do

7 Exod. 40:35.
8 Rev. 11:19-12:1.

with downplaying sex – a fact underlined by the doctrine of the Immaculate Conception, which makes clear that there is nothing intrinsically problematic about sexual generation. The Virginal conception has everything to do with creation out of nothing. And this means that what Mary was being invited to do by the angel was to allow herself to be the link place, the portal, between the Creator out of nothing and the coming into being of everything that is. That is, she was to be in historical fact what the Holy Place had prefigured. It is certainly beyond my imagination to figure what it must have been like for this woman to find that she was becoming the gateway of Creation; that one of the angels which ministered to God before the creation was addressing her, inviting her to become the living portal; that she was to become the incarnation, the permanently contemporary seat, of Wisdom, the feminine figure which accompanied God at the creation of all things; that she would in fact become the one our near worship of whom would correct and fulfil the worship of the goddess whose cult was alive in Jerusalem before Josiah's reformation of the First Temple. This is how Luke says it:

> But she was greatly troubled at the saying, and considered in her mind what sort of greeting this might be.[9]

This is the understatement of the ages!

Of course, there is a biological mystery here: from where did the necessary extra chromosome come which alone enables a male child to be conceived? And the only answer I know is a negative one: not from any human paternity, or from within any human structure of desire, parentage, male possessiveness, need to control or propagate. Rather it came in the same way that Creation comes: as something out of nothing. But to be fixated on the biological mystery, which seems to have been of little concern to the ancient authors, is to miss the point of what Mary is being asked to live out. She is living out virgin creation, new, fecund, fresh, ripe with constantly birthing possibilities, not run by men, not tied down into property or chattelage. And instead of doing so in the midst of a

---

9   Luke 1:29.

huge and heavy sacred structure, such as the Temple, she is doing so as a living human being, who needs protection in her vulnerability, as is shown when Joseph offers her covering from the potential honour-killing which could easily have been the lot of an unwed mother.

So, here we have the Holy Place made suddenly alive as the Creator prepares to vest himself with flesh. In the non-canonical Protoevangelion of St James, Mary is depicted as being involved in weaving the veil of the Temple when the angel comes to her for the Annunciation. However historically inaccurate this may be in terms of where Mary was actually living, it shows at least that the symbolism was well understood at the time: what Mary was doing in the nine months of her pregnancy was in fact weaving the veil of flesh which would enable us to see YHWH come into the world. But it is from *her* flesh that she was weaving, and it is her flesh that is thus inextricably caught up with the making new of all things.

This lived-out creative performance by Mary continues when she arises and goes to visit her cousin Elizabeth. When Elizabeth heard her greeting, John the Baptist leaped for joy in her womb. The verb in Greek is ἐσκίρτησεν and it appears in two significant places: it is the same verb which, in Hebrew, describes David dancing about, skipping (מְרַקֵּד), before the Ark in 1 Chronicles 15. The arrival of the Ark was greeted with great shouts, and the verb ἀναφωνέω is used of both the Levites greeting the Ark and Elizabeth greeting her cousin. Even more significantly, the same Greek word, σκιρτάω to leap about, appears in Malachi 3:20 (4:2) where the gender of the protagonist is normally mistranslated but should be:

> 'But for you who fear my name the sun of righteousness shall rise, with healing in *her* wings. You shall go forth leaping (σκιρτήσετε) like calves from the stall.'

Now please notice what has happened in Luke's Gospel: what had been cultic objects, used for occasional symbolic acts, have become fulfilled by someone, Mary, beginning to live out, slowly, painstakingly, in time, what those cultic objects had been pointing to. What Luke is showing is how Creation out of nothing is becoming history, a real performed, lived-out history, over time. And it is this real, performed, lived-out history over time, soon to be opened out through her son's protagonism so that we may all become its performers and livers-out, which will itself be the crowning perfection of Creation.

Thus we have in Luke's Gospel, as in the others, moments of tension between Mary and Jesus, times when she does not understand, times when she is anxious, times when she has to tuck things away until what they mean can become clearer. And yet this space that includes learning, tension and interaction is the space within which Wisdom, who gives form to creation, allowed Jesus to grow up in Wisdom and in stature. Please notice that these moments of tension, of misunderstanding and so on, are not, as it were, embarrassing lapses in what ought to have been a perfectly uninterrupted motherhood, lapses put in so as to test our faith in the Immaculate Conception. They are parts of the creative tensions of the performance, which was being brought into being by real human beings over time; by real human beings interacting with each other.

It is the whole of that interactive performance which is made alive for us as something *for us*, as something we can be relieved by, not stressed out by. It means that we can reconsider, to give but one example, that very particular fleshly human reality: the bodily eyes of a mother whose expression over time is moulded by her interaction with her child, being patient when the child is impatient, alarmed when the child is over-confident, tired of the child's mewling and puking, stretched and aged by the whole business of caring at all. There is here all the tension that is proper to Wisdom accompanying creation and making of creation a lived story. And we can consider that it is fully appropriate for us to see all the grace of God available for us through exactly those same time-enriched eyes, which are entirely specific to a woman. Incarnation without living interaction wouldn't be incarnation, and the living interaction then becomes, very properly, part of what the incarnation gives us.

I think this is brought out specifically by John in his treatment of the relationship between Jesus and Mary. In John, Jesus does not talk about 'Our Father' as though he has a father in common with any other human. He talks about 'My Father' or 'The Father'. It is only at the end of the Gospel, after the Resurrection, that he becomes inclusive in his language, saying to Mary Magdalene:

> 'Do not hold me, for I have not yet ascended to the Father; but go to my brethren and say to them, I am ascending to my Father and your Father, to my God and your God.'[10]

In other words, John seems to be pointing to a sense in which, until Jesus has gone to his death, and then, in his Ascension, created that new space which is death-lived-in-as-moot-for-humans, the real paternity of his Father couldn't yet be shared in by others. It is in his going to death that he makes available that paternity.

It is also curious that in John's Gospel, although the Evangelist is happy to refer to Mary, Jesus' mother, as 'his mother', Jesus himself never does. When he addresses her, it is in the seemingly formal vocative – γύναι – 'woman!'. This is the term he uses at Cana[11], and from the Cross[12]. And I would like to suggest that, as usual, John is giving us more than seems to be the case. It is as though until Jesus' death, Mary is still in gestation of him, and not giving him birth, but that in his dying, he gives her, in the person of the beloved disciple, a son, the first of many brothers, and names her *that disciple's* mother for the first time. The stretching effect of the interaction between Jesus, Mary, the disciples and the circumstances of his death is seen as opening up both a new shape to paternity and a new shape to maternity, and this is seen as something creative and deliberate[13].

What I particularly like about this, is that it does seem to make sense of the oddity of the Miracle at Cana. For there, Mary, off her own bat, and without anyone asking her to intervene, points out to Jesus that 'they have no wine'. Jesus appears to rebuke her for

10 John 20:17.
11 John 2:4.
12 John 19:26.
13 Tina Beattie pointed out to me that some commentators have seen in John's use of γύναι a sign that Jesus is designating his mother as Eve, the original woman. This would mean that from the Cross he is the new Adam designating Mary as the new Eve, the mother of all the living.

jumping the gun, as though she is pushing him into doing something before he is ready for it:

'What have you to do with me? My hour has not yet come.'

However, she is not put off, and tells the servants to do whatever Jesus would tell them, which they duly do. I have long been curious as to why Jesus thought Mary was jumping the gun here, in what is solemnly reported as the first of the signs he worked. And there may be a clue in the book of the prophet Isaiah. As Margaret Barker has pointed out, the Hebrew text of the Qumran manuscript of Isaiah 7:11, the earliest version which we have extant, and one contemporary with Christ, reads not, as the (later) Masoretic text has it: 'ask a sign of the Lord your God' but, with one letter's difference: 'ask a sign from the Mother of the Lord your God'. We may have here a not-yet censored relic from the religion of the First Temple.

This does at least suggest a reason why Jesus should have thought that Mary was jumping the gun. No one had asked her to produce a sign, and yet there she was trying to get her son to produce one. And Jesus' hour – which, in John, means the hour of his death – had not yet come. Might it not be that it is only in his creatively occupying the space of death, when he will bequeath to her the first of many disciples who will call her mother, that she will properly be called 'the Mother of the Lord your God', and thus one who can properly be approached to ask for signs? It is of course typical of the sort of lived performance that I have been talking about, that the reality of the abundance and the fullness of what was to be given exceeded its proper place in what the characters imagined to be the script, and came rushing out anyhow, giving even more than the author intended.

There is a point here about the shape of what Jesus was bequeathing to us in his going to his death. He was making available the paternity of God as something that could be shared in by others who were not he, but would be becoming he over time – hence the ease with which he speaks of his 'brethren' after his Resurrection. But this paternity was not simply something celestial and removed. It did also include the being inducted into a family, a living family of faith, with a real woman who is to be mother of all beloved disciples, a motherhood that is a proper part of the making available for us the celestial paternity.

It is this element of family I would like to bring out. The interactions in the Gospel story show that there was something rumbustious, slightly out of control, about the family relationships being described. And this I think is a good and proper part of our life in the Church. No matter how po-faced and sententious, ordered and obedient, are the dreams of some ecclesiastical males, Mary seems to have a centre of gravity all of her own, one which isn't pulled in by, and submissive to, ecclesiastical constructs of what her Son would want. And God persists in gifting us with that tension, that sense of more than one centre of gravity as a relief and a freedom from the consequences of our own monistic, univocal and frightened visions of what is acceptable.

This I think is worth attending to: the 'mono' in monotheism can have at least two valencies. One of them is restrictive, zealously hygienic let us say, because God is in rivalry with other gods and needs everything to be narrowed down and made more exact, since the danger of idolatry is everywhere. The other is not in rivalry with anything at all, and is seriously concerned that we will not have enough joy and freedom and happiness unless we are set free from our fear of death and enabled to dare to participate in the life of the Creator. And the more signs of our being loved and encouraged and enabled to belong we can get, the merrier. It is this rumbustiousness of God, whose monotheism is decidedly unhygienic, whose oneness is nothing at all like our monisms, trying to get through to us that we are loved, which means that the shape of the life we are being welcomed into tends to spill over into our world through the prayers and protagonisms of the saints and, chief among them, of course, the portal of the new creation herself, Our Blessed Mother.

So, as we turn over the next few days to matters of ethics in the light of Mary's hymn of praise, may I ask you to remember that non-monistic rumbustiousness whose different centres of gravity save us from our univocal pictures of God – a rumbustiousness which is kept so much better alive when we are dwellers not in ideological cages, but in a hugely extended family household of spacious dwelling places, and where the heroism and the struggle for the good which we must learn can never entirely swallow the sensation that we are safe, that we are held, that there are others reaching towards us and that, whatever may be the immediate appearances, we are in much more of a playground and much less of a war zone than we are inclined to think. Maybe then we will be making room for *Mary*'s soul to magnify the Lord.

Recommended reading:

Tina Beattie: *God's Mother, Eve's Advocate* (London, Continuum, 2002)

Tina Beattie: *New Catholic Feminism: Theology and Theory* (London, Routledge, 2006)

Charlene Spretnak: *Missing Mary* (New York, Palgrave Macmillan, 2004)

Margaret Barker: *The Great High Priest* (London, T&T Clark/ Continuum, 2003)

Margaret Barker: *Temple Theology: An Introduction* (London, SPCK, 2004)

ARCIC: *Mary, Grace and Hope in Christ: An Agreed Statement* (Harrisburg/London, Morehouse/Continuum, 2005)

CHAPTER 3

Wrath and the gay question:

on not being afraid, and its ecclesial shape

I would like to start by comparing two stories[1]. The second, just to show catholicity of taste, and in case there are any adults present, will be Shakespeare's *The Merchant of Venice*; but the first is DreamWorks' 2005 film, *Shark Tale*. Lenny is a great white shark who happens to be a vegetarian. His brother Frankie is a perfectly normal, meat-eating shark. Their father Lino is the mob boss of the sharks, who prowl around the reef for food. Having a vegetarian son would be a very serious blow to Lino's mob boss prowess and family values, and his vegetarian son is understandably not keen to 'come out' to him. Alas, Frankie, the red-blooded, meat-eating brother, is killed when an anchor, casually dropped from above by a ship, hits him on the head. Now Lenny has to live up to all his father's expectations, which he can't do since he is a vegetarian and wants to dress up as a dolphin. So he escapes to the reef, whose inhabitants are initially terrified of him, as they are of all sharks. However, he is eventually befriended by the fish he is supposed to eat, and together they concoct a plan to ward off Lenny's marauding relatives. You will be glad to hear that all ends happily: Lino is eventually brought to a place where he can accept his son as a vegetarian and tell him that he loves him however he is, and Lenny is able to get a job at the swim-by whale wash, along with all the non-carnivorous fish, turtles and the like. Perks of this job include both being able to dress

---

1   This chapter was born as a talk originally prepared for the Salisbury Diocese Clergy Conference in July 2006, and for Mount St Agnes Theological Center for Women, Baltimore, in October 2006.

up as a dolphin and to wear what looked to this viewer suspiciously like a Village People uniform to hold his barnacle-scrubbing gear.

I must say that I was pretty stunned, when I saw this film, at how brazen it is. For a gay man, it all seemed astoundingly obvious. I mean, *puhleeeze*: a vegetarian shark, as vivid an illustration of *contra natura* as you can get; his fear of 'coming out'; a moronically macho father who wouldn't accept him; the son wanting to act like a dolphin, and dressing up like the Village People; and the overall message that 'It's OK to be different, and your daddy will eventually get round to liking you'. All this seemed to be a classic example of modern American, preachy advocacy. We all know that Tinky Winky from the *Teletubbies*, and *SpongeBob SquarePants'* friend, Patrick the Starfish, have been denounced by the usual suspects as subversive, crypto-gay characters, further assaults on the psyche of America's children. What amazed me was not that *Shark Tale* suffered the same fate, which eventually it did, but that its detractors took so long to point out something which was so blatantly obvious. The overall story line seemed to me to be 'It's OK to be different, and being a vegetarian shark or, for that matter, a gay son, is just a form of being different, and you too can be a hero and end up being accepted by your family'.

So far, so good. It sounds as though the film has the right sort of storyline to fit in with a group of people who are facing issues of 'living with difference', or 'tolerance and diversity'. But now I would like to turn to my other story, *The Merchant of Venice*, and, although there is in *Shark Tale* an elderly Jewish shark[2], called Don Feinberg, whose voice-over is done by Peter Falk of *Columbo* fame, he is not, as it happens, the link around which my comparison works.

Let us turn to Shylock's famous speech from Act III Scene 1 of *The Merchant of Venice*:

> Hath not a Jew eyes? Hath not a Jew hands, organs, dimensions,
> senses, affections, passions; fed with
> the same food, hurt with the same weapons, subject
> to the same diseases, heal'd by the same means

---

2   I guess this figure was included so that DreamWorks couldn't be accused of Italian Mafia stereotypes.

> warm'd and cool'd by the same winter and summer
> as a Christian is? If you prick us, do we not bleed?
> If you tickle us, do we not laugh? If you poison us,
> do we not die? And if you wrong us, shall we not revenge?
> If we are like you in the rest, we will resemble you in that.

In a romantic presentation of Shakespeare, we could imagine this as another moment of preachy advocacy, as the moment when Shylock gets to stand up in front of the Doge and say 'Yes, I am a vegetarian shark, and you know, that's a tough thing to be; we have a tough time too, our own form of heroism, and why can't you learn to accept us and live with difference?' But, of course, Shakespeare is not a romantic[3] and, although our romantic expectations can deceive us into not noticing what Shylock does say, he does in fact say exactly the opposite of this. What he says, and repeats, and repeats is, in effect 'I am the same as you, exactly the same as you'. And he is roundly ignored by all the other characters for whom his 'difference' is very important.

Shakespeare, however, agrees with Shylock, even to the point where Portia has to have Shylock identify himself, for to the untrained eye he looks just like any other Venetian[4]. Shakespeare underlines, and repeats and repeats that all the people in the play are obsessed with money, all their values entirely materialistic. Their every prospect of happiness or sadness, even their understanding of marriage and of having children, is dependent on their relation to capital, theirs or their patrons'; to whether their ships come in, or are wrecked by storms; to what we would call the vagaries of the market. Every single feature which they, and the mediaeval stereotype into which they buy so mercilessly, attribute to the figure of the Jew, is a dominant feature of their own lives. If there is any distinction at all between Shylock and the other characters, it is that Shylock is almost autistically honest and straightforward in calling a spade a spade, and is too little sophisticated to be able to cope with

---

3 My reading of *The Merchant of Venice* is entirely dependent on that of René Girard in 'To entrap the wisest', which can be found in Chapter 28 of *A Theatre of Envy: William Shakespeare* (New York, OUP, 1991).

4 'Which is the merchant here, and which is the Jew?' Act IV Scene 1.

the elegant guile and hypocrisy of the other Venetians who run rings round him.

I would like to suggest in fact that Shakespeare's emphasis on sameness, rather than DreamWorks' emphasis on difference, is the more profitable route for us to pursue in looking at the gay question in our Church and our society now. For what Shakespeare suggests is that the insistence on difference is a way of blinding those who insist on it to what is really going on. Think of it this way: if the Venetians didn't have someone like Shylock, onto whose tiny difference from themselves they could project all the things that were most awful about their society, they might have to think about who *they* were, what really ran them, what 'being Christian' really meant (as opposed to merely 'not Jewish'), what 'the quality of mercy' really meant (rather than a feat of cruel forensic prestidigitation conducted in drag), how their lives had become the symptom of an economic system characterised by the ever-present threat of a wrath which they could only temporarily escape by playfully, and hurtfully, coming up with someone whose difference they could hate.

In other words, the emphasis on 'difference' is part of a conjuring trick, the keeping alive of a delusion, under cover of which forces that are as destructive of Christians as of Jews work out their ways. This, I think, is part of the sadness which underlies the play, a sadness announced by Antonio from the first line of Act I[5]. It would have been comparatively easy for Shakespeare to play to the mediaeval caricature of the Jew. Another possibility would have been for him to turn the caricature on its head, making Shylock a romantic hero, as DreamWorks did with Lenny. Instead, Shakespeare does something altogether less visible, less entertaining, and more suggestive of truthfulness. He shows how a mechanism of projection works in creating a scapegoat, choosing someone who is no better, but no worse, than the other characters in the play, and that the only result of this, apart from making life miserable for poor Shylock, is to blind everyone to their similarity with him, with the result that the apparent contentment of their happy ending is merely a

---

5   'In sooth, I know not why I am so sad ...' Act I Scene 1.

cosmetic putting-off of dealing with what is really running, and ruining, them all – a guarantee against them ever growing up and
becoming responsible.

What I would like to do now is to explore the workings of whatever it is that is going on in the background, whatever it is that is
swirling around in the Venetian society of the play, and in our own
society, and which tempts us to come up with 'differences' so as
to create temporary shelters of identity, violence and 'playfulness'
by contrast with them. In other words, I want to explore with you
what I call the workings of 'wrath'. In doing this, I want to bring
into polite adult discussion something which is not normally allowed there, but is relegated to the backroom of fundamentalist
discourse, where its misuse is a mirror image of its exclusion from
enlightened discourse.

In enlightened discourse, there is, of course, no 'wrath' in any
theological or anthropological sense. There is progress, and development, and, on the way, there is conflict. Conflict is shown as
something painful, but necessary: steps on the way towards the next
phase, no omelettes without breaking eggs, and similar sentiments.
In fundamentalist discourse, that conflict and those 'steps on the
way to the next phase' are personally and cosmically significant, and
victory and defeat in them are part of the mysterious workings of a
divinity, certainly something far greater and more important than
anything the 'wise' and 'enlightened' of this generation could know
about. Part of the attraction of fundamentalist discourse, and this
fundamentalism can be Christian, Jewish, Muslim, Hindu, Marxist
or secularist, is the way it allows partially self-selecting 'outsiders'
from mainstream culture (and we are all such partially self-selecting 'outsiders' now) to see themselves as secret 'insiders' with a
direct line in to What's Really Going On.

For the enlightened, it is perfectly obvious that there is no violence in God, if there is a God at all; while, for the fundamentalist,
the violence is always associated with God, directly, or through
those charged with interpreting 'His' (and it usually is *His*) message.
In fact, without the violence there would be no sign of God's activity in the world, which effectively means there would be no God.

What I would like to do is rescue the notion of wrath by attempting to show how there is indeed no violence in God, but that the phenomenon which religious language has described as 'wrath' is very real, and worth taking seriously. Not only that, but it is rather important for our contemporary ability to live the Gospel that we overcome the schism between the enlightened and the fundamentalist, two positions which are, in my view, very much enemy twins, by recovering a sense of the anthropological effect in our midst of the covenant of peace to which the Scriptures refer[6]. By recovering, if you like, the ecclesial shape of Christ making his covenant for us and enabling us not to be afraid.

There seems to be something odd going on when the same person, Jesus, both promises his followers:

> 'Peace I leave with you; my peace I give to you; not as the world gives do I give to you.'[7]

And yet says:

> 'Do not think that I have come to bring peace on earth; I have not come to bring peace, but a sword. For I have come to set a man against his father, and a daughter against her mother, and a daughter-in-law against her mother-in-law; and a man's foes will be those of his own household.'[8]

These latter verses would have made great sense to Shylock, one would have thought, when his daughter ran off with a Christian, taking with her a good deal of her father's money. Or consider these verses from the book of Revelation:

> Then the kings of the earth and the great men and the generals and the rich and the strong, and every one, slave and free, hid in the caves and among the rocks of the mountains, calling to the mountains and rocks, 'Fall on us and hide us from the face of him who is seated on the throne, and from the wrath of the Lamb; for

---

6   Isa. 54:10, Ezek. 34:25 and 37:26.
7   John 14:27.
8   Matt. 10:34-36 cf. Luke 12:51.

the great day of their wrath has come, and who can stand before it?'[9]

I would like to trace with you the way in which there is both no violence in Christ, and yet the result of his coming includes violence; to trace the process by which 'the wrath of God', something literally attributed to the divinity in parts of the Hebrew Scriptures, becomes the anthropological reality known to Paul as 'wrath', and can even be referred to as 'the wrath of the Lamb'.

Let me give you some background: in a classic lynch murder, such as that described in Joshua 7, where 'all Israel' gathers against Achan and 'stoned him with stones', the wrath of God is simply, and straightforwardly, associated with the group's loss of morale, and the subsequent build up to anger which turns them into a lynch mob. First, the anger of God is detected in the collapse of morale, the melting hearts, of the sons of Israel who have just undergone a minor military defeat. So God provides Joshua with a lottery to determine at whose door responsibility for the defeat should be laid. When the lottery achieves its purpose of finding a suitable culprit, all Israel discharges stones, murdering Achan. In their very act of ganging up together, unanimously, against poor Achan, of whose guilt they convince themselves through the liturgical mechanism of the lottery, they create peace among themselves. And, in that very moment when their stones are all discharged, then 'the Lord turned from his burning anger'[10]. Of course he did: the shifting patterns of fear and mutual recrimination which had riven the people have been overcome by their triumphant and enthusiastic unanimity. From their perspective, it feels as though 'peace has been given them'. This is, in fact, peace in the way the world gives it, the peace which comes from unanimity in righteous hatred of an evildoer. But it is misperceived by the participants as peace flowing from the divinity thanks to the right sacrifice having been offered.

The power of this experience is very real, and can still be detected when human lynching has found its substitute in animal sacrifice. It appears that the role of the priest in early forms of atonement

9   Rev. 6:15-17.
10 Josh. 7:26.

sacrifice was to cover the participants with the blood of the animal; it was as though the blood sprinkled over them wove a huge protective covering against wrath. The Hebrew letters כָּפַר from which we get 'Yom Kippur' and our word 'atonement', designate a form of covering. It does not take a huge stretch of the imagination to see that the freedom from wrath which came with the successful production of unanimity in the murdering of a victim, and which probably involved the participants being splattered with blood, could then be reproduced liturgically. The priest slaughters the animal, sacrificing it to the divinity, and then sprinkles the blood over the people, unanimously gathered to receive the fruits of the sacrifice. In the liturgical unanimity that occurs under the cover of the blood, the assuaging of the wrath is remembered and made newly present.

Interestingly, Israel does not seem to have stuck only with this model of sacrifice, but also had the very special Day of Atonement sacrifice, where it was YHWH himself, through the High Priest, acting 'in personam Yahveh', who offered his own blood, symbolized by a lamb, for the people, who were then covered with it, this blood being taken to restore Creation from the various forms of ensnarlments with which humans had distorted it. Here we begin to glimpse the notion of the victim performing the sacrifice for the people which will be brought to fulfilment in the New Testament.

When we get to the New Testament, we see that the question of wrath is very much on people's minds. John the Baptist assumes that the coming of Jesus is to produce wrath, since he tells the Pharisees and Sadducees who come to be baptised:

> 'You brood of vipers! Who warned you to flee from the wrath to come?'[11]

He then goes on to compare what he is doing with what he imagines Jesus is going to do, which will be a baptism with the Holy Spirit and with fire:

---

11 Matt. 3:7.

'His winnowing fork is in his hand, and he will clear his threshing
floor and gather his wheat into the granary, but the chaff he will
burn with unquenchable fire.'[12]

And yet, curiously, when Jesus does come, he doesn't seem to act in
the way that John thinks he is going to. In fact he is so little wrathful
in his appearance that John, from prison, sends to ask:

'Are you he who is to come, or shall we look for another?'[13]

Yet Jesus *does* warn that the effect of his mission *is* going to be to
produce wrath, in the passage I have already quoted to you. And he
then gives himself to the sacrificial mechanism, in a way which the
Gospel writers point to as being the way proper to the great High
Priest, and becomes the lamb of sacrifice. In fact, he reverses the
normal human sacrificial system which started with human sacrifice and is later modified to work with animal substitutes. Jesus, by
contrast, substitutes himself for the lamb, portions of whose body
were handed out to the priests; and thus, by putting a human back
at the centre of the sacrificial system, he reveals it for what it is: a
murder.

Now, here is the curious thing: it looks for all the world as though
Jesus is simply fitting into the ancient world's views about sacrifice
and wrath but, in fact, he is doing exactly the reverse. Because he
is giving himself to this being murdered, and he has done nothing
wrong, he brings about an entirely new way to be free from wrath.
This is not the way we saw with Achan, where the temporary freedom from wrath comes with the outbreak of unanimous violence
that creates singleness of heart among the group. What Jesus has
done, by substituting himself for the victim at the centre of the
lynch sacrifice, is to make it possible for those who perceive his innocence to realise what it is in which they have been involved (and
agreeing to drink his blood presupposes a recognition of this complicity). These then begin to have their identity given them not by
the group over against the victim, but by the self-giving victim who
is undoing the unanimity of the group. This means that from then on

12 Matt. 3:12.
13 Matt. 11:3.

they never again have to be involved in sacrifices, sacrificial mechanisms and all the games of 'wrath' which every culture throws up. They will be learning to walk away from all that, undergoing being given the peace that the world does not give.

So there is no wrath at all in what Jesus is doing. He understands perfectly well that there is no wrath in the Father, and yet that 'wrath' is a very real anthropological reality, whose cup he will drink to its dregs. His Passion consists, in fact, of his moving slowly, obediently, and deliberately into the place of shame, the place of wrath, and doing so freely and without provoking it. However, from the perspective of the wrathful, that is, of all of us run by the mechanisms of identity building, peace building, unanimity building 'over against' another, Jesus has done something terrible. Exactly as he warned. He has plunged us into irresoluble wrath. Because he has made it impossible for us ever really to believe in what we are doing when we sacrifice, when we shore up our social belonging against some other. All our desperate attempts to continue doing that are revealed to be what they are: just so much angry frustration, going nowhere at all, spinning the wheels of futility.

The reason is this: the moment we perceive that the one occupying the central space in our system of creating and shoring up meaning is actually innocent – that he actually gave himself to be in that space, then all our sacred mechanisms for shoring up law and order, sacred differences and so forth, are revealed to be the fruits of an enormous self-deception. The whole world of the sacred totters, tumbles and falls if we see that this human being is just like us. He came to occupy the place of the sacrificial victim entirely freely, voluntarily and without any taint of being 'run' by, or beholden to, the sacrificial system. That is, he is one who was without sin. This human being was doing something for us *even while we were so locked into a sacrificial way of thinking and behaviour that we couldn't possibly have understood what he was doing for us, let alone asked him to do it*. The world of the sacred totters and falls because when we see someone who is like us doing that for us, and realise what has been done, the shape that our realisation takes is our moving away from ever being involved in such things again.

Now what is terrible about this is that it makes it impossible for us really to bring about *with a good conscience* any of the sacred resolutions, the sacrificial decisions which brought us, and bring all societies, comparative peace and order. The game is up. And so human desire, rivalry and competition, which had previously been kept in some sort of check by a system of prohibitions, rituals, sacrifices and myths, lest human groups collapse in perpetual and irresoluble mutual vengeance, can no longer be controlled in this way. This is the sense in which Jesus' coming brings not peace to the earth, but a sword and division. All the sacred structures which hold groups together start to collapse, because desire has been un-leashed. So the sacred bonds within families are weakened; different generations will be run by different worlds and give their loyalty to different and incompatible causes, the pattern of desire constantly shifting. All, in fact, will be afloat on a sea of wrath, because the traditional means to curb wrath, the creation by sacrifice of spaces of temporary peace within the group, has been undone forever. The only alternative is to undergo the forgiveness which comes from the lamb, and start to find oneself recreated from within by a peace which is not from this world, and involves learning how to resist the evil *one* by not resisting evil. This means: you effectively resist, have no part in, the structures and flows of desire which are syn-onymous with the prince of this world, that is to say with the world of wrath, only by refusing to acquire an identity over against evil-done-to you.

I hope you can see now why I love the image of the 'wrath of the lamb'. There is the lamb, permanently and forever standing alive, as one slain, on the altar in heaven, his blood given to us as we accept this purely peaceful self-giving and allow ourselves to be moved out of the whole 'old creation' dominated by wrath. But the fact that this peaceful, life-giving lamb is standing there, slain, has effectively pulled the plug on the whole system of social order. It offers people a choice, one which most of us do not want to make: follow the lamb, and so become liable to be treated as the lamb was treated. Or, resist what the lamb has revealed and so be involved in ever-increasing wrath without the means of handling it. But, from then on, everything would be in flux, no order would hold, until the end of time. And the new Jerusalem coming down is coming down from heaven, without a Temple, with nothing of the old sacred in it, because the light of the lamb, standing in the place of, and rendering pointless, all sacrifice, is everywhere. This new Jerusalem is coming down in the midst of the overthrow, collapse and vanity of all kingdoms, empires, powers and rule.

So, to recapitulate: Jesus reveals that there is no wrath in God, but the effect and the shape of his coming opens up the possibilities of wrath for those who do not receive him in ways which could not be imagined. The workings of 'wrath' become a measurable, detectable, anthropological reality as the innocent lamb exposes to us our own responsibility for what we, deceived by the hallucinations of our own mob behaviour, thought of as the anger of a divinity.

Paul, of course, takes this even further. He comes to the question of wrath from a very particular perspective. He had been an agent of wrath in the way he belonged to the party of the Pharisees. He knew the way in which zeal for the Law had made of him an enemy of God, because God had revealed himself to him as the One whom he was persecuting. So it is not surprising that he, in his treatment of the Law, is eager to point out the anthropology of wrath. The way wrath works is to get people to set themselves up with an airtight system of goodness. In a system of goodness, the Law (whatever form it takes) becomes a way of creating difference. It enables you to know how to be 'in' by comparing yourself with those who are 'out'. The more zealous you are, the clearer will be your sense of the boundaries of your group and, of course, the narrower and more incorrigible your righteousness will become.

Jesus notoriously had refused these boundaries of in and out. He had in fact faced down the party within Hebrew religion that was tending towards the creation of an ever more zealous and textual religion based on purity and difference; instead, he recovered many of the traditions of more ancient Hebrew voices which had fought against that. Finally, he had substituted his body for the Temple, thus fulfilling the Law and making it moot for ever. For anyone at all with any sense of the need to maintain a system of goodness, this was a disaster. It brought down any system of goodness forever. It would make of goodness something given by the Holy Spirit without any of the comforting crutches of sacred separations. And Saul had to stop it.

One of the amazing insights which he learned as a result of his conversion from 'fiercely loyal bulwark of the system of goodness and differences' to 'apostle of the new creation emerging in the midst of the collapse of all differences' – and that is what 'apostle to the Gentiles' effectively means – was the way in which belonging to a system of goodness destroys you. It tells you to love your neighbour as yourself, but then it creates a whole class of neighbours who aren't really neighbours: people who are cursed through not obeying the law, and thus become irredeemably different. This means that, with the best will in the world, you find yourself caught in a double bind: you must love, but you must hate in order to love. Because of this you are divided against yourself and find yourself unable to do the good that you know you should do, but find yourself instead doing evil things that you should not do, but which the system of goodness actually drives you to do. In other words, rather than your being a free adherent of a system of goodness, the system of goodness runs you to produce wrath.

You can imagine then the passion of this former 'righteously innocent' perpetrator of wrath, as he tries to persuade those who might be tempted to go down the route of reinforcing the system of goodness: the game's over! And you can imagine why, when they will not accept that Christ has become the curse of the law, and thus that the game which ran the system of goodness has been shown up, that he regards them as retrenching into a system of goodness, and thus becoming ever more fully denizens of wrath. But please, this is not Paul the convert becoming anti-semitic, or even anti-nomian. It is the person who realises that systems of goodness are all the fruit of, and agents of, wrath, and that only the Crucified One can get us out of wrath, and only the Spirit which he gave can take us into the New Creation.

I hope it is perfectly obvious that we are acquiring again in our modern world a sense of what 'wrath' is about. And it also needs very few reminders in this company that one of the symptoms of 'wrath' in our world, and it is indeed only one of the symptoms, and a comparatively unimportant one at that, is the emergence in the midst of all of our societies, whether we like it or not, of the gay question.

It is also obvious that one of the ways of dealing with this is to attempt to come up with some formula such as: 'Look, we're discovering that people we used to regard as weird and even evil are just different. But, since they are functional to the way modern society works, just as we are, let us learn to live with our difference.' The key phrase here is: 'they are functional to the way modern society works, just as we are'. And this means that it is modern society, its structures of desire and survival, which get to run the show, because it is modern social structures, and their financial and corporate systems, which get to determine what 'likeness' is. This means the 'living with difference' is not really living with difference at all; it is really living with a sameness dictated by certain patterns of desire. And part of the way we protect ourselves against having to take seriously whether these patterns of desire really come from God, or are the pomps and splendours of this world, is by having decorative 'difference' in the midst of all this sameness, and feeling proud of ourselves for being so broad-minded.

Well, I want to say: 'No!' I am not at all interested in being given a post-modern identity that is in fact merely functional to the particular shape of wrath in our time. I am interested in becoming a son and heir to the whole of Creation through the arduous discovery of my likeness with my sisters and brothers. I understand how it is one of the delusions of wrath that it is able to point to the growing visibility and public and legal acceptability of gay people and their lives and relationships, and see this as an attack on the 'family' and the 'divinely given order of society'. But it *is* a delusion of wrath, like that of the Venetians against Shylock, because all it does is disguise from all of us quite how much the unleashing of desire, which continues apace in our world –our capitalist, globalising, technological world – does in fact subvert from within and change every form of relationship, including family relationships. It disguises from us how much we are all already run by these things, and how arduous it is for any of us to receive holiness of life, of desire, and of relationships, in the midst of all this. And it sets things up for us to fight about this, rather than to help each other out of the hole.

So here, rather then defend anything, I would like to be tentatively vulnerable about my pursuit of becoming a son and heir in the midst of all this wrath. And I want to do this by indicating that there is still something, it seems to me, which eludes us in all our discussions about the gay question. It is what I call the shape of Christian story as discovered from within by lesbian and gay people, and as able to be shared and recognised to be a pattern of story that is the work of the Holy Spirit.

Let me try and explain what I mean. Over the last century or so, in English speaking countries, gay men and lesbian women have started to find a voice. I do not mean only a political voice, I mean a story-telling voice. By a story-telling voice, I mean one which other people have been able to vibrate with from within, even when they have not had the same experiences or got the words for it. Not for nothing did Lord Alfred Douglas' phrase 'the Love that dares not speak its name' travel so well. Something like this, it seems to me, was at work in the public reception of the film *Brokeback Mountain*. Daniel Mendelsohn, in the *New York Review of Books,* rightly insisted, against mainstream media attempts to 'de-gay' the film, that this is first and foremost a specifically 'gay' film, since the overarching reality of it was the closet which destroyed the lives of all it touched. Yet, having conceded that, there were elements of the film with which anyone could vibrate: I think specifically of the tragedy of Ennis Del Mar's paralysed inability to dare to act on his love in any meaningful way, and therefore his inability to dare to live, whatever the consequences. This sort of paralysis is surely not gay-specific, even if the setting which made it available in the film was entirely so.

The real challenge, it seems to me, is not for gay people to learn to tell a different story, but to find ourselves able to tell the same story, the Christian story, which is the deepest and most extraordinary narrative available to us in any culture, and which is the story of living trapped by desire in an illusion, finding oneself torn through the consequences of that illusion, and being brought to a place of peace and new life through that. It is the story of *Don Quijote*, of *A Winter's Tale*, of Raskolnikov, of Alyosha Karamazov.

For far too long, and it is not in any way surprising, gay and lesbi-an people have had to scrabble about for elements of story floating around, since the one story that was not available and open to us was the Christian one. The Christian story was specifically presented to us as one within which we could only inscribe ourselves by agreeing to mutilate our souls. I think of how sad so many gay literary stories seem, apparently wedded to the morbid, the dark, the faux hero-ism of a romanticised classical past, the dignity and love brought out in the shadow of death in many AIDS novels so often refusing interruption by grace. The quirkiness of desire, its double-binds and contradictions are well brought out, but how little is there of a sto-rytelling which lifts the soul on wings.

This is scarcely surprising. Famously, black people are born into and brought up by families composed of black people, Muslims into families composed of Muslims, Tagalog speakers into families comprised of people who speak Tagalog. So, whether those groups are majority groups or minority groups in any particular situation, their common stories are usually grown into as a normal part of infancy and childhood. Gay people are one of the very few minori-ties to be born into and brought up by families who can offer them no tribal song which makes any sense to them. So, while being gay does not appear to be learned behaviour, receiving the beginnings of an identity, becoming a viable and a truthful storyteller or be-ing socialised into a capacity for relationships, these indeed have to be learned from other sources, often sources which include ele-ments of exile, shame and having to learn to imagine the possible where all the voices you most respect are insisting that what you are looking for is something impossible, that what you are is some-thing that is not. Harry Potter had the comfort of discovering that the Muggles who were bringing him up and forcing him to live in a closet under the stairs were simply an inferior race, not available to magic and enchantment. Many gay kids must have identified with the imagery in the film. But the magic and enchantment we must learn in our gay Hogwarts is only good magic if it helps us return to our own mugglehood as a contribution to the enchantment of all muggledom.

So I am aware that what I am saying, in lamenting that we have not yet come up with an ability to inscribe ourselves within the Christian story, sounds awfully like a stern demand to a people inhabiting an exile: 'Sing to us, they said, one of Zion's songs'. But sing it with the constant background presence of emissaries from Zion insisting that any song you could possibly sing couldn't really be a song of Zion.

Well, I am not a novelist, and lack both the bravery and the talent to be able to pursue this discovery of story in a way to which any reader would be able to say: 'Yes, you know, there is in this story that quality of sameness, even though told by someone who is not me, that I can find that his story illuminates with sympathy elements of my own. I can receive what he tells me as a gift which helps me discover my own vocation more fully.' That, I think, is what I am looking for in gay writing and which I have not yet wholly found.

However, instead of being a novelist, my vocation seems to be that of a priest and a theologian, and as such I do try to explore elements of the grammar which might one day make such stories strong. There are two particular elements of grammar in this area which I have pursued. One is the coming down of the Holy Spirit on Cornelius and the Gentiles after Peter has spoken to them, and before they are baptised in Acts 10. Indeed, what I have been talking about, when I talk about gay people learning to tell a story, is precisely raising the question of what is the shape of the Holy Spirit coming down upon a group of people who, it has long been assumed, have been outside the bounds of holiness. And my concern is far more with attempting to develop that new shape of holiness, including the new possibilities of life-giving and life-sharing narrative which will flow from that, than with convincing Peter of the need to baptise us. When Peter sees that our stories are in fact filled out by the Holy Spirit, he will recognise our likeness, and that the Holy Spirit has already been given us.

What seems to me to be important is not to be so concerned about getting Peter's approval that it becomes a substitute for the hard work of finding ourselves on the inside of God's story. And that means the hard work of discovering ourselves loved, being able to face up to the terror, the sense of annihilation, the fear of loss, the powerlessness and frivolity, and the continuous sense of shame which have been our lot. This is where I have begun to find a second element of grammar, also related to the Holy Spirit. In the Christological accounts of the giving of the Holy Spirit, it is something Jesus does which makes it possible for the Holy Spirit to be given. The Holy Spirit cannot be given without Jesus doing this something, and it is in his doing it, something that he alone could do, that we see the shape of the Holy Spirit which will then be breathed on us all.

This 'thing' which Jesus does is to go to his death, or go to his Father, and, in the long Johannine description of this, these terms apply to the same reality. But what Jesus is doing is very especially occupying the place of shame, and of wrath. And he is doing so in such a way as to detoxify it forever. When he pronounces himself the Gate of the Sheep, he is referring to the gate by which sheep were led into the temple for slaughter. He indicates that the Good Shepherd does what the shepherds of Israel never did: he goes in as a sheep, with the sheep, into the sacrificial space. They are not frightened of him since they recognise that he is the same as them. The Shepherd is thus able to lead the sheep in and out to find pasture, something previously impossible. No one ever led sheep *out* from the Temple abattoir. It was as one-way a track as the railway line to Treblinka. Only one who was not affected by death could lead sheep in and out of the place of shame, wrath and sacrifice, so as to find pasture. So, by himself becoming the abattoir door, the Shepherd makes the sacrificial space no longer a dead end, no longer a trap. He even points out how different this is from the thieves and hirelings, easily recognisable ways of referring to the religious and political leaders who ran the Temple and the system of goodness. Such leaders never went into the Temple through the abattoir door, but rather through another way, and then, from above, they took the sheep for sacrificial slaughter[14]. But when there was any real religious crisis, whenever wrath threatened, or the wolf came, they could be guaranteed not to stand up for their sheep, not to dare to go through the same door as they insisted the sheep go, but

---

14 θύσῃ John 10:10.

rather to flee and leave the sheep to be scattered, the prey of every wild beast. And this, of course, is true of any system of goodness to this day, such as the ones that give sustenance to those of us who are 'religious professionals'.

It seems to me that what Jesus is doing in 'going to his Father', 'going to Death', 'occupying the space of shame and of wrath', being both Shepherd and abattoir door, is making the place of shame, of wrath and of sacrifice into a pasture. And that means a place where we can be nourished, and find wholeness, health and story to live by. The giving to us of the Holy Spirit is, then, the giving to us of the whole dynamic, the whole power, by which Jesus was able to occupy this place of annihilation, shame and wrath without being run by it. And this does seem to me something very powerful for gay and lesbian people. I wonder whether our ability to be able to sing one of Zion's songs, to find that, in our hearts, are the highways to Zion[15], does not at the moment pass through our ability to be able to occupy the place of shame without being run by it.

This is a difficult notion, since shame produces flight. To be able to live in the midst of shame, by which I mean that space of shame, which has for so long been so toxic for us, without being run by it, may turn out to be a hugely positive feat. This is the space where – because one no longer has anything to lose, is no longer frightened, knows that the only thing left that they can take away is your life, and that is already in the hands of Another – one can develop a tender regard for those who are like one, and a tender regard leads to a creative imagination, and a playful generosity of heart.

This is where I suspect that the Holy Spirit may be beginning to produce gay and lesbian stories that will turn out to be irrefutably Christian; where Jesus has made us not ashamed and not frightened of occupying the space of shame. Where he has enabled us no longer to be run by the wrath which has so defined us in past generations, there we will be able to discover our likeness with those others who have needed us to occupy that position because it is the only way they think they can keep wrath at bay.

---

15 Ps. 84:5.

You see, I am not sure that anything, any power at all, can resist shame held delicately in tenderness. And I am not sure that anyone can predict what creativity, gifts and life will emerge from such a peaceful place.

Rather than seek to convince you of anything, to plead with you as a vegetarian shark seeking the tolerance of difference, or to belabour you with sameness like some poor Shylock furious that you cannot see the obvious, I have chosen to try something a little different: to share with you a space of shame, of incompletion, of story not-yet-forged, a sense of being in a pit and not yet knowing a way out of it, in the hopes that, as you reach to help me, you will discover that my pit is the same as yours, and that, as we realise this, we may find ourselves turning this valley of weeping into a place of springs[16].

---

16 Ps. 84:6.

❖❖❖❖❖❖❖❖❖❖

CHAPTER 4

Discipleship and the shape of belonging

I dare to call my work that of preacher, and teacher[1]. My major undertaking over the last few years has been to try and come up with
an adult introduction to the Catholic faith, an inductive, twelve-
session course, following the thought of René Girard. I have been
attempting to gave an account of our faith in such a way as makes it
both attractive and easier to pass on, one that is entirely orthodox,
and yet fresh. In fact, I have given this course, still in the process of
development, in a number of different settings, and hope to do so
again before long. And naturally, there would be no point to such
preaching and teaching if it were not to lead to some sort of discipleship in those who hear it. Discipleship not of yours truly, but
of the One at the heart of the preaching.

One of the things which people who have either heard me teach,
or read my stuff, sometimes say to me is: 'We get the Christianity
bit, and we even get the bit about which you are adamant, about
how there's no following Christ which doesn't bring with it a certain ecclesial belonging. Now can you tell us how to survive the
Church that is actually there! We notice that when people belong to
anything, they can take seriously the bits that are to be taken seriously, ignore the silly bits and not be scandalised by the really bad
bits. That is to say, they know how to love what they belong to and
somehow grow in dignity and purpose through their belonging. But
how do we do this in the Church nowadays, where the language of
excommunication rains down so easily, and where some find it so
easy to qualify others as "not really Catholics"? How do we find both
the sense of belonging and the capacity to relativise things, to get

---

1   This chapter was born as a participation at a conference on 'Discipleship and the City' at Villanova
     University, Pennsylvania, 'in October 2006.

them in their proper perspective, which is the sign of adulthood? How do we make sense of the bizarre, alternative, shrinking universe of the clergy, and the strange double-messages which emerge from the Vatican, or at least are fed to us as if emerging from the Vatican? How do we cope with the information overload which is supposed to be teaching us, and yet which tends just to flatten everything out so that war, contraception, the love of God, clerical celibacy, the death penalty, liturgical translations and altar girls flow mind-numbingly by, like a conveyor belt with game-show prizes which you get to take home if you remember them all?'

This sort of question is one that anyone who hopes that the result of his or her preaching is discipleship is going to be faced with sooner or later. Any healthy ecclesiology must nowadays include not only the traditional questions of Church Order, and the life of the sacramental signs resulting from Christ's foundation of the Church, but also some treatment of the structure of desire and imagination in the members with relation to the sort of institutional life which is their current Church order. And that, for me, is at the heart of the questions concerning discipleship at which we will be looking over the next few days.

Here, however, I must mention not only my gratitude for the chance to think about this with you, but also my trepidation. And this is because there is, of course, no realistic way of talking about our discipleship of Christ without being self-implicatory. All priests in the English-speaking world have passed down to us, like an heirloom, Chaucer's pithy reminder of what a good priest is about, in his portrait of the Parson. He received the highest praise any of us could aspire to:

> But Cristes loore and his apostles twelve
> He taughte, but first he folwed it hymselve.[2]

---

2   The concluding lines of the Parson's portrait, from *The Canterbury Tales*.

It would be lovely to be able to say, as St Paul could, 'Be imitators of me, as I am of Christ'[3], but many of us, lay or clergy, are at least as much obstacles to the following of Christ as we are encouragements. And, of course, by our preaching or teaching we are not merely supposed to be passing on ideas, or information. We are attempting to get across that a Happening has irrupted into our world; that It matters; that we are at least beginning to find ourselves altered by exposure to this Happening; and that therefore at least part of the truth of what we are talking about should be able to be detected in the way we are undergoing something. This bearing witness to something by becoming a sign of it having happened, and which points towards it, often in ways of which we are not aware, but which other potential imitators can pick up, is rigorously inseparable from any talk about discipleship.

Anyone who takes some responsibility for this business of pointing another towards the way of Christ has to become aware that he or she can get in the way of the imitation, can get in the way of the discipleship and can become a scandal, a source of stumbling to the one who would follow Christ. And learning to avoid giving scandal to such potential followers is a great deal of what discipleship is about. Giving scandal is where I am not giving an example which will lead the person imitating into an uninterrupted following of the One who we are all called to follow: the One in whom there was no guile, no double-bind, the One who allows desire to become uncomplicated and untrammelled by fear and death. Instead of facilitating this, I am pointing someone down a route which will lead only to their confusion and unhappiness, their being locked into constantly bumping their souls into double-binds which paralyse them and lead them into fear and death.

Given that you have offered me the privilege of participating in discussion of this subject in a Catholic University, I would like to issue the equivalent of one of those health warnings by which the Surgeon-General beautifies cigarette packets. Not, I hope, 'This theologian can cause impotence if inhaled', but rather: 'This theologian occupies uncertain ground. Do not be quick to follow him.' I

---

3   1 Cor. 11:1.

feel that I should say this since, just when the Pontifical Theological Commission is getting round to acknowledging the non-existence of limbo, I find myself occupying a place which is uncommonly like limbo, and I do so both as priest and as theologian. Let me explain.

I am a priest, but, as far as I can tell, am of no juridical standing. Which is an anomaly, since one is supposed to have juridical standing, some line of accountability, in order to function as a priest. I wish I did have, but I do not. And I do not know where to start in finding a proper line of accountability. I aspire to be a theologian, then, but effectively work as a freelancer. This too is an anomaly, since theology is an ecclesial discipline, presupposing structure, collegiality and oversight, so to be a 'freelance theologian' sounds to me very much like a contradiction in terms. However, that is my reality: I inhabit not one, but two non-places. And I would be loath to think that I am trying to persuade any one to imitate me in this. I am well aware that I am treading on what might turn out to be quicksand, and I do not want to encourage anyone to follow me onto it until it is pretty clear that it is part of the safe space, the rock on which to build, offered to us by the Gospel.

My reason for inhabiting these non-places, for beginning tentatively to build on what may be a dangerously firm-seeming crust rather than the rock I hope it will turn out to be, is fairly simple: I have come, after a long time of search, study and struggle, to believe that the current characterisation of gay people held by the Roman congregations is not true. Although this is not in itself a very important matter, it is one that does go to the heart of the way the clerical set-up runs in our Church. In my case, it means that I have discovered that, since my vows and promise of celibacy were taken at a time when I was bound by a false conscience, I have no valid vows or promises, but am nevertheless validly ordained, and indeed, love being a priest, a preacher and a teacher. I am not sure that I can properly make such promises or vows within the juridical context offered by the Church while it continues to insist on what I regard as a false characterisation of the one making the vow or promise. Which is why I think that the Vatican was probably right to say the Church should no longer try to induce gay men into priestly life, since it cannot at this time offer an honest gay man a limpid context for vows or promises. I agree with them that we should not lead people into double-binds.

And the same is true with relation to being a theologian. I take very seriously that becoming a theologian, and especially a priestly theologian, is an ecclesial vocation, and indeed hope that I show signs of being ecclesial in my writing and teaching. I do not want to make a living by being a theologian in a secular faculty, where being a priest would mean nothing, and where the mode of production and system of rewards is determined by the regard of the Academy, itself just as full of rules, anathemas, rivalry and ambition as any ecclesiastical set-up. Others less suggestible than I have shown themselves able to avoid these temptations, but I fear that in my vanity I would be unable to avoid the temptation to 'make a career' and to 'become someone' in the eyes of my secular employers and colleagues, making of them, effectively, my 'Church'. And that would be the death of my vocation as a Catholic theologian.

On the other hand, since I am open in my disagreement with what I take to be a third-order teaching in the Magisterium's current hierarchy of truths, it seems to me fair enough that until, and unless, there is a sufficient clarity that my opinion is one which can legitimately be held by Catholic theologians without causing scandal to the faithful, or until I can be disabused of my opinion by evidence that it is not true, I not be invited to teach in a Catholic theological faculty, even though that is what I aspire to. So, I find myself hoping that my ecclesial vocation as a theologian will bear fruit through my accepting being a non-person in the regard of the Church for the moment, rather than aspiring to become a 'someone' through the regard of those outside it. But that is my hope, nothing firmer than that.

Well, excuse me for this detour, but it seemed to me that not to set out warning flags around the ground this presenter occupies would be a failure to take seriously the way in which any presentation on discipleship must implicate the presenter, and challenge them to come into the light, so that be it may be seen whether what they do is wrought in God[4].

---

4   cf. John 3:21.

So, to the matter at hand: My guess is that when you heard the word 'discipleship' in the title of this conference, and of this lecture, you intuited, for however brief an instant, that it was 'Christian discipleship', or 'discipleship of Christ', that was to be discussed. And, at least as far as this talk goes, you were right. But is it not strange that a word that is in itself object-neutral has come to acquire a quick-flash association with Christ? In principle, at least, discipleship could be of any model at all: Ho Chi Minh, Ethel Rosenberg, Marian Anderson or Saladin. What is odd is that because the followers of Christ are called his disciples, so discipleship has come to be particularly associated with him, as though there is a special form of religious following called discipleship which is an especially good thing and different from any other form of following. Well, my hunch is that when ordinary words become 'religious', it is time to take them to the laundry. Because what has usually happened is that they are being taken out of their normal field of application in interpersonal relationships and given a patina of specialness. This 'special' quality then often mystifies at least as much as it illuminates.

So let us go the inverse route. Let us look at the ordinary before we look at the special. I would like to suggest to you that there is no such thing as *not* being a disciple. Discipleship is not, in the ordinary run of things, a voluntary option. It is, on the contrary, a necessary precondition for being a viable, socialised adult human being. We are massively competent imitating machines, and from the very first time our mirror neurons get fired in our infancy, which they do by adults doing things we can see, we repeat, and imitate endlessly. It is others, whom we imitate, who induct us into gestures, into language, into developing a memory, and thus having the beginning of a sense of self over time. It is others who fire off in us what enables us to develop the very elaborate forms of social interaction that constitute human culture[5]. And, in fact, so advanced and successful are we as learners and imitators, that we often do not perceive quite how many automatic responses to actions of others we engage in without in any way feeling that our autonomy is threatened. We

---

5   cf. the article on mirror neurons in *Scientific American Mind* Volume 17, Number 2, April/May 2006.

avoid collisions in crowded spaces, we yawn when others yawn, our facial gestures communicate reactions which are quite non-deliberate, and over which we have limited control. In all these situations, the social other is prior to the self. It is not, if you like, that there is simply a stable 'I' who am interacting with others from a position of freedom. Rather, the relatively stable 'I' is a symptom of the massively successful prior social interactions which bring it into being and sustain it[6].

This, of course, goes with something which seems counterintuitive but, as far as I know, is simply true about this species of ape which we are: what we call the 'self' is in fact something received *through the eyes of others*. It is what we see reflected back at us in the eyes of another that calls us into being. And this is something which developed over many thousands of years among our pre-human ancestors: our eyes not only see the other members of our race, but these eyes of ours see *them seeing us*, and learn from what they pick up *reflected in them* who *we* are. Our 'selves' are reflexive. Which means that what we call our 'self' is not a given which grows inside us autonomously. It is, if you like, the making viable in this body of the one who is being called into being by the interaction of the social other with this body over time.

The social other that calls us into being is not simply an individual other, looking at us very hard until an individual self 'takes' in us. We do, for the most part, have individual others, parents or guardians, who do look at us and talk at, and then to, us for a long time, and it is very hard work for them. But we are, if you like, far more absorbent, or promiscuous, in our learning than to be able to be formed by so few people. We pick up not only what people want us to pick up, but also far more than what they know they are communicating to us, what they know they are hiding from us and what they don't know they are hiding from us, about themselves, and about the world. We are, as a race, astoundingly adept at filling in the dots, at providing as known things we intuit between the

6   cf. Henri Grivois: 'Adolescence, Indifferentiation, and the onset of Psychosis', in *Contagion*, Volume 6, 1999, and his reference to Paul Dumouchel's work *Émotions: essai sur le corps et le social* (Synthélabo, Le Plessis-Robinson, 1995).

gaps of what we see or are told. In fact, incredibly fast, we become socialised into the whole pattern of desires which runs our wider social group, and of which our parents and guardians are themselves symptoms; symptoms who partially go with the flow, and partially react against it in an effort, which becomes increasingly vain as we become more viable, to protect us from its stormier waves. Our 'self' is in fact an extraordinary exercise in negotiating the many different 'others' which have formed it, and which are built into it automatically. The relation between that 'other' which is the self, and the 'others' which have formed it and are still imbued in it, is of course absolutely vital to our health, stability, sanity and so on.

I hope this makes it clear why it is that we are all, and without thinking about it, prone to discipleship. 'Show me who I am!' is not a stupid question, asked by the dumbest kid in the class who can't work it out for him or herself. 'Show me who I am!', whether spoken or not, is a driving dynamo of desire in all of us, and asking it is a sign that the ability to be a disciple has not yet got caught up in the adolescent fear of being noticed to be an imitator, when the really cool thing is to be 'so not into imitating other people, their hairstyle, their fashions'; cool, like ... well, that's the give-away: the maximally cool person is the one who seems to be completely in-different to the desires of others. But that maximally cool person is in fact entirely dependent on the others imitating him to keep up his apparent poise and self-possession, and will quickly come to have a contempt for those who imitate him, since he is half aware that there is nothing 'there' beyond a negotiating ruse. The contempt itself will betray the dependence on the other. Or, should a bigger star swim into the galaxy, one capable of exercising a stronger gravi-tational pull, so that the regard of the others becomes redirected, watch Ms Cool's self-possession and poise disintegrate!

Please notice that I am speaking to each of you as if each one of us is not only an individual person, which we are – we are *this* body, with *this* life history over time – but also as though in each one of us the set of relationships between an individual and the crowd is already inescapably present. Each of us is a 'we' as well as an 'I', and in fact when we use the word 'I', it is usually a particular in-flection of the 'we', a particular statement of the state of relations between the 'we' and this body over time which is negotiating in their midst. None of us says 'I am' in the absolute. Each one of us is the space of negotiation over time of a multiplicity of different possible identities.

Now I would like to take this a step further, and say that this search for 'Show me who I am!', this 'Notice me with approval!', is not only fundamental to all of us, but it guarantees both such stability as any of us enjoy, and our sense of 'belonging'. In other words, discipleship, imitation in view of being given an identity by someone else, and belonging, are intimately linked. Someone *belongs* whose sense of being is peacefully dependent on the regards of those with whom they live. You cease to belong if you begin to feel the draw of a different regard, one from a different group, and especially one that is in some rivalry with your current group. You cease to play happily with other ten-year-olds when you start to feel the draw of a group of older kids whose regard teaches you to despise the kind of things you have been doing quite happily until recently, and teaches you to aspire to a new belonging, with new sorts of games. Or, you can cease to belong if, for whatever reason, the negative regard of the weathervanes of your belonging is turned on you. Your parents, in all innocence, bought you the wrong-coloured sports bag, or the wrong brand of jeans, and you know what this means: that the disapproving regard of all those with whom you aspire to be will be directed at you, and you will be cast into outer darkness for ever.

But mostly, there is a certain stability to belonging. The stability is actually a constantly shifting stability, and it requires constant energy to stay still, but we know how it works. We imitate, and then we fall out, we find new models to imitate, or people imitate us. We learn the rules of surviving in the group, and they are really quite simple. We can sum them up normally in one word: reciprocity. I give, and I expect to be given. I invite, and I expect to be invited. If I do something hostile, I expect hostility to be meted back to me, so I take measures to avoid it, or shift responsibility somewhere else. There is, in fact, a constant circle of reciprocity going on in any form of belonging. Even negative reciprocity is a kind of belonging, and groups can form, like Montagues and Capulets, whose negative

reciprocity is very important for their belonging. Take them out
of each other's orbit, and they will collapse into meaninglessness,
since their belonging depended on having the other who was a sign
of what 'not belonging' meant, being near at hand. If one can talk of
a golden rule of belonging in this sense it is: don't break reciprocity,
and don't allow the exchange of favours to be transformed into an
exchange of blows; but if it looks as though it is going to be, antici-
pate the change of wind and get your strike in first. Or, in other
words: do unto others as they do to you and, only very occasionally,
and when you're quite sure you're among friends, stand back and
wonder what it is that you would like them to do to you, and do that
to them instead, in an effort to create a more positive reciprocity.

The ideal person in this sort of world would be the person who
could switch on and off their imitative capacity at will. They would
be able to imitate, which is how they would learn an enormous
amount very fast, and so be enabled to belong, become socialised,
learn how to play the game. And yet, at the first sign of the cycles of
reciprocity turning nasty – which means the threat of vengeance –
they would be able to turn off their imitative capacity and no longer
be run by such revenge and rivalry. Imitation would always be for
learning and never for rivalry. But, in fact, there are no such ideal
persons. For, in exactly the same way as we imitate, we find ourselves sucked into rivalry without, as far as we can tell, ever doing
anything wrong. It only needs the tiniest hint of disapproval in the
eye of a much-admired model for us to redouble efforts to please,
and end up imitating them so well as to be seen as a threat: imitation will be interpreted as rivalry which means that the whole of
the reciprocity will turn negative, and the exchange of favours will
become an exchange of slights, a mutual casting out into the outer
darkness with each party being convinced that it was the other who
started it.

As a general rule, we humans are pretty good at setting up the
rules to protect ourselves against ourselves within this sort of belonging. We come up with laws to limit the right to revenge to what
is strictly proportional to the damage done. And we seek to avoid
the immediacy of vengeance by the sleight of hand of having relatively impartial law enforcement agencies whose job it is to ensure

that the heat of reciprocity is slowed down by introducing ever less partial-seeming ways of determining what happened, whose fault, if anyone's, it was, and how compensation is to be adjudicated. We have a knack of making sure that the sort of people who get it in the neck are the sort of people who will not have the power to retaliate. And thus, most of the time, in most cultures, do we keep the peace, and have forms of belonging which keep us, if not happy, at least engaged in relatively harmless-seeming games of prestige, dignity and respect, the bitterer edges of which we are very good at ignoring in as far as they do not bite too close to home. As King Lear says in an idyllic moment, thinking of an imagined retirement with his daughter before the final fury of the play turns all such hopes to bloodied dust:

> So we'll live,
> And pray, and sing, and tell old tales, and laugh
> At gilded butterflies, and hear poor rogues
> Talk of court news; and we'll talk with them too –
> Who loses and who wins, who's in; who's out...[7]

Well, into this world of relative stability, of mostly controlled imitation and rivalry, hospitality and vengeance, Christ comes crashing like a comet which has strayed out of some distant galaxy. And his invitation to discipleship is a terrible gash, forever ruining the relative stability of the party. If I have taken my time to get around to talking about discipleship of Christ, it is because I wanted to bring out just how weird a thing it is. For its key feature is that it undoes the central rule of logic governing all induction into belonging: it undoes reciprocity.

Let us start from the end, which is in itself odd. Mostly we imitate people who are, just as we aspire to be, 'on the way up', growing, becoming more successful, more beautiful, richer, stronger, more prestigious and so on. By definition most of these people are not yet 'at an end'. It is their glamour, not their cadavers, which we imitate. In the case of what Christ is offering us, it is just the reverse, for the central thing that he is offering is living without death, something

---

7   *King Lear*, Act V Scene 3.

which no one else, before or since, has ever offered or made available. And the form of this offer is not to push his contemporaries towards some heroic act of sacrifice, assuring them of celestial rewards, while quietly watching from the sidelines. It is to have undergone death in advance for us, in quite specific circumstances, so as to remove forever the fear of it, and the way it drives us. It is, if you like, to create spacious mansions of being indwelt by the living God, there where others would see only death and loss.

I want to stress this, since it is really what is absolutely central about the discipleship of Christ. He makes no demands from us until he has created something for us first, and it is only then that he asks us to imitate him: 'As I have loved you, so love one other'[8]. This means that never, at any stage, will we be in rivalry with him, or with anyone else in order to survive, since survival is not what it is about, nor do we get anywhere by trampling on anyone else. There is nowhere to get to, since the whole purpose of the imitation is to undergo death in advance of our biological finitude, so as to live thereafter as if death were not, or, in the phrase of my friend Sebastian Moore, 'with death behind us'.

So, the first rule of reciprocity is already pre-broken. Gratuitous benevolence has started to turn reciprocity on its head. He has done something for us that no one could ever repay, or return. And he is not remotely interested in our repaying or returning it anyhow. What he asks us to do is to multiply the gratuity, by doing other gratuitous things to and for others without any hope of repayment. Notice what this looks like: a command to create gratuity rather than expect reciprocity, so:

> 'When you give a dinner or a banquet, do not invite your friends or your brothers or your kinsmen or rich neighbours, lest they also invite you in return, and you be repaid. But when you give a feast, invite the poor, the maimed, the lame, the blind, and you will be blessed, because they cannot repay you. You will be repaid at the resurrection of the just.'[9]

8   cf. John 13:34, 15:12.
9   Luke 14:12-14.

And also, the reverse of that – a command not to engage in expected negative reciprocity, but instead to be gratuitous:

> 'You have heard that it was said, "An eye for an eye and a tooth
> for a tooth." But I say to you, Do not resist one who is evil ... You
> have heard that it was said, "You shall love your neighbour and hate
> your enemy." But I say to you, Love your enemies and pray for
> those who persecute you, so that you may be sons of your Father
> who is in heaven;'[10]

And, of course, this is massively destabilising to any form of human belonging. In fact, it reveals quite to what an extent all our discipleships and all our belongings, all our constructions of identity, are based on, dependent on – which means secretly run by –death, and its fear. But this is where we start in discipleship of Christ: we start from death having been rendered moot as a factor in our construction of identity, by Jesus having occupied the place of shame and death without being run by it, and having been witnessed on the third day and thereafter as being a dead man who, without ceasing to be dead, was alive.

Discipleship of Christ is the process by which that protagonism of gratuity which he inaugurated by going to death for us, and which we sometimes call the giving of the Holy Spirit, reaches us and enables us to start to live as if death, fear, ignominy and shame were not. Which means that it first reaches us, and can only reach us, as a certain rupture of our stability, a certain enabling us to stand loose from our previous belonging and a certain breaking of heart which usually goes by the name of 'the forgiveness of sins'. Discipleship of Christ presupposes us being in the process of being forgiven as our access to being re-created.

Now, I am aware that I do not have time to do this properly, but I would like to look briefly at four different moments in the process of our becoming disciples. I call them 'moments' rather than 'stages' since I am not talking about chronological succession; indeed, elements of these moments can be simultaneous. I mean something more like: four different dimensions of a process of Life in the Spirit

---

10   Matt. 5:38-39a, 43-45.

that does develop through time. I call these four moments: 'stripping away', 'spluttering creativity', 'turning' and, finally, 'belonging'.

'Stripping away' is the process of loss of reputation and being held in the regard of others. Without this stripping away, there is, as I see it, no discipleship of Christ. The most difficult thing, I think, for any of us to be weaned of, is the need for the approving regard of others in order just to be, and to belong. Jesus teaches this quite clearly when he teaches on prayer. In order to receive rewards from our Heavenly Father, which is to say, in order to receive that 'Well done, I'm sooooo pleased with you!' which is what we all want so desperately to hear (and which, in Latin, is 'Magna cum laude noti-tia', and is St Augustine's definition of glory in heaven), we need to learn to let go of all the forms of reputation and regard, good or 'wicked', which we struggle so hard to get and to keep. So, we are not to do our good deeds, or say our prayers, so as to get a good reputation from others, since the trouble is that if we do that, we will be too easily satisfied: we *will* get a good reputation from them, and then we will be run by them, and will play any number of games of hypocrisy, violence and treading on others to keep that good reputation, because in that reputation is our identity. So, we must pray in the one room[11] in the house where no one can see us, not because we are essentially private individuals, but because we are essentially public puppets, and are run by the desires of others, and need to spend a lot of time in detox from the desires, voices, patterns of reward and expectation from those others in order to begin to hear the voice of One who is totally outside reciprocity, and is totally gratuitous.

Our Lord says very much the same thing again in an entirely different set of circumstances: talking to a group of religious leaders, he says:

> 'How can you believe, who receive glory from one another and do not seek the glory that comes from the only God?'[12]

---

11 cf. Matt. 6:6.
12 John 5:44.

The group identity that is built up by mutual regard is impervi-ous to the regard of God. Or, stated differently, reciprocally-given identity is a closed system, and it is only through undergoing a loss of reputation, which means a loss of identity, which means a certain form of death, that a gratuitously-given identity can break through.

Please notice the link between reputation, identity and death. Learning to let go of depending on the approval, or disapproval, of others as part of discovering who I am is an immensely painful ex-ercise of stripping away of identity, and risking not being anyone at all, so as to trust that an 'I' not yet known to me will be called into being by the regard of God. This is, and can only be, experienced as a certain form of dying. And it is able to be gone through because the one we are learning to follow was able to occupy this space of shame, loss and bereftness without being run by it.

The second moment is what I call 'spluttering creativity'. It is an infantile place. Part of the process of dying is giving up deriving identity over against anyone else at all; no longer reacting against them, or provoking them. Cheap shots of meaning, bits of junk identity, can always be got by reacting and provoking, by taking up 'positions' over against others. But this is futile, and there is nothing creative about it. What is odd is that when the old 'self' has finally given up the struggle, finally died, there is the curious sensation: 'Well, how on earth am I to be creative of anything, if there is no longer anything for me to be over against? What on earth does it mean to be creative *out of nothing*? For it is only the things which are created *out of nothing* which have real meaning, stability and being. Anything created reactively is entirely dependent on what is already there, and is going out of being. But how long am I to be stretched over this abyss of nothing, during which I hope to find myself called into being out of nothing through being given a creative project out of nothing, but where I am spluttering around somewhat frus-tratedly and not seeing what on earth I could actually do, or what indeed it would look like, to love?' Well there is, I think and hope, a certain moment of what I call 'faffing around', trying to be creative, that precedes one actually finding that one has been called without knowing it into doing something, and that something out of nothing has already started to emerge. It is part of learning that time is not my enemy, but is very spacious, and I do not need to succeed immediately, or to order, because it is eternal life that is behind the hints of creativity which are being born.

Again, the direct opposite of this is pointed out by Our Lord, describing a normal form of religious discipleship:

> 'Woe to you, scribes and Pharisees, hypocrites! for you traverse
> sea and land to make a single proselyte, and when he becomes
> a proselyte, you make him twice as much a child of hell as
> yourselves.'[13]

The 'normal' form of discipleship works by people eagerly looking for others to be like them, to join their group. And when a convert joins the group, of course the first thing they want to do is become as much of an insider as possible: there is a massively thirsty 'Daddy, daddy, tell me who I am, and tell me quickly!' Now the easiest thing to imitate in a group are the distinctive things, the things which make us 'us' and not 'them', and so it is no surprise that a new convert quickly becomes the most ardent exponent of every one of the group's 'over againsts': he or she picks them up in a fantastically hungry absorption or osmosis. This means that such proselytes too are being infantilised into becoming simply a function of the worst features of the group, creative of nothing. If the group is of any worth at all, then there will also be wiser heads that are embarrassed by this cheap identity, and who try to get the convert to see that in time he will discover for himself how much like other people and other groups they all are, really. But that wiser head will have to be grounded on something other than group identity if that is to work.

The third moment is the one I call 'turning', and I use this word deliberately with its connotations of the Hebrew שׁוּב which can translate 'return', 'turn back', 'repent'. But I think I am referring to something rather odd here. It is as though the self is being turned round and sent *back* to the world of previous belonging, but with the whole internal wiring system being run in reverse. This is not

---

13 Matt. 23:15.

at all the same thing as a stripping away, but it is a strange sense of being run by somewhere else, and so being able to start to return to life in the places and even groups of the old belonging without being frightened by them, or feeling reactive to them, or having to survive them. I think that it is here that the whole running of one's body starts to acquire a new dynamic, so that, for instance, property I may have becomes something which is mine, but as if it were not mine, able to become part of a gratuitousness towards others. My sex life becomes something which is no longer agitated, moved, by the pushes and pulls of others, and so becomes part of a way I might give myself to someone else, or not, over time, put peacefully and sensitively to their needs, my body for them, not theirs for me. I rather think that it is this sense of being sent back, empowered by the gift of self-control, which is the way we are given back our bodiliness, so no longer run by fear and necessity, that enables us to find that we are being turned into 'Ambassadors for Christ' – emanations of a different power, being sent into the midst of the power of this belonging and its identities and rivalries, but in the disguise of nothing at all special. What *is* special is that we have been 'turned' and are approaching the whole of what we face empowered by a spaciousness which does not know death, and thus we are unwitting creators of signs of the power we represent. It is here, I think, that we start to find ourselves actually loving and liking people, groups, things, with the eyes which are being given to us by One whose love is not run by the need to succeed, to get things right, to perform to order. This new loving regard is being born in us by our being stretched towards that from which before we would have run away.

My fourth and final 'moment' is 'belonging'. And this is very definitely a continuation of the previous moment, the sense of someone else gently turning you, rewiring you, and sending you back. Interestingly, if you go to the Greek New Testament and look up all the places where you expect to find a verb corresponding to the English 'belong', you will find nothing of the sort. The Greek invariably says simply 'am of' or 'is of', and this is, I suppose, straightforward and clear. When *we* talk about 'belonging', we usually refer to some comfortable sense, of being 'at home', or of feeling 'OK with our surroundings'. But if we strip away the sentiment, what we are left with is something pretty naked: 'Who are you of? Of whom are you? You belong to whom? Who owns you?' There is no belonging without a 'to whom'. So our normal sense of belonging is something much more like 'I'm comfortable with being run by this lot'. But please remember that this 'I' that feels 'comfortable being run by this lot' is the space of negotiation with the others, interaction between whom and this body causes 'me' to be. And it is, as we have seen, this 'I' that is stripped down and rendered dead by the loss of regard of significant others during our induction into the discipleship of Christ.

One of the things which the Apostolic Witnesses are absolutely clear about, and I am thinking particularly of John and Paul, is that the 'I' that is reborn out of the rubble of that stripping down, and is called into being by an entirely new form of interaction and negotiation with the others, a creative, gratuitous, untroubled, unhurried, spacious, 'I', is quite literally, the 'I' of Christ[14]. His going to death enables his 'I' to be born in us, through our being conformed to him over time in our being sent out into doing the same as he did 'and greater works than these'[15] because it will be he who is doing them, and there is no rivalry between the One who made the space available and the spaciousness which erupts from it.

This form of belonging is not the 'jealous ownership' of the owner who ties you down and makes sure that you do not do anything wrong, so that you do not show him up. He does not want to possess you to diminish you. On the contrary, it is much more like the sort of ownership of one who does not care about being seen in himself at all, but wants to be recognised in the ones he has made vibrantly alive, creative, and caused to flourish. This is the sort of ownership by which an excited parent publicly owns their child who is excelling in the school swimming race, pointing out excitedly to other parents 'That's MY child!' This parent has a vested interest in the excess glory of the ones he owns. And it is because that owning 'I', the 'I' of Christ, is indistinguishable from the 'I AM' of the One who makes all things out of nothing and holds them

14 'it is no longer I who live, but Christ who lives in me;' Gal. 2,:20.
15 John 14:12.

in being, that we know that the culmination of our discipleship of Christ is to find that our being 'of Christ', publicly owned by him, rather than publicly shamed by him[16], will reveal us as interior to the 'I AM' that is God, and so equipped to discover that everything, everything at all, belongs to us.

16   Matt. 10:32-3.

CHAPTER 5

Sacrifice, law and the Catholic faith:

is secularity really the enemy?

I would like to start by thanking you, Madam Editor, and with you the board of directors of the Tablet, for having invited me to give this lecture, and for having given me a free hand as to choice of subject[1]. I was more surprised than I can say, more honoured than you can imagine, and even a little frightened, as I will explain in a moment, when it dawned on me what kind of gift you have offered me.

Our faith requires that over our lifetimes we leave many different homes and families – many an Ur of the Chaldees, many a household of the Pharaoh. And I have had the privilege of experiencing this 'leaving home': in the first place in order to become a Catholic; then in embracing the thought of René Girard as something inspiring life-changing attention; then as I try to fulfil the charge given me at my priestly ordination; then, and much more precariously, in daring to think it might be part of my vocation to have a shot at becoming a truthful gay man within a mendacious environment. Your invitation frightened me because it beckoned to me as a certain sort of homecoming, a 'welcome back' into an English Catholic world in which I had not expected to be asked to belong. And, with that, there comes the need to learn how to speak not with the freedom and insouciance of the foreigner, for I mostly work abroad, and speak to those in cultures not my own, but with the delicacy of one who is learning how to greet long lost relatives, one who is a little nervous of what they will show him of his roots, of who he really is, but who is deeply warmed that they should be curious to have him

---

1   This chapter began life as the 2006 Tablet Lecture, the annual such lecture organised in London by the English Catholic periodical, *The Tablet*.

among them at all. For all the rest, as they say, there is Mastercard, but an invitation like this … priceless.

When we met, you and I, Madam Editor, to talk over possible subjects, I suggested that I would like to talk about something that seems to be missing in current public discourse. This is the way in which, contrary to easy talk about 'rampant secularism' and 'shoring up our religious identity', it is and always has been a proper part of the Catholic faith, and the life of the Church, that it tends to generate a relatively benign secularity; that. far from the 'secular' being our 'enemy', it is in fact our 'baby'. A fragile baby; one whose birth and development is well worth protecting. Nowadays, our contemporaries are inclined to use the word 'religious' as though it were synonymous with the word 'sacred', and the word 'secular' as though it were synonymous with 'common', 'normal' or 'profane'. Nevertheless, to regard those definitions as fixed is, I am afraid, the result of a mixture of historical ignorance, cultural tone-deafness and the fact that thinking in dichotomies is a great deal easier than anything more subtle.

In fact, the concept of the 'secular', as it comes to us from St Augustine, was born as a new form of historical time and culture brought into being by Christian faith in which there is no longer anything or any people who are properly 'sacred', or anything or any people who are properly 'profane'[2]. Instead, there is a time when the patterns of desire leading to holiness and patterns of desire leading to destruction are to be found side by side, intertwined, and not to be uprooted by human agencies. They are present both in apparently 'ecclesiastical' and in apparently 'civil' spheres. The Church, which, with regard to its varying organisational structures, is as much part of the secular as is the civil, political, imperial or democratic realm in which it lives, would, at its best, be the regime and discipline of signs, made alive by God: signs pointing towards, and actually being, God's bringing about of his Kingdom by reconciling all humans together; signs tending to summon forth certain shapes of human desire, interpretation and living together, rather

---

2   For further reading on this see Robert A. Markus' *Saeculum* (Cambridge, CUP, 1989), or his more recent *Christianity and the Secular* (Notre Dame, University of Notre Dame Press, 2006).

than coercing people into sacred structures. The driving force behind this is the Spirit, breathed forth by Jesus in his dying. This alone, this breath of a crucified criminal, unjustly put to death by the breathing together, the con-spiratio, of the sacred and the profane authorities of the time, this breath which cannot be tied down, is the holy power which turns apparent dregs of failed humanity into astounding witnesses of the holiness of God.

Since Catherine[3] and I met in August, I am very glad to say that these issues have at last been raised publicly, forcefully and to varying degrees of incomprehension, by none other than, in short order, both the successor of Peter and the head of the Church of England. For those who like alliteration, that's Ratzinger in Regensburg, and Rowan in Rome. In the case of the Archbishop of Canterbury, I am referring to his 2006 lecture to the Pontifical Academy of Social Sciences[4]. Both leaders are reminding people, in Rowan's words, that 'a certain kind of secularism has direct Christian and theological roots' or, in Pope Benedict's words, that 'the West has long been endangered by this aversion to the questions which underlie its rationality, and can only suffer great harm thereby'[5]. They say this as though it were obvious that our scientific rationality has long been recognised as originating in, and not against, our Faith. And for those of us privileged to have had graduate-level Catholic theological education, so it should be.

However, I fear that for many of our contemporaries, the notion that the Catholic faith engenders a relatively benign secularity, not by accident, but as its proper offspring, and that our 'enlightened' world, in its aversion to recognising and examining what it is that gave birth to it, is constantly in danger of cutting off the branch upon which it sits, seems so counterintuitive, that I would like to use this space to fill in, as it were, the gaps which my elders and betters could take for granted. I would like, in short, to give a quick trot through why it is that Catholicism is not really a religion in the ordinary sense of the word, and how it is that it holds in tension the

3   Catherine Pepinster, editor of *The Tablet*.
4   www.archbishopofcanterbury.org/sermons_speeches/061123a.htm
5   www.vatican.va/holy_father/benedict_xvi/speeches/2006/september/documents/
     hf_ben-xvi_spe_20060912_university-regensburg_en.html

various elements of what normally passes as 'religion' with a view to generating something quite, quite different. I will do so, as will surprise no one who has ever heard or read me before, by applying the thought of René Girard, since it is his thought which seems to me to offer the possibility of recovering for twenty-first century Catholicism both the advances of the enlightenment, and the pre-modern patterns of thought which sustain them and can alone make them lasting.

Happening

I would like to start in the least promising of places to begin an approach to secularity: by claiming that the centrepiece of the Catholic faith is a divine happening breaking through into our scheme of things, in the form of a very particular sort of priest perform-ing a very particular sort of sacrifice, and thus opening up a new Creation. This does not sound at all like secular language. So, in order to envisage with you where our perception of this happening leads us, I would ask you to imagine a crime scene in an American cop show. While scenarios of this sort are common to many such shows, I myself am thinking of a particular episode of the series called *CSI: Las Vegas*. In this episode, our investigators are called to a large, almost empty barn, riddled with bullet holes from high up on all four walls right down to floor level. On the floor is the body of a teenager, very recently dead. Our investigators' job is to piece to-gether what happened so as to hold somebody accountable. They do the classic thing, tracing back from the bullet holes in the walls to pinpoint where the gun was fired from, using a mixture of rods and laser beams. The first problem they discover is that the bullet that went through the standing teenager and then hit the barn wall was clearly coming at a steep downward angle, passing through him and then hitting the wall somewhere below his standing height. In other words, the bullet had to have been fired from above the boy, from considerably higher, in fact, than any other human could have fired, unless they were standing on some structure in the middle of the floor. But there is no forensic evidence of any such structure having stood in the middle of the floor. At this stage, a trigger-happy Tyran-nosaurus Rex would just about fit the crime scene, but little else.

It then becomes clear that, though there is no structure standing in the middle, the bullets were all fired from different heights, some downwards, and some upwards, but all from roughly the middle of the barn. However, there is no platform, let alone a moving platform, upon which someone might have stood to fire the bullets, nor was there time to remove such a platform between the boy's death and the arrival of the investigators.

Finally, the investigators find some evidence that friends of the boy were at the barn with him. Through tracing them, questioning them, and breaking through their lies and cover-up, the investigators are able to work out and envisage exactly what happened. The kids were playing a game of 'dare'. The dare consisted of one of them climbing up onto the roof of the barn, and then lowering down a twisted rope from a hole in the ceiling. This youth then allowed a machine gun, with its trigger jammed into firing mode to spin down the rope, jerking slightly as it moved, and spraying the walls all the way round as it moved down. The other kids, so as to avoid being 'chicken', had to stand, or dance around, on the floor of the barn, 'dodging' the random bullets. Amazingly, only one of them was killed. In other words, the investigators are able to determine that the 'happening' which they are investigating was not a murder, but an accident in the midst of a crazily dangerous form of 'extreme adolescent dares'.

The reason I tell you this story is because of the analogy it offers. What we have, at the root of our faith, is the claim that something happened in the midst of a group of humans. Something huge, scarcely able to be put into words, something breaking through normal schemes of description and something seen as opening up an entirely new perspective on being human. Such a happening is too mobile and subtle to be seen in itself, it can only be detected in the various bits of evidence it left behind. In our cop show scenario it was impossible for the crime scene investigators to see 'the happening which had happened' in itself; they had to use a mixture of the forensic evidence and the effects on the emotional lives of the friends of the dead boy to posit as the most rational, and ultimately the true, explanation: a highly complex, evolving and mobile 'happening', which they could then repeat if they wished, to see whether it did in fact have the effects which, according to their reconstruction, it should have. Just as the 'happening' itself, which is the root of our faith, cannot be seen in itself. It can be glimpsed and posited through a mixture of the patterns of bullet holes peppered on the walls, which we have in the words of the Apostolic Witness-put-into-writing which we call the New Testament, and the effects in the lives of the witnesses themselves, about which we know something from other sources.

I ask you to hold onto this analogy because it is very important indeed, in order to understand the generative function of Catholic faith, that we be able to distinguish between the 'happening' and what one might call the 'crime scene'. It is important for us that, once we have distinguished the happening, we be able to imagine it as something which can in principle be detached from that particular barn, that particular gun, those particular bullets and those particular teenagers. In fact, the 'happening' can be reproduced wherever, and the original barn and evidence will be a normative pointer to whether we are right in detecting the happening at work again. This is what we mean when we talk about Christ giving the Holy Spirit, and the Holy Spirit turning us into other Christs, summoning us into living the same happening in a wide variety of 'pock-marked barns'. If the dynamic of the happening in the new circumstances is such as to produce an analogous trail of evidence, we will know that we are indeed talking about the same happening. And if not, we will know that something else is going on; a different sort of happening not organically the same as our original happening, and not to be confused with it.

Sacrifice

As far as I can tell, it is the Catholic understanding that the best shorthand to describe the 'happening' is to call it a sacrifice. The 'happening' consisted in the complex and mobile event of God himself coming into our world, as an act of communication with us which was designed to show that the Creator of all things likes us and wants to prove to us that he can be trusted as wanting our good, wanting us to be free and to share his life. He set about proving his goodness, his 'not out to get you' nature, by offering himself to us, in what looked like something entirely familiar to us: a sacrifice. However, this sacrifice was curiously subverted: instead of it being us offering something to God, it was God offering himself to us. What God was doing was in fact showing us what we do when we sacrifice: ultimately we kill another human being as a way of keeping ourselves feeling safe, secure and good; dressing up a murder as something holy. And the point of God's act of communication was not to leave us feeling 'accused' by this piece of knowledge of what we are like, but to show us instead that though we are inclined to behave like that, we are not really like that, needn't be like that and that, if only we will let go of the world of false security and group self-congratulation at having 'got' the bad guy, we can be moved into a much bigger world, one in which we can be free, not frightened of dying, not having to grasp at security, but able to trust in a benevolence that wishes to take us into something much more alive than we can imagine. As we allow ourselves so to be moved, so we will discover amazing new and liberating possibilities of life together – including new scientific possibilities – which we just could not have imagined while 'hunting for another victim to sacrifice' seemed to be the solution to our problems.

Now this is a very complex 'happening'. It involves a particular historical act by a particular historical protagonist – a going to be crucified, a dying and then a being seen in an identifiable but mysterious form, an act both drawing from, and making newly available, an inherited network of texts and interpretations and a network of interpersonal relationships among those chosen to be witnesses. And the evidence we have of this hugely complex, dynamic, meaning-stretching happening, is the pock-marked barn wall of the texts of Scripture. These only make sense at all in as far as they enable us to begin to sense the parameters of the sheer richness, fullness and dynamic nature of the happening whose symptom they are, and then re-imagine ourselves undergoing that same happening which is working itself out in our midst, in our culture, and in our language.

I have emphasised this because the happening is, in principle, relatively free from the words that are the pattern of bullet holes it has produced. The texts of the Apostolic Witness are not the centre of the happening itself, they are the evidence from which the shape and dynamic of the happening can be scoped out and understood by us. But in principle, the same happening can happen anywhere where the same human dynamic of sacrifice is available to be subverted from within. In other words, the act of divine communication that is at the root of our faith is a radical interruption of, and reinterpretation of, a key element of human culture present, as far as we know, wherever there are humans. That element is our tendency to create group unity, togetherness and survival by resolving conflict through an all-against one which brings peace and unity to the group at the expense of someone, or some group, held to be evil. Every culture will partially hide and partially describe what it is doing, and will use different words to justify its group unity over against another. So, in every culture, the linguistic bullet marks of the happening as it unfolds in the midst of that culture will be different, but the dynamic of the happening will be the same, and we will know it by comparing the normative pattern of bullet holes seen in our New Testament barn with the pattern of bullet holes as they emerge in the cultures concerned.

In other words: the Catholic faith is of its nature syncretistic. Whatever culture it comes across, it will gradually subvert and change from within. This it does, not by imposing a set of laws, texts or norms, not by making a particular set of words, or a particular language, sacred and thus normative. Rather, it does this by making available the 'happening' through preaching, liturgy and example in such a way that whatever is 'sacred', or taboo, or demanding of sacrifice in that culture, ceases to have a hold on people as they come to lose their fear of death. This is when they start to be able to witness to the freedom that comes when one is no longer run by death and its fear, when one is able to make plans for people's long term good lasting beyond one's own lifespan, and when one is not afraid to stand up against sacred consensus in order to make truth available.

Please notice what this means: in any seriously 'religious' culture, the Catholic faith will, quite properly, be regarded as 'not religious enough'. Inevitably, as the Catholic faith permeates, various things will start to become unimportant: there will no longer be any good reasons for sacred rules concerning food, for particular sorts of food which may not be eaten, or for special cultic killing rites for meat, for religiously-required forms of dress[6], for beliefs of impurity or impropriety concerning women's menstrual cycles. It is not that these things will suddenly be abolished, but that in every case the same realities will gradually come to be looked at differently: is such and such a food good for you, or for us?; is such and such a form of dress appropriate?; might we not agree on such and such a communal fast for those strong enough to do so? In other words, it is the pattern of desire at work in us: whether we are seeking attention or acting modestly; whether we are deliberately scandalising and provoking those of bound conscience, or trying to help them move beyond their fears; whether we are strengthening our desire for God through prayer or fasting but without seeking to impress anyone with our holiness. This pattern of desire becomes the central thing to which we attend. It may very well have outward forms, but it is the pattern of desire, and not the outward form in itself, that matters.

Phrases like 'everything is permitted, but not everything is convenient', or 'to those who are pure, everything is pure', or 'the letter kills, but the spirit gives life', could be quoted by anybody, and sound the rankest of secularising remarks. And they are. They are all phrases by which St Paul sought to make the oddity of the un-religion which he was preaching available to people[7]: the subversiveness of the pattern of desire, unleashed by the sacrificial death of Christ, proving God's goodness to us when faced with any 'sacred' religious observance.

As Catholics we carry around with us, as it were, a mobile crime scene, in the form of the Mass. Please remember that the structure of the Mass is suspended halfway between being an ancient sacrifice or murder, and a modern community meal. And, taking advantage

---

6   It may, for instance, be perfectly reasonable to fight for the civil right to wear, or not to be forced to wear, a particular item of clothing or jewellery – a crucifix for example – in this or that public forum. But, since Christian faith makes no demands concerning what we wear, it would be misleading to claim that it is an infringement of the Christian faith that someone be prohibited from wearing a particular article of clothing or jewellery.

7   1 Cor. 6:12, Titus 1:15, 2 Cor. 3:6.

of that suspended state, the One who constantly wants to get through to us so that we can be free makes the sign alive, empowers it to be both the remembrance and the actual living presence of 'the happening'. This is so that we can simultaneously undergo being set free from fear and death, and enabled to stretch out in a new set of interpersonal relationships. In other words, what we have as the source of holiness is the portable crime scene that encourages the happening to incarnate itself in us again, to keep us constantly undergoing that crime scene.

This centrality of a flexible form of worship, which acts as a sign of the 'happening-having-happened' happening again in our midst, is as vital for what it is *not* as for what it is. It is not a text. It is not a law. We are not a people of the book. We are a people of Spirit and Sign. And the criterion we have for who God is and what God is like is given us by God *doing* something in our midst as human, something detectable at a purely anthropological level, something in flexible imitation of which we are invited to be swept up.

Here is what is bizarre: any normal account of the 'secular' would posit that the world of sacrifice is the direct opposite to the world of the secular. And that a religion based on a text or a law is much more likely to be secular than one based on a sacrifice. In fact, the reverse is true: unless you face up to the universality of the human tendency to scapegoat and sacrifice, text and law will merely create new forms of sacred as you impose them on others, and become much more tough, rigorous and likely to sacrifice those who fall foul of them. If you do face up to the universality of the human tendency to sacrifice, then any text and law you have will gradually come to be interpreted by your facing up to that tendency, and so will become comparatively toothless.

This is for the simple reason that the more you resist the tendency to sacrifice, the more the interpersonal relationships within your group will be de-sacralised, and the more it will become possible to learn who people really are. If you simply replace sacrifice with a book, you will recreate the same dynamics of sacrifice within your group, sanctifying those dynamics with the words of your text, while hiding from yourself that you are involved in sacrifice. If we have Jesus giving himself to us as sacrificed out of love constantly before our eyes, then there is a goodish chance that we will remember how prone we are to participating in such things. If, instead of that, we say 'that's over – now I'll go by the book', then we may fall into the terrible trap of seeing ourselves as the righteous, and others who don't go by the book as outsiders, sinners and so on. In other words, we will participate in the creation of a new sacred instead of allowing the Holy One to make us ordinarily holy. This ordinary holiness is found in the changing of our pattern of desire in the midst of the new time that has been brought about by the gradual undoing of the violent sacred.

So please remember this: the Catholic faith is not a rival sacrificial system among many. It is the undoing from within of all sacrificial systems, wherever they may be.

Law

Another way of looking at the same dynamic is to look at the Law. One of the first pieces of evidence that the happening had happened was that it became possible to detect that systems of goodness are terribly dangerous things. This was Paul's great insight concerning the Law. He wasn't being anti-Semitic. The space created by his own relationship to Torah was merely the particular barn within which the bullet marks of the happening had happened. He had perceived something about all sacred systems of goodness. And this is that they are traps. A system of goodness works by having rules which determine who is in and who is out. If some of the rules are hard to keep, so much the better, since that gives the impression that what is in fact a tragically easy form of goodness is, rather, heroically difficult. Paul's insight is that systems of goodness do not counteract people's desires that are run according to the familiar mechanism of gathering people into unanimity against an evil one to be expelled. On the contrary, systems of goodness depend on that mechanism, and they fall prey to it tragically easily, so that the most 'virtuous' within systems of goodness become those clearest about who is in and who is out.

What Paul understood from this is that, in practice, systems of goodness which give the impression of being chosen voluntarily do not really work that way. Their adherents are driven by them and become functions of the crystallised group violence which underlies them. So you get people who want to be good, and know that goodness looks like loving your neighbour as yourself, but because they are trapped in a system of goodness, they become unable to see their neighbour as themselves, and end up in fact hating their neighbour and perceiving them as something unclean, or outside, or not quite human, so as to be able *not* to love them as themselves. This is how you end up with people who are convinced that their religion is a religion of peace, yet who are quite unaware of how completely the system of goodness of which they are part jerks them about. This system makes them, in fact, incapable of creating peace. Paul discovered this very clearly:

> For I do not do the good I want, but the evil I do not want is what I do. [10]

Here, he is talking quite specifically about how the system of goodness runs people, and also about how the only way out of it is the realisation that, because God had occupied the place of one 'cursed by the Law' by undergoing the death of a despised criminal, the system of goodness has been rendered moot forever. From now on, the shape of goodness is the slow learning how to live without being dependent on a system of goodness. It involves instead our becoming aware of how much we have been loved by someone who is our victim. Because of that, we can become good, as we are loved in our most vulnerable places, rather than by forcing ourselves to cover up our vulnerability and be good so as to be loved. This means that the only sort of goodness we know is that of the penitent. It is only as undergoing being forgiven that we can possibly start to be good. And that means being daringly patient about forgiving others, not holding things against them, seeing them as the same as us before offering to put them right and so on.

This means that over time we can actually learn that some things that seemed to us to be good and holy and just are not so, and some things that seemed to us to be impure and evil and profane are not so. And this is because the question of whether we are allowing ourselves to be forgiven by our victim, and whether, in the light of that forgiveness, we are learning to treat our neighbour as though we are the same as they are, *this* question gradually comes to supersede all other questions of morality which a system of goodness would impose on us.

Let me give you both an ancient and a modern example. It might surprise you to know that the first written records we have in European history of people standing out against, and questioning witch trials, came not from enlightened sceptics but from people whose religious understanding led them to be highly sceptical of the craziness of the systems of goodness which were leading people to the pyre. Of the first four voices, two (1549 and 1612) were Spanish Inquisitors who understood perfectly well that their job was to introduce the boring secularism of due process into areas which would otherwise have tended to exciting lynch deaths. These Inquisitors would have been considered 'not sufficiently religious' by those at the time who were run by systems of goodness. Those for whom belief in the real evil of the witches was at that time what belief in the magical capacity of gay people to destroy the fabric of society is now: the dividing line between 'true believers' and the advancing secularity offered by the due processes inspired by Catholic faith. The truth was that the Inquisitors knew, within all the limitations of their time, that goodness after Christ's sacrifice looks like introducing boring intermediary forms of process and protection, and insisting on rules of evidence other than what is derived from torture, given how easy it is for us to ignore that Christ's sacrifice has happened, and instead to recreate it in a dangerous bid for goodness.

For a more modern example, look at the pictures published in the US media of José Padilla[8] in 2006. This man, a full US citizen who is a Muslim, was arrested, held without proper charge or trial for several years in a US prison, tortured, incarcerated and treated as though he were toxic waste by the American legal system, at the instigation of that champion of a system of goodness, John Ashcroft. All the evidence produced against him has been revealed to have been fabricated, so as to give the Administration the electorally

8   www.thesmokinggun.com/archive/1204061padilla6.html.

convenient weapon of 'a Muslim manufacturing a dirty bomb'. So much has the balance of his mind been altered by the torture and deprivation that he has suffered that, although it is clear that none of the evidence against him has stood up, it is not at all clear that he will ever be able to tell his own story or mount a defence. The reason I ask you to look at a picture of him, going back to websites in order to do so, is that, of the pictures of him that have been released, one stands out. It shows him chained, handcuffed in an orange jumpsuit, with goggles on (apparently so that he can't blink some signal in code to his alleged Al Quaeda colleagues). It shows him being pushed around by some quite extraordinarily overdressed and over-armed military figures, who look as though they have just rushed into a scene of extreme danger. In fact, they are about to escort a totally helpless, mentally unstable, rather small man towards a visit to the dentist in a prison in South Carolina. But what leaps out about the photograph is that it is exactly the same picture as a mediaeval representation of Christ being blindfolded, tortured and beaten by the Roman soldiers in Pilate's palace.

Anyone who sees that knows what is going on: a terrible system of goodness is torturing and destroying someone for whom Christ died. Yet it is the cursed one to whom we must reach out. It does not matter whether he is a Muslim, or a Jew, a Hindu, a Christian or a Communist. He is the one who is our neighbour because he is our self. It does not matter whether he would do the same to us if he had the chance. It matters terribly that we recognise that all systems of goodness have been interrupted by Christ, and that the apparent secularity, the boring due process, of the justice system seems to have been suspended by those who, thinking themselves good, are in fact being run by the evil of a sacred system of goodness to produce the usual, lethal, sacred results. And it matters not only for Mr Padilla, but it matters for all of us: for as long as we continue to find, torture and blame people like him, just so long will we remain in ignorance of what the real threats and dangers to any of our societies might be, and unable to take the small-scale, rational, proper precautionary measures to protect ourselves and others.

So, please remember this: the Catholic faith is not a system of goodness. It is the introduction into the world of a constant undoing of all and any systems of goodness such that a genuine, difficult, tentative goodness can begin to be elaborated by those who are becoming aware of how terribly dangerous 'goodness', and our need for it, is. But the perception that systems of goodness are terribly dangerous, and our very proper, modern suspicion of them: these are not enlightened, sceptical positions. They are the working out, over the time in which we have learned to suspend easy, sacred solutions, of a quite specific divinely-given tradition: the Catholic faith.

Faith

Again, it is difficult to imagine that it should be *faith* that is the gateway to a relatively benign secularity. Faith, surely, is the ultimate sacred ideology to be held to by those creating religious forms of togetherness and those who are in or out. But again, this is not so! The word 'faith' has come to stand in for 'religion', which is a blinding muddle. For most religions, faith is not particularly important. It is some or other form of practice, or act of acceptance, that is important. That the centrepiece of the Catholic faith should be exactly that, *faith*, a habitual confidence given us by Another in whose hands we can relax, is something far too little commented on. It means that what causes us to belong is a pattern of desire produced in us by someone we cannot see who is giving us the strength to live in the midst of this world as though death were not. And the access to this faith is desire: that we should *want* the gift of eternal life. It is the giving to us of this desire which we normally celebrate with that inverted religious rite called baptism. In this rite, we agree to undergo death in advance, so as to live thereafter with death behind us. It is an inverted religious rite, since it is not the crowd which gathers to drown the victim, but the candidate, not frightened of becoming a victim, who walks through the waters of being drowned so as to emerge on the other side into the welcome of those who are already living with death behind them.

It is for this reason, being dead in advance, that with baptism there comes a complete loss of identity given by any human forms of belonging: your parents are now your brother and sister in Christ; the only form of hierarchy which need matter to you is the hierarchy of service made available through signed members of the community you are joining (made available by us signed-ones more or less incompetently, to be sure, and with greater or lesser admixtures of an ability to relativise the way the world does 'power'). You have no king but Jesus, no prophet but Jesus and no priest but Jesus. And Jesus was a crucified criminal. Now you share that kingship, that gift of prophecy and that priesthood. Indeed, you are charged to make it present in the world by yourself incarnating and recreating the 'happening' which we looked at earlier.

But this means that no form of earthly belonging is sacred: your family, your tribe, your clan are not sacred, and you may have to stand up against them in order to live the truth; your homeland is not sacred, and you may have to be considered a criminal or a traitor by it in order to live the truth. Your only form of belonging is invisible except by sign. It is for this reason that there is no Christian Holy Land, only lands where the usual mixture of holiness and destruction is lived out, but where political frontiers can only be pragmatic matters, able to be negotiated over time, never sacred ones. There is no Christian Holy City, Rome's status being a purely historical and pragmatic one, and there being absolutely no sacred imperative that the Bishop of the Church in that city should also be a secular head of state. There are purely contingent and pragmatic considerations, always up for negotiation. It is genuinely indispensable to being a Catholic that we have a direct relationship to the successor of Peter. Yet that relationship is, in principle, entirely independent of whatever *secular* power structure adorns, or blackens, the Petrine office. And it is quite right that it should be secular affairs that give the context within which our relationship to Peter is lived out in each generation. The same reasoning lies behind the fact that there is no Christian Ummah – not because the West is somehow enlightened, decadent, and has lost its religious roots, meaning the remnants of Christendom, but because the whole point of Christianity is to bring down the sort of wall of protective sacredness which makes universality impossible by having a necessary 'other' over against whom we make ourselves 'good'.

The premise of the Catholic faith is that *there is no real other* in any meaningful religious sense; that is, 'another' who can be seen as so unlike us that they could not learn as we have learned, that we are victimisers and must learn not to be, and so belong to the same sign as we. There are only humans, who, starting from where they are, can have desire reformed in such a way as to learn not to create identity over against anyone else at all. Whenever we come across an apparent 'other' and start to get frightened and retrench into identity politics, we are not becoming *more* Catholic, but much *less* Catholic. When Catholic bishops intervene in the political forum, seeking to maintain a sacred right to discriminate against gay people, I am deeply saddened. However, this is not because I am a gay man, but because I am a Catholic. It is because I am a Catholic that I recognise that anyone playing identity politics with a victimary slant is functionally atheistic.

Is not identity politics a refusal to allow ourselves to undergo the happening that might teach us who our neighbour is, and empower us to grow into being not-over-against-anyone at all? Do not such politics tend to produce cheap togetherness and junk goodness? When I see this identity politics with a victimary slant from other groups in our society – and Lord alone knows there are enough of them from throughout the spheres which we call 'religious' and 'secular', both left and right – I am sorry for them, but how can I judge whether they know better? They are genuinely sheep without a shepherd. But when I see a Catholic authority doing this, I am really, really sorry, because we are without excuse. Catholics cannot complain about being treated victimarily, since at the centre of our faith we have agreed to be treated victimarily in advance, without ever seeking it, so as to be able slowly and patiently to work towards the truth and wellbeing of all our sisters and brothers with all that victim stuff already behind us. We have agreed to lose our identity in advance, so as to receive the much, much bigger, stronger identity of being contributed to by others who, whatever *they* may think, are not really over against me at all. That is what 'love your enemies and pray for those who persecute you' means!

Desire

Well, there is much, much more to say in this vein – I would love to have developed more fully the secularising effect in our midst of the doctrine of Creation as made full and complete by Christ, but time and space will not allow it. What I hope to have done is merely reminded you of something counterintuitive: that anything solid and lasting in what we call Enlightenment values of liberty, equality, fraternity and the birth of the scientific spirit, comes from a quite specific set of circumstances, brought into being and kept fragilely alive, with many a betrayal and backwards step, by the happening that is at the root of Catholic faith. It is the keeping alive of the sacrifice having happened in our midst, the imperative not to do it again and the realisation that it is only by creating social forms of togetherness such that we do not automatically resolve things by scapegoating, that we can have the space and freedom to discover and work out how our world really works. In other words, our ability to overcome scapegoating by having been empowered to live as if death were not, the realisation that this means one can stand up for the unpopular in order to make the truth shine, and our having started to forge a culture where this is a matter of common sense: this is a necessary precondition for science, for knowledge and for the possibility of humans coming to live together universally.

Of course, the downside of all this is that the happening is not our invention, and the power which has undone the roots of our scapegoating culture is not our own. The normal results of the undoing of a scapegoating culture, or of a system of goodness, are wrath, anger and violence out of control. Because the fragile bulwarks holding that society together have been undone, and there is less and less belief in the authentic 'sacredness' of whatever might put them together again. In the midst of this, the slow, patient forging of holy desire, and of the intermediary, negotiable institutions that encourage peace and foment flourishing, is very difficult, and very fragile. We are quite extraordinarily lucky to find ourselves on the inside of the happening. The Catholic faith enables us to navigate the wrath produced as sacred structures and boundaries collapse from within and a new creation emerges. How we make available to others the uniqueness of this strangely un-religious gift, without falling into the trap of allowing that uniqueness to seem like merely another rival form of exclusivity, is one of the great challenges of living and preaching the faith in our time.

CHAPTER 6

'Like children sitting in the market place':

a teaching on Wisdom, vanity and desire

Imagine yourselves, please, in a dusty market square in the Middle East[1]. Children are playing. They are involved in a traditional game of 'Weddings and Funerals'. In this game, the boys lead the way in calling the group to take part in a mock-wedding, for, in their adult world, playing the music at weddings, and dancing, was principally the work of the menfolk. So the boys play on pipes and penny whistles to conjure up the ambience of the wedding, and the girls respond, also being drawn into the dance. After a bit, the girls take over as the music shifts shape to become more mournful, and soon it is their shrill ululations, wailings and beating of heads and breasts in mock despair that powers the dance, and the boys for their part join in with mock weeping. The girls are imitating the adult womenfolk they will become, women whose role in leading rituals of mourning by extravagant gestures has become sadly familiar to us from endless pictures, televised from the Middle East, of funerals amidst human and architectural devastation. And back and forth the game will go.

As in all really good children's games, the point is not to get anything done. The point is the game itself, the fun of swinging to and fro between the different 'parties', the shift from wedding-type music and dancing to funereal music and wailing, and back again, the being involved in endless, apparently pointless, repetition. For this endless, apparently pointless, repetition is in fact a form of learning and socialising. Through it, the boys and the girls will become the

---

1   This chapter was born as the third William H. Shannon Lecture, delivered at Nazareth College, Rochester, NY, in February 2007.

adult actors in the culture for which their childhood is rehearsal time. Thus do play and culture reinforce each other.

Now imagine this scenario gone wrong. For some reason, the game has broken down. For the game to work, a certain reciprocity was needed, a certain give and take, so that each 'party' allowed itself to be sucked into the rhythm of the other. But that reciprocity has failed. The boys are sitting in the square, when they should be on their feet, making music, and they are shouting out to the girls 'we piped to you, and you wouldn't dance'. And the girls, also sitting, in another part of the square, are shouting back 'we wailed, and you would not weep'. In other words, each group is refusing to take part in the bit of the game which was dependent on the other, and each group is blaming the other for having started it first. A certain sort of reciprocity has collapsed, the benign reciprocity of each agreeing to be pulled into the game of the other, so as to make the whole thing more fun in a constant back-and-forth. And, instead, what looks at first glance like a simple failure of reciprocity has started up: each group is paralysed by its inability to enter into the game of the other.

In fact, however, this does not lead to a simple failure of reciprocity. The groups have not fallen silent and collapsed into glum introspection. Each group is still as resolutely dependent on the other as before, but the game has turned from a dance game into what we would call 'the blame game'. So each is calling out to the other 'it's your fault, you started it by not joining in with us', and 'no, it's your fault, you started it by not joining in with *us*', as though there could possibly be a beginning or an end in the game of weddings and funerals. This is the ultimate 'chicken and egg' situation: if you stop to argue about which came first, then you are left with neither. The culture you are rehearsing and learning how to repeat is one which has ground down into the futility of constant recrimination.

This children's game, as you all know, is the image which Jesus used[2] in order to say something about his contemporaries and about how Wisdom was working in their midst. The context of that teaching

---

2   Luke 7:31-5; Mt 11:16-19. I give the full text of the Lucan version as Appendix I.

is far richer than we are accustomed to hearing, so I would like to fill it in for you, in the hopes that we can find how we fit into the narrative. This is one of those places in the New Testament where, if we scratch the surface of the text, we can get a glimpse of an extraordinary teacher giving a scriptural master class in the midst of a group of his contemporaries. A clue that this is what is going on is to be found in the verse Jesus puts into the mouths of the opposing groups. One shouts

'We piped to you but you would not dance!'

while the other group shouts back:

'We wailed, and you did not weep!'

Now any listener with a sensitive ear to words could have picked up the allusion. And many of those in whose midst Jesus was teaching would have had long-honed recall of the sacred texts. Jesus is alluding to the text of the book of Ecclesiastes, one of whose best known sections is a list of things for which there is a proper time:

> For everything there is a season and a time for every matter under heaven:
> a time to be born, and a time to die;
> a time to plant, and a time to pluck up what is planted;
> a time to kill, and a time to heal;
> a time to break down, and a time to build up;
> *a time to weep, and a time to laugh;*
> *a time to mourn, and a time to dance;*[3]

Jesus links the quote and the children's game to point out that something has got out of kilter. In the book of Ecclesiastes, part of the Wisdom of Solomon, to whom it was traditionally ascribed, you get an indication of how things should be, as set out by Wisdom. When Wisdom orchestrates, there is a time for dancing and a time for mourning: each has its proper place, and they flow into each other, like the children's game when it is working. But, when vanity gets in the way, and vanity is described as like the wind, going round and round, going nowhere, you get the breakdown of the

---

3   Eccl. 3:1-4. I give the full text of Ecclesiastes 2:18-3:4 as Appendix II.

proper time for things, and people shouting at each other instead. So Jesus is pointing to something about how 'this generation', his contemporaries, have got bogged down into vanity, going nowhere at all, with their culture breaking down into mutual recrimination. Yet, nevertheless, he says, Wisdom *is* at work, bringing all things to be in a way that is artful, full of meaning and vitality– the very opposite of vanity, where everything goes round and round in ever more cantankerous circles, grinding down into paralysis.

It is not merely that Jesus asserts this about Wisdom; he shows himself fulfilling it by interpreting a situation he himself had provoked, and it is here that we begin to see quite what an extraordinary teacher he must have been. He takes advantage of something his audience has just seen, and must have been wondering about. In both Matthew and Luke (and it is the Lucan version which I am following), the passage about the children in the marketplace, with its Ecclesiastes reference to the proper time for dancing and for mourning, is immediately preceded by an account of the visit of some disciples of John the Baptist.

John was in prison, but had not yet been executed. He had been toiling in the desert, preaching a baptism of repentance, so as to prepare the way for one coming after him. This had been a popular religious phenomenon, leading to mass pilgrimages of multitudes of the 'simple faithful', including lots of people widely regarded as 'bad', to the Jordan. The religious professionals of the time had thoroughly disapproved of this: it was too extreme, too fundamentalist, too crude and too undiscriminating, so not really from God. During his baptising, John had even identified Jesus as the one for whom he had been preparing. Yet, now, in prison, and facing an uncertain future, which would in fact be his execution, John wondered whether he had really been right to point to Jesus as the one who was to come. So he sent some of his disciples to ask whether Jesus really was the one for whom he had been preparing, or whether they should be waiting for someone else.

Jesus replies to these visitors by pointing out the signs which he had just been performing, and of which there was ample evidence and talk all around him: people cured from diseases, from being bound by evil spirits, sight being given to the blind and so on. And then he tells John's messengers to consider what they have seen and heard; but he does so, again, by allusion to a series of passages from Isaiah[4] which tell of the coming of the Lord and what will happen on the day that he comes: the blind will see, the lame will be made whole and so on. Please notice that this 'coming of the Lord' is not prophesying the arrival of a miracle worker, it is announcing the arrival of the Creator who is fulfilling Creation, turning bits of 'futile' or 'vain' creation into Creation made fully alive and rejoicing. So Jesus answers John's question by saying 'I'm not going to answer you directly, for what you were preparing for is arriving as something on an entirely different level from what you expected, and you can infer what that is from what your messengers report to you of what they see: signs of the Creator in the midst of his people, fulfilling Creation'.

It is then that Jesus turns to his audience and asks them how they thought of John. His audience was composed of two different sorts of people: the kind who had gone out to take part in John's baptism, people who had been happy to take part in what would have been something like a popular mourning party, as crowds poured out for a penitential pilgrimage; and, on the other hand, the religious professional kind who had not gone, thinking all such vulgarity beneath them. What Jesus then does is quite masterly: he plunges his listeners into a ventriloquised performance of a central chunk of the book of Ecclesiastes. He has just been approached by the messengers from John, and what John had effectively been asking was 'Have I been in vain? Has my ministry been worthless?' And Jesus has assured him that far from it: the very reverse of vanity, Wisdom making Creation alive and filled out, is now at work.

Jesus then turns to the audience and, by allusion, puts into John's mouth the following passage from Ecclesiastes:

> I hated all my toil in which I had toiled under the sun, seeing that *I must leave it to the man who will come after me*; and who knows whether he will be a wise man or a fool? Yet he will be master of all for which I toiled and used my wisdom under the sun. This also is vanity. So I turned about and gave my heart up to despair

4   Is 29:18-19; 35:5-6; 61:1.

over all the toil of my labours under the sun, because sometimes
a man who has toiled with wisdom and knowledge and skill must
leave all to be enjoyed by a man who did not toil for it. This also is
vanity and a great evil. What has a man from all the toil and strain
with which he toils beneath the sun? For all his days are full of
pain, and his work is a vexation; even in the night his mind does
not rest. This also is vanity. There is nothing better for a man than
that he should eat and drink, and find enjoyment in his toil. This
also, I saw, is from the hand of God; for apart from him [*Hebrew*:
me] who can eat or who can have enjoyment? For to the man who
pleases him God gives wisdom and knowledge and joy; but to the
sinner he gives the work of gathering and heaping, only to give to
one who pleases God. This also is vanity and a striving after wind.[5]

This is the passage immediately leading into the Ecclesiastes passage
I quoted to you above, about there being a time for mourning and
a time for dancing!

Do you see what Jesus is doing then, when he asks the crowd:
'Whom did you go out to see?'? 'Did you go out to see a reed blowing in the wind – as though John really were a symbol of the vanity
of the wind blowing? Or did you go out to see the flip side of that
vanity: the vanity of the soft-clothed courtier to whom everything
appears to have been given, the one who can 'eat and have his enjoyment'? In other words: was this trip out to the Jordan simply a
mimetic function of crowd desire, which one moment fixates on
an ascetic celebrity, so as, moments later, to fixate on a luxurious
celebrity? Or was there something more than this there? And then
Jesus answers for them: 'Yes, there was more to it than just crowd
desire. John really was a prophet. There was in his message and his
ministry something that really was from God. He was in fact fulfilling Malachi's prophecy of the messenger, or angel, who was to
come before God himself came. John's ministry was not a function of vanity, for Wisdom; which is to say: the ordered pattern
and bringing into being of creation really was at work in preparing
people by penitence, even though what was coming, the wedding
feast, was going to be so different in kind, not merely in degree,

that, great though John was, what is coming about now is of an entirely different order.'

Well, as you can imagine, upon hearing this, there was an outbreak of partisan spirit among the listeners: Jesus was apparently justifying those who had gone out to John, those who had been easily moved. He was saying: 'Yes, there really was something there, this was not simply vanity'. And of course, this enabled, as it always does, those people to crow victoriously over the uptight. The uptight took themselves more seriously than to allow themselves to be swept up in such things. They looked down on the easily-moved. The up-tight had more serious things to be about: it was their job, after all, to preserve the bride spotless for the wedding, to prepare the wedding feast when the Lord would come and marry Israel, to be the friends of the bridegroom. And, of course, if your job is to keep the bride spotless, you need to purify her constantly by getting rid of sinners and other diluters of holiness from the midst of you. So you engage in constantly fencing around desire, to make quite sure that you are sinless. And you can clearly see that the sort of people who are easily moved are just the sort of people who are easily run by desire, carried hither and thither by every wind of fashion. These are just the sort of people who get in the way of the Lord coming to his marriage feast, so we must discount them. If they go off after something, you can pretty much guarantee that it is not the sort of thing the friends of the bridegroom ought to be about: so we can easily discount the baptism of John as not having been from God.

The really interesting thing here is that Jesus, contrary to what we might think of this story at first blush, does not simply side with the 'easily-moved' over against the 'up-tight'. He does something far more subtle. He notes the reactions of both groups to his insistence that John was a prophet, and what he sees is the 'easily-moveds' celebrating and rejoicing in the discomfort of the 'up-tights' who are pooh-poohing the whole notion. And then he stands back from both groups and says 'You know, you're really as bad as each other. You up-tights, you would-be friends of the bridegroom, have been trying to get everyone to dance to your tune, trying to make the whole culture into a preparation for the wedding entirely on your terms, and completely despising those who don't dance to your tune, making it more and more difficult for them to be part of the wedding. You regard them as easily-moveds, so that when they started wailing with a funeral-type dance, following John the Baptist, you wouldn't take part in their dance, by going along and weeping with them. By being up-tight you make it more difficult for yourselves to be moved, for sure, but that makes it far more difficult for you to be moved towards what is good, as well as towards what is bad.

'And you easily-moveds, you found it easy to be swept up in the dance of repentance which went along with John, but you don't seem to be aware that there is no point to that repentance dance if it doesn't lead into the wedding dance. Will you be able to follow me as I lead you into the wedding dance? At least the up-tights have it right about it being fundamentally a wedding dance, even if their childish rehearsal for a wedding falls as spectacularly short of the real thing as your childish rehearsal for mourning falls short of the real breaking and remaking of hearts which is to come with the Holy Spirit. You refuse to join in their dance, just as much as they refuse to join in yours.'

But what is key here, and it is a feature of Jesus' teaching in all the Gospels, is that being an 'up-tight' is no different from being an 'easily-moved' in terms of desire: both are equal and opposite pathologies of desire which play into each other. The up-tights need the easily-moveds so as to compare themselves with them and feel good about themselves by contrast. And the easily-moveds need the up-tights because the up-tights are so obviously inhuman and screwed up in comparison to 'us good, plain common folk, with none of your lah-di-dah airs and graces'. Each stakes out his own petty 'goodness' over against the other, and neither enters into real goodness which requires no comparison against the other, but a common-being-sucked-into-a-common game, building each other up in readiness for the real wedding. A society and a culture is functioning well when its masters of the 'good' as well as its masters of 'getting on with things, making mistakes and getting up again' are sufficiently in harmony with each other that there is an easy flow between the two elements. But it has broken down when the two elements are made into each other's enemies, grinding each other down into futility.

Now, of course, it is true, as Jesus points out in other passages, that it is much easier for the 'easily-moveds' to make it into the Kingdom than it is for the 'up-tights', and he warns the religious leaders that prostitutes and tax-collectors are making their way in easily, while the 'righteous' stand scandalised outside. But, and this is important: this is not a populist point of the sort 'the people, *el pueblo unido*, are the good guys versus the religious leaders, who are the bad guys'. Jesus is not a populist teacher, and crowds and their patterns of desire are not good things in the Gospels! Jesus is observing something much more straightforwardly anthropological: of the two equal and opposite pathologies of desire, being easily moved has the advantage that it is easier to get out of. If you are the sort of person who is easily moved, it has the disadvantage that it makes it awfully difficult for you to be consistently and constantly involved in a project over time, and much easier for you to swept up in a fashion, or for a little slip-up to progress rapidly into a major vice. But it has the advantage that it is much less hard for you to be able to recognise that you have screwed up, and to respond to help when it is offered.

Whereas, if you are one of the up-tights, you will be unaware of how much your own needs and desires, including your reactions to the crowd, are enmeshed in your long-term making of yourself good. And, because you are less likely to have a major slip-up, you are also more likely to avoid the humiliation which goes along with being confronted by your pathology, and you are much less likely to appreciate such help as you are offered. In other words, it will be much more difficult for you to be stripped down and refitted for entry into the Kingdom. And we all know this: Alcoholics Anonymous groups abound, so too do Narcotics Anonymous, and groups for those with sexual addictions, but I am not sure that I know of any support group for addicts to righteousness, for those who have become enmeshed in and paralysed by their own highly danger-ous pursuit of goodness. Unless, of course, we remember that the

Catholic Church, when it is faithful to what it is about, is largely God's own attempt to set up a worldwide association of 'Fundamentalists Anonymous'.

To finish his teaching, Jesus does indeed then turn specifically to the up-tights, to the Pharisees and lawyers, who are, of course, the members of his audience who will have best understood what use he is making of Ecclesiastes. He points out to them their own stuckness of desire, their own paralysis and inability to enter the Kingdom. They look at John the Baptist, and they see an extreme ascetic, and they say to themselves: 'Oh, that's much too much – that's religious desire wound up to a crazy, or even a demonic, pitch. We should have nothing to do with this.' And then they look at Jesus, who has none of these ascetic practices, and is perfectly happy to keep thoroughly impure company, and they say to themselves: 'Oh, that's far too little – that's religious desire which is far too relaxed and unconcerned about purity and holiness. We should have nothing to do with that.' So they are in a perfect double bind, unable to move this way or that, but unaware that in this double-bind, they are as much moved by desire as the crowds they despise, just moved into constantly painful stuckness.

Jesus' final salvo goes back to the Ecclesiastes text which he has been illustrating consistently throughout. In Ecclesiastes 2:18-20, which Jesus puts into John's mouth, the speaker effectively says: 'Here I have been toiling away in impossible circumstances, and all that I have done will be left to another. Has it all been in vain?' Jesus has already answered this question: 'No, it was not vain. You were not vain in your ministry. You worked with Wisdom and knowledge.' Now, the very next verses of Ecclesiastes, 2:20-22, imagine John putting a second question: 'OK, let us suppose that I *am* a man of Wisdom and knowledge; even so, might I not have left everything to be enjoyed by someone who didn't toil for it, and wouldn't that also be vanity and great evil? In other words: Wisdom might be justified in my work, but not in the work of the one who comes after me. What do you say to that?

Well, what Jesus says to that is: 'I'm doing what it says in Ecclesiastes 2:24-25, where it says "There's nothing better for people than that they should eat and drink and find enjoyment, and far from it being a matter of my being a drunkard and a glutton, these things are from the hand of God." In fact, apart from *me* (and you can imagine the frisson in his listeners as they realised what he was implying), how could they eat or have enjoyment? For God gives wisdom and joy and knowledge to whom he pleases, eating and sharing enjoyment with them. So, not only was John a child of Wisdom, but so am I, and so are those to whom I give Wisdom by sharing in their meals – Wisdom is justified by all her children, and doesn't that leave those of you who think of me as a glutton and a drunkard in the position of sinners who are gathering and heaping in vain, while God gives his riches somewhere else?'

Luke's Gospel does not give an account of the reaction of the Pharisees and lawyers to Jesus' teaching here. But I hope I have given you enough of a glimpse of what that teaching style might have been like to see that they would have been simultaneously amazed at the freedom and authority with which he interpreted Scripture; admiring and, I should imagine, not a little jealous of the way he was able to bring together both events as they unfolded around him, and the perfect set of scriptural texts from which to make sense of those events. They would of course, have been left challenged and discomfited by the open-ended questions he was leaving as to where they themselves fitted into the Scripture – not necessarily where they would have liked to have been. But some of them, I suspect, would have been left with a more speculative curiosity. For Jesus wasn't merely being playful, though he was that, and you can almost hear the rabbinic playfulness beneath his handling of these texts, or you would be able to if I knew how to handle them less clunkily

Jesus was suggesting, in a quite coherent fashion, something about the relationship between God, creation, desire and the present time. Let me have a go at trying to bring this out, because it illustrates something which is both fundamental to our faith, and yet something about which we are little accustomed to think.

The great Jewish breakthrough concerning monotheism is something to which we Catholics give far too little attention. And yet, without it, nothing in our texts make sense. The Jewish break-through into monotheism was not simply a matter of having worked out that all the other gods were either silly, or better considered as different faces of the same god, so that it was more hygienic, and more grown-up to have one god. It was not a speculative matter at all. If it were a speculative matter, the ancient Hebrews would have found themselves worshipping one god, with a small g – a projection of their group unity and togetherness. This god would have been a function of their pattern of desire, and their worship of this god would have in fact been an imprisonment in a form of totalitarianism; a form of totalitarianism in which they would have enclosed themselves, thinking themselves superior to others, at-tributing their imprisonment to the limits of created order as set out by their one god. Their worship of their one god would have been what kept the order of creation going and would have given them goodness, and, of course, enabled them to identify who the bad guys are.

However, this was not what happened at the great Jewish break-through into monotheism. Indeed, something almost exactly the reverse of this happened. The Ancient Hebrews made the discovery, or underwent the revelation, which are two ways of referring to the same thing, that far from god being a projection of theirs, trapped into being part of the order of everything that is, as a guarantor of order and prop to their group goodness, they and everything that is were projections of God, who is not part of anything that is. This is not, as it were, *an addition* to, or *a perfection* of, religious under-standings of God available in other cultures, but it is a complete turning inside out of any religious understanding available in any culture, and, once made, it cannot be gone back on.

Let me give you a somewhat crass image to help make sense of this turninginside out. I would like you to imagine a brown paper bag from a bakery. Now, imagine that this bag is upside down, so that the open bit is at the bottom, and the closed bit is at the top. Let us imagine that since this is a pretty classy bakery, there are all sorts of quality crumbs, of an energetic nature, and these crumbs are clustering inside the closed top of the bag, pushing and shoving the edge of the bag, trying to stretch its limits, trying to see out through the bag, which they can a little, since a brown paper bag *is* slightly see-through, and yet lends a mistakenly sepia tint to every-thing you see through it. Well, of course, the more the crumbs push and pull, all they do is push and pull the bag more firmly around them, and everything they see is in fact a function of the bag and its being pushed and pulled around by them.

Now imagine something they cannot see properly, but which starts to happen: a giant fist comes out of nowhere and slowly and gradually pushes in the top of the bag, against which all the crumbs are pushing upwards. This fist which seems at first to be an enemy, pushes on and on – it is much stronger than the crumbs, and in fact it pushes the bag right through, with the crumbs still pushing against it, and gradually, and without the crumbs noticing it, what used to be the inside of the bag has become the outside of the bag, and the fist has become hidden inside the bag. The fist turns and starts to raise itself up, with the crumbs still pushing against the crease. But they are now pushing downwards, and they are in fact on the top of and outside the bag, which is being gently held aloft by the fist within. Gradually a few of the crumbs stop trying to push down and turn round and look around about them.

For the first time ever, they have no sacred canopy, no protec-tive cover, nothing at all hemming them in, no sepia-tinted vision. And they can look outwards towards nothing, and then down at the paper bag and for the first time, look at it as if from outside anything that is. Which means that they can see themselves, as well, as part of everything that is, but with the extraordinary relativity which is made possible by being able to see that it is all contingent, not sacred, not part of any push and pull of their own. The moving fist, which they cannot see, is not part of anything that is, but what the fist has done is enabled them to see everything that is as open-ended, and not tied to a sacred order made in their own image.

When we talk about God as Creator, and as Creation, it is this huge turning inside out of worlds that is being talked about: the dif-ference between 'us being trapped in an order of our own creation which is a function of our own projections', and our discovering to our amazement that there is an unmentionably huge power behind everything that is, that we and everything that is are contingent to and projections of that power. With this there comes the extraordinary freedom of the realisation that there is an 'outside' to everything that is, so that everything that is, is contingent, and that means not tied down into sacrality, divine power struggles and so on. And, of course, apparently 'religious' people of every generation will try to reject the Creator and Creation, preferring instead a god who maintains a sacred order according to a set textbook. And the reason why is not hard to see: if you are outside the bag, and looking outwards, and the fist is hidden beneath you, as it were, in the bag, what you will see is: nothing, nothing all around. You will be considered an atheist by all, because nothing you see or can imagine is God. And everything that is will be open to exploration.

Well, so much would have been absolutely common ground between Jesus and the Pharisees and lawyers with whom he was talking. Any self-respecting Rabbi knows this: that when we say God is not one of the gods, we are saying that God is much more like nothing at all than like anything that is, because it is only by God not being anything that is, that everything that is can be a function of God. It is, however, not easy to keep this endlessly open-ended glimpse alive. And after you have got over the initial excitement of the great reversal, the perception that everything that is rests on God's constantly bringing it into and holding it in, being, a further, perfectly reasonable question asserts itself. This is the question of vanity.

After all, there you are, standing on the outside of the bag, you have undergone the great reversal, you are able to look about at everything that is and you know that this is all from God. So there is all this open-endedness that you cannot go back from. And yet, so what? Does not everything seem to be constantly grinding down anyhow? What is the point of it all? It does not lead anywhere, does it? There may be a fist in the bag, but since everything moves altogether, I cannot detect whether it is going anywhere. I have no sense that any of the power of the fist is able to reach through the bag and inspire me to look out with shining eyes. This is the regard of vanity: the eyes that could be making the extraordinary glimpse are seeing all that is as somehow not sharing in the vivacity and endless creativeness that is God. And it is a pattern of desire that forms those eyes. A pattern of desire that goes round and round getting nowhere. When St Paul talked about 'creation being subjected to futility', this is what he was talking about: we can look at everything that is, and yet not have it be bright for us, not have it reflect a glory not its own, or yield a loving intention. What *is* is not shot through for us with a creative desire that we can sense, a being pulled beyond itself into something more. It just is, and our hearts curve down with the sense of an arrow falling short of its mark, a disappointment at things somehow not being what they might.

The opposite of vanity in the Hebrew tradition was Wisdom. And Wisdom was what brightened the eyes, enabling the one making the glimpse to see that there was a point to it all; there was a 'this is going somewhere', 'this is meant for something', 'God does not make things in vain' and 'all this undetermined open-endedness is good and for something good, and good for you'. Now, the genius of a book like Ecclesiastes is how it sits on the open edge of what is and looks out in a way which can be read as tending down towards vanity, or can be read as tending up towards Wisdom.

But here is the point: if there really was to be Wisdom, then it must come from somewhere, and it must be the same somewhere as God, it must be part of the fist breaking through the paper bag into our own eyesight, or else it too is simply a part of everything that is, and cannot therefore be a criteria *by which* we can know that what is, is *for* something. And, if Wisdom comes from the same somewhere as God, and is to do with the holy desire by which 'everything that is' is held opening out into ever greater vivacity, then it too must be something living, eternal and contemporary, because Creation is always an eternal 'now'. From the point of view of us humans, such a holy, living, eternal desire, intelligence or dynamic, forming creation constantly from within, cannot only be something that is 'just out there', about which we know, but must be something that is coming, coming towards us, sensed as on its way. A Wisdom that was 'just out there', and did not have any 'coming towards us', would be just as much subject to vanity as everything else. For it would not be enabling us to break out of the vanity of our downward-curved regard.

Now this is where Jesus' discussion with his contemporaries gets really interesting. The notion of Wisdom as personal, almost a divine persona, when not actually a goddess, since feminine, who accompanied creation: this was part of the old priestly tradition of the First Temple. The religious leaders of the second Temple period, the ones who gave us the Pentateuch, and their disciples, had rejected huge elements of that Wisdom tradition. Creation has happened, and thereafter what we have is Torah. No visions, no incarnations, no emanations from God, angels are deeply suspicious; just Torah. So you should not look into mysteries, but merely study the Law of the Lord. That will give you all the wisdom you need. There is no need for prophecy to be fulfilled, for a divine spirit to be given, or for the will of the Lord to be made manifest in certain ways in history.

It is this that Jesus is challenging: he is not only teaching, but performing Wisdom coming into the world in and through a specific historical acting out which is happening now. 'These miracles are not simply the products of a wonder-worker. This is what happens when the Creator is in the midst of his people, making Creation alive, bursting with potential. This habit of mine of eating with sinners is not simply another example of eating well since there's nothing better to do, which would be a good example of 'what is' curving down towards vanity. By eating with sinners in this way, I am actually making of those meals a sign of the wedding feast that is coming, since that is what Wisdom is preparing: there is a point to everything, it is good and it will end in rejoicing. But please, if you reject the One who is coming in, you are in fact left with One whose will for you, and intention for you, you can't really know, and you will remain stuck in vanity. If you are too hygienic in your understanding of God, you will be left with a Creation which you will try to close down as being too much for you, and you will somehow be disappointed in it, whereas if you understand that the fist is, even as we speak breaking through the paper bag, that I am in fact a finger of the appearing fist, and that all these crumbs can themselves become fingers, able to become alive from within the meaning of what is and take part in making it something new and fresh, then, and only then, will you really be worshipping the Creator. Only then will you be a living part of the wild ride adventure of what is, from within.'

Well, I do not want to go on too long from here. I just wanted to illustrate how an ancient Jewish discussion about the Creator and a discussion of us being reached by a new pattern of desire starting from where we are is in fact the same discussion. Just as the Jewish discovery of Creation meant an ability to glimpse the contingency of everything that is, so Jesus' resurrection meant an ability to see the contingency, the non-necessity, the non-sacrality, even of death, thus setting us free to live as if death were not. And the giving of the Holy Spirit enables us to see the contingency and the non-sacrality of all human desire. Not something to be run away from, or protected against, but something which the Creator can curve upwards, away from vanity, towards up building, and indeed towards a fruition and a joy, starting in the permanent now, which is where we are.

Some of you, I am sure, will have noticed that, not at all unlike the people gathered to hear Jesus in the passage I read to you, we too know of, or we may be, 'friends of the bridegroom', whose desire to keep the bride pure causes them to engage in constant restriction of access to marriage. And we also know of, or we may be, those who, having been constantly told that they cannot marry, have given way to vain desire and all its sadness. We are probably, in fact, people who flit between being up-tights and flibbertigibbets. I hope that, perhaps, this evening, we will have been able to hear, breathing through the pages of our Scriptures, the voice of the bridegroom, laughing tenderly at our waywardness and summoning us, coaxing us, encouraging us, to come to the wedding.

CHAPTER 7

God and desire

There is a lovely Italian word to which I would like to introduce you[1]. The word is 'rovesciamento' and it means something rather like 'turning everything upside down'. It goes quite well towards describing what happens at the end of the first act of many two-act operas from the early nineteenth century. Typically, what has gone on during the first act is that the characters have come together, fallen in love, plotted, schemed, planned bold new enterprises, whatever. But at the end of the first act there comes a moment when the characters, and all their schemes and machinations, are completely caught by surprise as it is suddenly revealed that the nice young man – who appears to be a steady but boring suitor to the leading lady, who has her eyes on an elder, richer man, who has his eyes on the governorship of some improbable chunk of the globe, but needs the money of someone else's aunt to buy the post – is in fact the Czar of all the Russias, or, maybe, Mary Queen of Scots in drag, or, just conceivably, a wicked Eastern Potentate who is in fact the illegitimate child of the lady he is apparently wooing.

At the moment of revelation in the opera, there is an outbreak of musical shock, where everybody gathers and sings, usually quietly and with a stunned quality, words like 'Ah, qual colpo inaspettato!' – 'What an unexpected blow!' – which it is, of course, since the silly dears haven't read their programme notes. After this moment of stupefaction, there is then an increasingly mad and frenetic bit of singing as everyone falls out of shock, and begins to assess their new-found situation, which is entirely different from what they had imagined up until now. So each sings separately, and yet all together

---

1   This chapter was born as a presentation for the annual meeting of the English Gay and Lesbian Catholic group, Quest, held in Sheffield in July 2007.

and with increasing hysteria, words to the effect of 'What the f...
do I do now?' – delicacy requires that that bit of the libretto remain
in the original French. This is, of course, the moment the composer
has been looking forward to. Often the best and most striking bit
of music in the opera is this aggravated scene of three, or seven,
or eleven characters and, along with them, the chorus, seriously
losing the plot and storming off in different stages of fury, rapture,
jealousy, despair and scheming, their differing feelings all being expressed simultaneously and yet all kept in harmony and rhythm by
the composer.

This is what I mean by talking about 'rovesciamento'. What the
characters know, their ways of understanding each other, and all
of their forms of interaction, are suddenly turned inside out by the
emergence in their midst of a sort of revelation: that someone who
they had considered as part of their story in a certain way was in
fact not part of their story in the way they had thought of at all, but
was part of quite a different story, which they had not taken into
account. In fact, the whole of the story of each one of them, their
longings, intentions, relationships, schemes and plans, all of this,
has now been undermined from within by someone who they took
to be simply another agent within their own story, but who now appears as the protagonist of a different story, a story being driven by
power lines quite other than they had imagined, one in which each
of them is assigned a much more peripheral role than he or she had
bargained for. In the light of this 'turning upside down', the stars of
some characters will unexpectedly be in the ascendant, and others
who seemed to be powerful will find themselves very much on the
wane.

In an opera, of course, the second act will be the story of how
the characters learn to cope with this new reality, jostle together in
a new set of relationships with each other, and eventually, if it is a
comedy, the leading lady will be led to the altar of marriage while
all praise her virtue, and, if it is a tragedy, she will be led to the
block or the pyre to be sacrificed, while all proclaim her heroism
and innocence. Same difference, really, and you do not need to be
an old school feminist to wonder whether it is not the same altar at
the end of both versions.

However, I am going to ask you to suspend your need for the second act for the moment, and stick with the moment of 'rovesciamento', the 'turning everything upside down', at the end of the first act. Because I want to suggest that one of the reasons for the poverty of modern discourse about God, whether it be to deny God, à la Dawkins or Hitchens, or to affirm God, in the way that so many of our religious representatives do, is that all of these people seem to be talking about a character who is evident in Act I of the opera from the beginning, someone who is absolutely part of the deal-making, schemes and story-telling of the group, or is claimed to have set the boundaries within which such storytelling makes sense.

What I want to suggest is that this is a complete misunderstanding, both on the part of the deniers and the affirmers, since the God to whom at least Christian, and, I respectfully suggest, Jewish, theology is beholden, is only able to be talked about at all as the 'rovesciamento' gets under way, that is, from within the losing of bearings of everyone involved in the opera.

It is from here that I would like to begin to talk about God and desire, and, if you will allow me, I will stick with my operatic analogy a bit longer. What happens in the opera when the moment of revelation occurs is that all the characters start to become aware that their previous stories, their patterns of desire, their schemes and their relationships were all a lie. They were all based on taking for granted that what appeared to be the case, was the case, that the apparent holders of power were the real holders of power, that the character dressed as the Grand Duke was the real Grand Duke, and not in fact a valet dressed up so as to test them all while the real Grand Duke came amongst them disguised as a chambermaid. But, as the moment of revelation dawns, so it becomes clear that each one of the characters has taken for granted something that was in fact false, and has based and staked their life and their love, who they are, and who they are to become, on this fake reality.

The important thing about the revelation which turns everything upside down is not that someone who did not have power now suddenly has it — which would merely be a change within the story, a dramatic one, and a shocking one no doubt, but not a complete turning of everything upside down. – but that those undergoing the 'rovesciamento' are becoming aware that someone who they 'placed' in a certain way, as relatively peripheral to their plans and schemes, has *all along* been someone quite else, and that therefore it is not merely a matter of their adjusting themselves to a new reality whereby someone who was not important has become important, rather as newspaper owners switch sides when candidates they did not really like start to look unbeatable in the polls. Rather, it is a question of becoming aware that up till now they had been living a lie *all along* and that the only possible reactions to the revelation that has thrown their world are: on the one hand to storm off, determined to hold fast to the unreality of pretending that it has not happened; or, on the other hand, gradually to allow the whole pattern of desire which ran them to be brought into question by the revelation. This will mean their learning to recognise their own vulnerability to the whims and intentions of the emerging protagonist, including their vulnerability to his memory of their previous contempt for him, when they thought he was the chambermaid, and their beginning to allow themselves to be reconciled to the new way in which reality is showing itself to be.

Now, bizarre though it may seem, what I hope I have shown you here is an understanding of the relationship between God and creation such that the doctrine which we call Original Sin occupies its proper place within the scheme of Christian theology. The Christian revelation supposes that we start not at the beginning, or the end, of the opera, but in the middle. It presupposes that, as the beginnings of the 'rovesciamento', the turning of everything upside down, come among us, so we start to be able to look back and see that our stories up until now, the whole pattern of our desires and how we relate to each other, have been based on a lie, and that all along someone who seemed to be a particular bit player in our drama was in fact the real protagonist coming into the midst of the story and beginning to tell it from an entirely different perspective. So what we call Original Sin is not a mere fact about us, tediously installed into the beginning of Act I of the opera, as part of the normal ordered setting within which we think we are acting. The doctrine of Original Sin points always towards a backwards glance, made available as the 'rovesciamento' gets under way, a backwards glance provoked in us as we move out of what we thought of as normal into a new story, with a new protagonist. It's the 'Oh, so that's what I was caught up in!' as we become aware of beginning to be carried off somewhere else.

Well, I have started here, not because I really wanted to talk to you about Original Sin (though no Catholic discussion about God and desire can bypass the issue), but because it is my claim that the doctrine of Original Sin is an important piece of the grammar of how we talk about God. It is, or should be, a permanent reminder that we humans do not come to talk about God from a stable, fixed, starting place we can dominate by our discourse. On the contrary, if God is true, then the starting place for our discourse is always as those in the midst of undergoing something. We always start as those who, having thought of ourselves (depending on our self-importance) as minor or major protagonists, in a narrative which we thought we understood, are always having that narrative blown apart by the emergence of another narrative in which someone else is protagonist, and we are peripheral in a way which turns out to be surprisingly reassuring. Or, in other words, the kind of 'we' that has brought each one of us into having the unsteady and instable thing we call a 'self', an 'I', over time, *that* 'we' is being radically restructured, and each of us is finding ourselves losing a certain sort of self so as to be given a quite different one in relationship to quite a different sort of protagonist.

I hope it will not come as too much of a surprise if I say that what I am trying to do here is to highlight the difference between 'a god' and 'God'. And I am trying to do so in a way that makes clear that the difference is not to do with the size and importance of the divinity in question. Rather, the difference is between something that is part of the universe we assumed we were in, in Act I, on the one hand; and on the other hand, an emerging protagonist who is provoking the 'rovesciamento' we are undergoing, and, in the light of which, Act II will look entirely different from Act I. So, for ease of description, 'a god' is always a character in Act I, while God is in principle not a character in any act at all. God is, from the standpoint of all of us involved in Act I, the entirely unexpected and random-seeming power behind the 'rovesciamento' which led to the possibility of there being an Act II; an Act II which is an entirely different story from what could be imagined from within the confines of the characters' view of what might happen starting where they are in Act I.

What I am trying to do here is to bring out something odd about the difference between 'a god' and 'God', since it is too easy, in discussions of 'the advent of Hebrew monotheism', to find ourselves talking about different sorts of 'it' – on the one hand, gods, which are 'its', objects, projections of ours, or of our social groupings, slalom poles within our negotiation of the piste which is our universe; and, on the other hand, 'God' which is a much bigger and more definitive sort of 'It'. One that sets everything up, gives rules to go by, and cannot be negotiated round. Well, the trouble here is that both the little 'its' and the big 'It' share in the same essential quality of 'it-ness' – that is to say, they are objects which are, to some degree or other, within our ken.

However, the whole point of the advent of Hebrew monotheism is that it does not fit into this picture at all: in fact it completely reverses it. What the advent of Hebrew monotheism looked like could, and can, only be detected in the radical reversal of desire which it produces. It is not that a new 'It' begins to open up *before* our gaze, a gaze brought into being by the relationships that have taught us who we are and shown us what we can see and desire. Instead, 'I Am bringing everything to be'[2] starts to emerge, as it were, from *behind* our capacity for gaze, behind everything that is, by producing profound alterations of the patterns of desire which enable us to be 'selves' at all, such that we find ourselves ceasing to be self-grasping 'I's' who share in the creation of 'its' by rivalry, defence, paranoia and projection.

So what it feels like to us to undergo 'I Am bringing everything to be' is much more like a loss of all those sacred projections and 'its' on whom we could depend and over which we could fight. And in their place, there is nothing at all in our gaze, no god at all. This is

2   Exod. 3:14.

because the new pattern of desire which is calling us into being is without ambivalence, conflict, scarcity or danger, and so the new 'I's', the new 'selves' which will be the embodied symptoms of this new pattern of desire, rest peacefully upon their own given-ness by another. It is not *what* we see, but our capacity for gaze itself that is undergoing transformation as we find ourselves being given an equality of heart so that we see as we are seen and we know as we are known[3], without distortion, because 'I AM' is enlivening us into being.

Please just think of the difference between referring to God as 'He' or 'She' on the one hand – an object *about whom* we can talk, and referring to 'I Am who causes all things to be'. The ancient Hebrew custom of not pronouncing the Name with anything like ease seems to me to be very sane: it is a protection against us instrumentalising a protagonism which cannot be instrumentalised, for indeed we are part of the instrument, and something quite outside our range of protagonisms is at work. To use the familiar analogy[4]: were a clay pot capable of being conscious, it might, with very great difficulty, start to understand itself well enough to be able to posit something about its maker from its own shapeliness, beauty, contours, etc. However it could not possibly grasp the creative intellect, skill and power of the one who brought it into being since there is nothing of it that is not the symptom of that skill and power, and symptoms are always external to their causes. An eye can see everything before it, but it has no direct access to the structure of optical nerves behind it which enables it to see, or to the pattern of relationships which has informed its dwelling on this or that object as of value or importance.

What I am attempting to say is that 'I AM' happens at, within, amongst us, and what that happening looks like is the emergence of a protagonism which is not from anywhere at all, so there is no handle we can get on it to fit it into our scheme of things. 'I AM' is not in any way part of the stories we have been telling ourselves during Act I, part of the push and pull of power, success and failure.

---

3   1 Cor. 13:12, Gal. 4:9.
4   Isa. 29:16.

Rather it subtly relativises all those things, and gradually unties us from being involved with them as we were before. In other words, it enables us to detect our own idolatry and start to relate to each other without idols.

I stress this, with all the awkwardness of language which comes with such things, because unless we undergo this very strange de-centring, this 'being born again from above' which Jesus described to Nicodemus, and was shocked when Nicodemus, a master in Israel, did not know about it[5], then it is not God we are talking about. Because if it is God, then we are talking about an entirely new sort of protagonism, which is showing us how completely contingent, dependent and peripheral we are to what is being brought into being. And the more we realise this, rather than it diminishing us, the more we find ourselves and others, and everything that is, of worth.

Now you may have noticed that I said earlier that God is, in principle, not a character in any act at all, but is the power behind the 'turning upside down of everything', and I hope that little bells might have gone off in your head, causing you to think: 'But what about Jesus? Surely Jesus was God and is a character emerging in Act I, even if it is only to provoke the 'turning upside down' which makes an Act II conceivable? Someone has to be the downtrodden valet in Act I and then be revealed as the Czar of all the Russias as the 'rovesciamento' gets under way.' And I want to say: 'Yes, that's right, though curiously what Jesus was about was God coming into the world so as to give himself a name by which we might know him.' So Jesus, qua human, is a character in Act I: a teacher and wonderworker condemned to a shameful death as a blasphemous and seditious wrongdoer. However, he himself is the making present of the 'rovesciamento' in our midst, the making available of the real name and presence of who God has been all along, and he is entirely consumed in that. So he is not a character in Act II at all, but has become the condition of possibility of *our* being characters in Act II. He has become the name that God gave himself, the idea being that *we* become his person, his body, over time[6].

5   ·John 3:10.
6   John 16:23-28.

I want to make something very clear here, because it has been possible to talk about the 'rovesciamento' as though it were a bad trick played by God on the Hebrew people – as though they are the Act I, and we Christians are the infinitely superior Act II. However, that is to miss the point completely: Act I is the human condition as we know it, and it is Hebrew monotheism that is the beginning of the 'rovesciamento' of which we understand the full shape finally to have emerged when Jesus was given the name that is above all other names, the same name, incidentally, which the High Priest wore on his tiara for the Atonement ritual. The 'rovesciamento', which is sometimes referred to as the 'inbreaking of the Kingdom of God', has always been a reality, palpitating just outside the human condition and, as it were, gathering shape so as to break in. Just so was the Holy of Holies in the Temple taken to be a place 'outside creation' from which the Holy One might break out into the midst of created matter.

In other words, the 'turning upside down' began when the prophets and priests first began to suspect that the One speaking to them was not just another god, but was 'the real thing' quite outside any of the existing categories, and that therefore nothing would ever be the same again – a complete turnaround was on the way. Naturally enough, this 'turning upside down' took time to emerge. It is rather as if each of the prophets were different tectonic faults, sensitive to the gathering power of 'I Am' as 'I Am' gradually began to make a volcanic eruption in the midst of a landscape, which would thereafter be totally altered.

And of course, each of the prophets gathered glimpses of the turnaround that was to come, which is why they associated its coming with wrath, and why so many of their prophecies do point towards the in-breaking of God as to do with wrath. It is why such care was needed in approaching the Presence in the Temple, since the potential for turning everything around was so threatening. And it was why the sprinkling of the faithful with the blood of the lamb in the Atonement rite, symbolically performed by the High Priest who 'was' the Holy One of God, and bore his name, was taken to be a covering, protecting the worshippers from wrath.

In other words, it was as though throughout Act I there were constant, barely underground, rumblings of the great 'rovesciamento' sometimes bursting through, and giving a sense of the shape of what was eventually to burst forth and turn everything round. I hope then that you can see something of the extraordinary quality of the explosion that is going on in the life and death of Jesus, and in that self-effacing gift being made available to the Apostolic Witnesses as the name by which the artist formerly known as 'YHWH' wants to be known among humans. The gift includes the Divine Presence, formerly known by the prophets and the people of Israel, glimpsed on a multi-wheeled chariot, having a face which shines and a presence which quickens, now being made available, ordinarily, to a whole people who have been ordained to the high priesthood, in and through the signs of self-giving to us which are the Eucharistic sacrifice.

Now I want to point out something rather special about the 'rovesciamento'. As people began to get a sense of it – they did indeed become aware that it would lead to a radical turning upside down of everything, and this of course is normally understood vengefully. Any of the actors in Act I of the Opera, as they begin to become aware of the fact that the apparent chambermaid, who they have been treating as a mere vassal, is in fact a heavily disguised Catherine the Great, knows that the normal thing that will happen when Catherine gets out of her wench's weeds is mass revenge: all the slights will be repaid a hundredfold. In other words, *because* they think of the turning upside down being part of a vengeful act by a formerly weak, and now powerful, player, so they will take measures to protect themselves from that. Thus it is no surprise that any announcement by the prophets of the breaking in of 'I AM' should have assumed that the mode by which 'I AM' would break in would be as one much more powerful than the powerful of the earth, but still on the same level as them, in terms of acting in the same sort of way.

What was clearly inconceivable until after it had happened, and is still scarcely conceivable now, is that the turning upside down should not have been produced by a former victim now turned powerful avenger, but that the real, complete and utterly different level of power of the one breaking in should be shown, not by a former victim now turned powerful, but by a contemporary victim kept alive as slaughtered victim, so as to enable those who perceive him as such to be forgiven. That is, to be let go from their Act I roles so as to recover the chance of a quite new role in Act II.

To put this another way: the prophets were entirely right to see that the breaking in of YHWH would produce a total turning upside down of everything. The victim would indeed be King. It was the shape of the kingliness which was a complete surprise. What had previously been impossible to imagine was that something far more powerful than a mere act of revenge was taking place. Instead, the shape taken by the strength, which was revealed as incomparably stronger than anything known to any of the actors, was that of an apparent weakness so strong that it did not need to show its strength, but by inhabiting weakness, shame and death, gently and deliberately, it pulled the plug on any story in which the storyline was run by revenge, tit-for-tat or ambition for power. All of those were revealed as futile. And the victim started, exactly as a forgiving victim who refuses to hold onto any sense of victimhood, to become King of an entirely new story.

Thus does the 'rovesciamento' take the form of inaugurating a quite new and unexpected Act II. Not one that is a mere reversal of Act I, but one where a quite new dividing line has started to emerge. One where there is an astoundingly strong presence, held weakly in being, and which is the power line of the new story, inviting people into losing their old selves by undergoing being forgiven, totally de-structured and re-structured, by the one who appeared to be a shameful dead transgressor and turns out to be I AM's named criterion for himself. 'You want to know what YHWH looks like? Here, like this executed criminal who occupied the place of pain and shame and death so that you no longer need fear it and, no longer fearing it, need no longer put anyone else there ever again, but might yourselves start to live as if death were not'.

There is, of course, faced with the emergence of this de-structuring protagonism, also the presence of an increasingly futile and pointless wrath going nowhere at all since being unable to escape from the meaningless-ness of a story whose only powerline is identity grasped over against the other, which is to say, revenge. But the wrath is not the wrath of the protagonist, it is the wrath produced by those bumping up against the protagonist, and yet not accepting that the storyline of Act I has been irremediably and absolutely brought to an end.

What I want to stress is that we are living in a world in which this strange form of presence, that of the artist formerly known as YHWH who has come amongst us giving himself the name IHS – this strange presence made alive to us through signs which constitute what we call the Church –is just there, as stronger than anything else which can be imagined, such that the whole world is, as it were apparently unchanged, but in fact with its axis completely reversed[7]. And the Presence, the Chariot Throne, the Lord seated on the Mercy Seat, which is the Crucified One shining out as live communication from our altars, is Presence as One forgiving, which means untying people from the way of being involved in futility which was ours before, and instead finding ourselves reprogrammed from within because we are daring to allow ourselves to be looked at with love by the One who is the victim of all of our stories.

As I understand it, the extraordinary and unique thing about being a Catholic is just this finding ourselves, through no merit at all of our own, being sucked through a veil which allows us to see and participate in the beginnings of an Act II that is already well under way, and which shows itself to us as being what Act I was really all about all along, but, while we were involved in it, we were too frightened ever to really get what it was about.

And, of course, what this means is that we find ourselves having, as it were, our inner workings, the way our patterns of desire were structured, being sucked out of us, often somewhat painfully, so that they can be turned around and given to us anew. The quiet, gentle, permanently forgiving regard of one who likes us is just there, and this is deeply disconcerting as we find that so much of us is formed by the need to run away from just such a person. We would love to be given hope without letting go of our security.

---

7   It is this that we celebrate on the Feast of the Ascension.

However, our holding on to security so dims our imagination and darkens what we can long for, that we can only hope as we let go of our security, because hope is the habit formed in us when another habitually inducts us into daring to want more with that daring buoyed up by the trust that we will actually get what we want. We would love to be able to be loved without letting go of our resentment, but, in fact, our holding on to what has been done to us – to 'whatever I am, I'm not like that', to comparison and rivalry so as at least to 'be someone' –makes it impossible for another to speak us into being, to join us in a journey of delight becoming something much more than we could dare to imagine.

My guess is that, as gay and lesbian Catholics, we may have found it particularly confusing to work out which bits of our lives are the remnants of Act I, still biting at us even though we know they are futile and going nowhere[8], and which bits of our lives are those being summoned, nudged, called, gazed into being by the Presence, empowered for Act II. One of the reasons for this is that part of the Act I of all of us has been Church authority of one sort or other making it quite clear that being gay or lesbian belongs to the mirage of false meaning proper to Act I, and that any of our desire that is gay or lesbian will be left behind as we find ourselves sucked through the veil into taking part in Act II. This was an Act I in which Church authority insisted that it was the gateway to Act II, it was itself part of the fruit of the 'rovesciamento' which led to there being any Act II at all, and it was giving us clear lines to discern what it was like to be in Act I, going futilely nowhere, and what it was like getting sucked into Act II, being quickened into real existence. And, very properly, we treated this with respect

Part of the problem has been that, not for the first time, it is beginning to look very much as though Church authority has been too quick to consider itself the fruit of the 'rovesciamento' and too slow to consider that elements of itself might also be part of Act I, and – in the process of undergoing the 'turning everything upside down' which the in-breaking Presence provokes – that those whom it

---

8   The traditional name for these remnants of Act I going nowhere is 'concupiscentia'.

considered sinners were in fact guiltless[9], and people it considered morally dangerous defects were in fact sisters and brothers, as capable of light and of darkness as everyone else. This is, after all, the way the turning upside down has been working since the breath of the crucified criminal was revealed to be the Spirit of God[10].

So the confusion has been: How do we know? How can we know? How do we know if the possibility of our being involved in Act II depends on us being *forgiven for being* gay or lesbian, meaning that in the story that is opening up we will not be gay and lesbian, but our pattern of desire will work in quite a different way, we will have become human in spite of being gay? Or, on the other hand, is it true that the 'rovesciamento' is beginning to make clear that it is not our repenting of being gay or lesbian that is the sign of our finding ourselves in Act II? Is it not rather the fact of our becoming able to forgive those who have hated us without cause, those who have blamed us and diminished us, which is that sign – the sign of our being sucked through the veil? And will we therefore be characters in Act II as humans, whose story of having had the whole structure of our desire turned round has a pleasingly gay or a lesbian shape to it, rather than that happening in spite of our being gay and lesbian people?

The only answer I know to this, and it is the answer urgently suggested in the first epistle of John, is to look for the testimony of the Spirit, and this is what I want to ask you to consider. We have amongst us an extraordinary range of years, of stories, of talent. What is the testimony of the Spirit? What sort of protagonism has it suggested into being in our midst? Has the Spirit – which is not one of timidity, but enables us to receive ourselves in that gentle power of self-control which enables us to be brave – had to put to death our being gay or lesbian in order to emerge, or has it given us back being gay or lesbian in a far richer way than we could have known as part of what we were invited into being so as to accomplish?

Has the Spirit confirmed in us that, unlike in our straight sisters and brothers, our sexual desire is not merely disordered, but is

9   Matt. 12:7.
10 John 19:30, Mark 15:37, Matt. 27:50, Luke 23:46.

122

quite simply a dead end? Not simply something in need of a process of humanisation so that it can be part of a relationship of bodily presence to another, tending to build the partner up, enrich and delight them as well as care for them, tend to them, and be stretched into age and death alongside them, but, instead, something that must simply not be allowed to be associated with any human other at all, not as a matter of a free choice, but as a matter of an intrinsic obligation? Or has it been through such intimations, disordered and insufficiently humanised as they may have been, of a process of bodily involvement with another that we have found ourselves being sucked into being given a self we did not know, but rejoice to see as something we are becoming, something holy?

And for me, perhaps the most important of all, and one which I find it very difficult to answer in my own case: has the Spirit prodded us, nudged us, into imagining new things to do, into longing for new projects to create, into desiring much, much more than we desired, into seeing more good in our enemies and being more sensitive to needs which we might satisfy as we have come to accept ourselves as gay and lesbian? Or, when we were reticent about accepting ourselves as gay or lesbian, thinking that that was only part of Act I, was there a livelier, more quickening, deeper longing, more attuned to others, more available for others, such that we can begin to glimpse that accepting ourselves as gay and lesbian has been an act of self-indulgence, a darkening of our minds, a diminishment of our horizons, a muddled retreat into Act I by people who might otherwise have been stars shining in the firmament of Act II?

This is the question which I would ask us to consider, through considering and sharing stories, allowing each other to be penitent where we find ourselves undergoing being forgiven, and peacefully joyful where we have been given joy and find ourselves flourishing. What are the signs of the New Creation in our midst? What is coming into being through us that is new, and solid, and for others? What is the testimony of the Spirit? How do we test the spirits? Because it is this testimony that is going to carry us through this strange, confusing stage in the history of the Church. A stage where it is genuinely not easy to tell whether, in matters related to being gay or lesbian, Church authority has been acting as a properly stern emanation of an Act II, which is indeed a real upheaval of desire; or whether we are not finding ourselves being given places and names of surprising honour[11] in the Act II which Jesus inaugurated, while some parts, at least, of Church authority, thinking themselves the owners of Act II, are refusing to let go of something which was in fact an element of the cruelty and futility of Act I, and are vainly struggling against the 'rovesciamento' which is breaking in amongst us all.

---

11 cf. Isa. 56.

CHAPTER 8

Strong protagonism and weak presence:

the changes in tone of the voice of God

It is the little words which always take you by surprise[1]. For example, think of the word 'so'. We are used to the Greek word οὕτως being translated 'so' when it appears in the phrase 'For God so loved the world that he gave his only Son, that whoever believes in him might not perish, but have eternal life.'[2] The 'so' sounds as if it is intensifying the desire, as if it were a psychological description of the depths to which the One who loves is moved. Rather as if I were to say: 'I so, so wish that she would call me', thus revealing my vulnerability in the face of the longed-for one's caprice.

However, οὕτως can be translated another way, and, despite my doubts about whether this translation will have the same public reception, it seems to me to be closer to the mark. This translation treats the word not as a way of making the love intense, but of demonstrating what it looks like: 'For it was in *this* way, you see, that God loved the world: that he gave his only Son so that whoever believes in him might not perish, but have eternal life.' We might even imagine the person pronouncing these words making a gesture which would give the sense of the colon and the 'that', which would also bring out the sense of the Greek word ὥστε.

With this translation, we have no access to a psychological movement in God, seen as underlying the action of giving his only son.

---

1   This chapter was born as a contribution to a colloquium entitled 'Post-modern or post-secular Christianity? Two interpretations of late modernity', which took place at the Universidad Iberoamericana, Mexico City, in September 2007. I have translated and edited this English language version from the original Spanish.

2   John 3:16 οὕτως γὰρ ἠγάπησεν ὁ θεὸς τὸν κόσμον, ὥστε τὸν υἱὸν τὸν μονογενῆ ἔδωκεν, ἵνα πᾶς ὁ πιστεύων εἰς αὐτὸν μὴ ἀπόληται ἀλλ᾽ ἔχῃ ζωὴν αἰώνιον.

Rather, everything that act of love means is made visible in what follows. It is as if we were to paraphrase the verse as follows: 'Do you want to know how it became manifest in the world that God loves it? Well, like this: in God's giving of his only Son so that everyone who believes in him might not perish, but have eternal life.'

My motive for beginning with a grammatical niggle is that it points towards something more properly theological. If we start with 'For God so loved', then all our concentration and effort goes into imagining the emotional intensity which lies behind the manifest activity. What is really interesting is not so much what happened, about which we can satisfy ourselves with the briefest of enquiries, describing it in very spare terms. What would really be interesting is the degree in which the act was intended, the push behind it, the emotional force with which the principal agent of this activity carried it out.

If, on the other hand, we begin with 'It was in *this* way that God loved', then we have no prior access to some supposed interior life of God, modelled on our own. Instead it is that which is visible, that which is manifest in the activity itself, which becomes the lure for our fascination. And it is only in the degree in which we allow ourselves to be pulled inside that activity, and what we can discover starting from it, that we begin to get some notion of God's love.

To my way of thinking, this second reading is preferable. And I have two motives for thinking like this. The first is having begun to notice the tendency in John's text for things to be said with such blinding simplicity and obviousness that they pass us by completely, while we look for a more complicated meaning. In John, time and time again, I have the strange sensation that the very simplicity of what he sets out so clearly and straightforwardly overwhelms us because we are convinced that we are dealing with something mysterious. Returning to the simplicity of what is actually said is a work of years.

My second motive is more properly theological. In the first reading we do not actually learn much about God, other than that God has emotions like ours; and that an example, perhaps an especially outstanding example, of God's emotive quality would be this act of love. In the second reading, our whole understanding of God, which we have to prune of all our projections concerning God's emotions or subjectivity, gets to be reconfigured starting only from what God has done. That is to say, it is what has been done which comes to be the criterion for who God is, causing us, bit by bit, completely to revise any other perception we might have of God. It is not a presupposition about God which gets to dictate how we are to understand what has happened.

My reason for starting with this is that it gives me a way in to what I would like to explore with you: some dimensions of the strange privilege which consists in being a Catholic theologian to-day, dimensions which are not sufficiently tied together yet, but which have in common, I hope, the intuition that something very interesting is being birthed in our midst, after somewhat of a glacial period for our discipline. A period in which our work tools were not up to the required theological task. Curiously, it seems to me that what some people call 'late modernity', with its post-modern nihilism, its post-secular reason, combined, at least in the English-speaking world with the strident populist atheism of a Dawkins or a Hitchens, exactly because it obliges us to look for more adequate tools for our labour, at the same time sharpens our intelligence for tasks which are much more our own, and makes much more agile our ability to focus on our properly theological mission.

The first dimension I would like to explore with you might be de-scribed as an inversion of something we take for granted. Typically, when we in the Church talk, or when Church officials pronounce, or when Evangelical or Muslim groups express positions in the pub-lic sphere, on the one hand we all give the impression that we are baying for a very strong presence of religion, of the divine, of what is sacred. On the other hand, it is as if we were constantly find-ing ourselves disappointed by a somewhat weak divine protagonism since, leaving aside the public religious noisiness of one camp or the other, God has a way of not showing up at rallies for his cause. And besides, those who talk about God with the greatest insistence have a way of understanding God as a back up for notorious public po-sitions which are perfectly comprehensibly described as springing from quite other motivations.

127

What I have begun to understand is that all this, the world of 'strong presence and weak protagonism', is very exactly the reverse of a properly theological vision of reality. That is because in the properly theological vision, divine protagonism is extremely strong, stronger it could not be; but the divine presence is exceedingly weak. And what is most curious is that this very weakness of presence is precisely what properly corresponds to the strength of the protagonism.

I would like to explore this notion of 'protagonism' – not necessarily a familiar word. The word is derived from the principal actor in the tragic or comic dramas of ancient Greece. The principal actor was the protagonist, the second was the deutero-agonist, and so on. Thus, originally, there was only one protagonist, in the same way as it would be curious in modern times to have an opera in which there was more than one 'prima donna', leaving on one side the 'prima-donna' tendencies of almost all artists, to say nothing of theologians. However, in all our modern languages the word 'protagonist' has ceased to have this strict usage, and we speak easily of the 'protagonists' of a drama, or an event, understanding by this 'those who have an active role in what goes on'.

Well, I would like to make a tediously obvious point, one of those which often are too obvious, and so escape us: if we really are monotheists, then we are very seriously committed not only to the existence of one God alone, but to there being only one protagonism. The two notions go together inseparably. To make a parallel: it is very difficult for us to talk about the 'existence' of God, who is not an object in the universe. On account of this it is less inappropriate to say that 'God isn't' than that 'God is', since the verb 'to be' inescapably has as its reference the universe of existing things amongst which we are, and which are at the same level as us. Well, in just the same way, it is difficult for us to talk about the 'protagonism' of One who is not at the same level of any of the created protagonisms, forces, actors or powers which we know, which move us and which move, *pace* Dante Alighieri, even 'il sole e l'altre stelle'.

However, in just the same way as our, very correct, negative theology of 'being' sometimes leaves us without any sense that 'behind' everything there is, yes indeed, an 'existing' – a splendour, a radiance, a power and a beauty which are so brilliant, real, and so on that in their light all the things which we know as existing, beautiful and powerful, are only weak sparks reflected from a great distance – our very proper recognition of the lack of similarity between our notions of protagonism and the protagonism that is God sometimes leaves us without any sense that 'behind' all acting forces there is a protagonism, one which is much stronger, more powerful and more deliberate than anything we can imagine.

I want to emphasise this, because in general I hear it mentioned little. We are committed to the notion that there is, in truth, a unique protagonism, by comparison with which all human acting out, and all the movements of the rest of everything that exists, completely real as they are on their own terms, are forms of deutero-agonism. And that this unique protagonism is real, is powerful, and that we are capable of detecting its intimations.

I would like to suggest that when we talk about this protagonism of God, we are not only talking about some long-term project, some notion of 'the history of salvation', but also of something that irrupts directly into our intimacy. If, when talking about that protagonism which is God, I am not talking about something that shakes up the stage on which I find myself, with my prima-donna tendencies, alongside many other deutero-agonists, then it is very greatly to be doubted that I am in fact talking about God. The fact that the protagonism which is God is at a totally different and incomparable level with all the forces that move me does not mean that it ceases to have a real incidence in my life. And if there are no signs, along the course of my life, and perhaps more easily detectable by others than by me, that I am coming to enjoy playing a secondary role, although a curiously enriched one, in the wake of a protagonism which is not my own, then it is to be doubted that I have been a worshipper of God.

It is this intimation of the protagonism of God which I would like to explore with you. And, of course, for it even to begin to make sense that we talk about this protagonism, I should say that I take it for granted that we are all 'on the same page' at least in this much:

that we are all within a process of becoming aware that *everything that is* is peripheral to a reality which is infinitely greater and more powerful; and that, even within our relational lives, we are all embarked on a process, one which is curiously enlivening of activity, even though it can only be described in the passive voice: a process of finding ourselves reconfigured, re-dimensioned and re-situated by that protagonism.

That is to say, I take it for granted that we are talking as people who recognise that we are far more profoundly recipients of something than we are protagonists, and that even our most active protagonism is something received by us in the very process of our activity.

If this is so, then it is rather an important part of our responsibility as theologians that we raise the question of the true nature of this protagonism. And this question is, at least as we start, the same as the question about the degree to which our projections onto God produce a real distortion in our capacity to receive that protagonism in our midst. And it is here that we touch on the matter to which I pointed in my subtitle: the changes in tone of the voice of God. I would like to stress that I did not give that subtitle as a mere piece of wordplay, understanding that of course God has no tone of voice, and that it is we who have to undergo the purification of our capacity to listen, sullied as it is by tones of voice which are human, all too human, so as to free ourselves from so many distortions and allow ourselves to sink into silence. No, I wanted to say rather more than that! The fact of undergoing this process of loss of idols is of itself a sign of our coming to hear a tone of voice which is the protagonism which is God, even though this be for us such a demanding process of learning that, in the light of where we stand now, it is almost unimaginable for us that it be a tone or a voice.

Allow me then to problematise some of the words which we habitually use in order to refer to the incidence of that protagonism which is God upon ourselves: words like 'will', 'desire' and 'law'. Of God we say, for example, that God has a 'will' which is directed towards us – for example, when we pray 'Thy will be done', or that God has a desire or a longing, as, for example, when we read:

'Have I any pleasure at all that the wicked should die? saith the Lord GOD: and not that he should return from his ways, and live?'[3]

or that God dictates a law which reflects him, as when we sing:

'I delight in your will, my God, your law is within my heart'[4]

or:

'Better for me is the law from your mouth than thousands of pieces of gold and silver.'[5]

Or what Paul says at the end of his homily to the Athenians gathered at the Areopagus:

'...Now God commands, παραγγέλλει all people everywhere to repent'[6]

and there is no doubt there of the force of the word 'commands', nor of the protagonism which it expresses.

In all these spheres, we are taking words that have their proper place within certain sorts of human protagonism. And, in each case, we are applying them to ourselves as being on the receiving end of these expressions of a divine protagonism. Along with each of these expressions of protagonism – will, desire, law – a whole series of associations come towards us. Associations, for example, from the field of ordering, of military commandments, of adults towards children or of the strong towards the weak. We all inhabit, inevitably, a whole ecosphere of such associations and power relations, with diverse protagonisms. And it would be very extraordinary if, alongside every use of these words which express a protagonism towards us, we were not to do what we normally do when we hear a word: we provide, or we furnish, in an act of extraordinary mental agility — which is in fact how we human beings learn – the whole network of associations which comes along with the word in its supposed application to us and to our life.

---

3   Ezek. 18:23.
4   Ps. 40:8.
5   Ps. 119:72.
6   Acts 17:30b.

This is to say that on no occasion, other than perhaps if we are learning a totally new language only from a book, do we come across a word by itself. Along with the word there comes inevitably a whole series of 'voices', detected by us and applied with subtlety and discernment, tones which insinuate, even verbal and auditory connections which have nothing to do with the word at hand, but have some similarity of sound. Or maybe an association is triggered by a word that we heard alongside the present word in a poem that 'reached' us at a certain moment, so that, when we hear the word now, it evokes those special circumstances. Put this another way: we do not only hear the words in themselves, but we also introject the logic, the silent patterns of working, the force fields, we might say, within which the words come ready set. And the more 'normal' is the way that setting reproduces itself in us, the less we notice it, since it seems to us that we are hearing the word, nothing else, and we give no mind to the network of protagonisms of which the word is a symptom.

Now I would like to suggest something: if the protagonism which is God reaches us through expressions which come from those worlds, then our whole imagination of what that protagonism might be will remain subordinate to what is dictated to us by those voices, with all their socio-cultural resonances. Unless, that is, part of what is produced by that protagonism which is God consists in a change in the tone of voice, altering the network of associations which those words bring along with them. However, that very act of altering the network also works through a human mediation: it is human happenings which give the basis for the genuinely changing associations starting from within which we begin to be able to detect the meaning of the words.

It is here, it seems to me, that we have something very important, special and difficult to grasp in the centre of our faith. And that is the fact that the protagonism which is God made itself manifest through the genuinely human happening known as a failure. A failure which at the same time was nothing more than that – a failure – and yet simultaneously brought along with it a whole series of connotations of an act of sacrificial self-giving proper to a world which was already considered archaic in the time of Jesus: that of the High Priest, the anointed Melchisedek. That is to say: on the one hand you have the violent death, at the hands of the colonising power instigated by the religious leadership and their acolytes, of a man held to be a seditious blasphemer. And, on the other hand, you have the deliberate path being trod of the fulfilling of texts and inspirations, dating from a very remote past, concerning a definitive atonement sacrifice to be carried out by the priest who would be the Holy One of God, the Son of God, titles which were given to the high priests of yesteryear.

It is very difficult to think of an appropriate way to hold these two descriptions together. There is the protagonism, freely undertaken and creative of meaning, of the One who understood what he was doing as the definitive priestly act. And there is a shameful putting to death, where the dead one is, by definition, an object, and not a subject; and, being an object, is incapable of exercising protagonism. The description is made more dense, rather than more simple, by the fact that, within a few days of this death having made it impossible that Jesus should exercise any protagonism that might be referred to God, God caused him to be seen by diverse witnesses from the group which had accompanied him. He caused him to be seen not only as dead but, along with being recognisably the same man as had died, the risen Lord was the subject of a demonstrable protagonism. And, curiously, his protagonism is not less, but much greater through the fact of his having died, since death could not contain him as merely an object.

The language of the Apostolic Witness concerning the Resurrection and Ascension revolves around the patterns of the Temple, where the Holy One of God, now sacrificed, is seated at the right hand of God. Which is to say that the protagonism of the victim who gave himself is revealed as being the very protagonism of God. And the foretastes of God, of YHWH, who makes appearances coming out from the Holy of Holies, find themselves fulfilled in this notion of the Presence of the One who is, at the same time, a human victim who was submitted to an atrocious and shameful death. This is the greatest sign of weakness that we are capable of imagining, and it is at the same time the fulfilment of all the promises of God concerning being present in and with his people.

During the same period in which the Apostolic Witnesses are undergoing all this, the same Spirit which Jesus had exhaled on the Cross is breathed into them. And so there begins to become accessible to all humans that strong protagonism of weak presence which we call Holy Spirit. And along with this, the very protagonism that is God begins to be the moving dynamic in the life of a whole series of people. People begin to find themselves within that protagonism.

Describing it like this is insufficient, because it does not point towards what is strange about this dense presence in our midst. And let us remember that this presence, which is, when all is said and done, that which is transmitted to us in the species in every Eucharist, and is the fulfilment of God's promise to be with us, is what is absolutely central in every Catholic and Orthodox liturgy. What is strange about this presence is that it is the presence of a rejected victim who returns to be in the midst of his group, showing them that, in fact, they have been forgiven, that he has nothing against them, and that if they accept him back, then they will find themselves becoming free and empowered for the building of new lives.

Please note the extreme weakness of this way of being present. Typically, in the worlds we know, our victims lack voice. We cannot hear them. The victim who can be heard is the one who comes back with a tone of triumph, seeking vengeance. But that is not the case here. Here, all the protagonism, all the creative power that is God, is present in *and as* that presence of the victim who returns and offers forgiveness. Please note here that it is not that God has different modulations in his voice – now strident, now majestic, and now merciful. No, something much more drastic is going on: the whole of that protagonism which is God is revealed to us in that presence of the forgiving victim. God has no voice apart from the one which emanates from the forgiving victim, the one which is the self-giving of the forgiving victim expressed towards us and on our behalf.

Well then, if that is so, then how do the faithful, and of course that sub-group of the faithful constituted by those of us who are theologians, listen? Of course, there is no way of coming to hear that voice which does not include going through the process of being forgiven. If God's whole way of being present in our world is precisely the strong protagonism of weak presence, then it reaches us as the process of our finding ourselves wrong, bound and tied to other protagonisms and other dynamics in the degree to which we allow ourselves to be addressed by the strength of that generous weakness. And it is starting from our reception of that being forgiven, which takes the form of us finding ourselves being set free, loosened for freedom, that we enter into the process of noticing the changes in tone of the voice of God.

Let me give some examples, taking as a basis those Bible verses which I just quoted. Let us listen to Paul again when he says

'...Now God commands, παραγγέλλει all people everywhere to repent'

And let us not change a word. But let us change, yes indeed, what I called the whole ecosphere of associations which come with the words. Let us first savour the phrase with the word 'commands' ringing with a military tone, the words 'all men everywhere' spoken imperiously, and the word 'repent' charged with moralism or even emotional blackmail. And now let us listen to this phrase anew, as flowing to its maximum extension from that weak presence which I have sought to describe. What is the tone of voice with which 'commands' is pronounced if it emanates from that throne which is a gibbet, and whose triumph consists in having rendered contempt non-toxic? In another place, Paul tells us that we are 'ambassadors' of that protagonism, and it is perhaps easier to understand the supplicant tone when it is explicitly *begging* 'be reconciled to God'[7]. Then again, how different does the word 'everyone' sound if it comes not with an imperious tone, but with affection, an equality of heart, a desire to embrace and enfold, since the one who is longing has always been beneath everyone, when not actually being trodden underfoot? And, how does the word 'change your hearts' sound if it reaches us as the personal dimension of an offer, made from below, to enter into a new 'we', made possible by the one whose similarity with me I did not want to see, afraid as I was of losing everything?

---

7   2 Cor. 5:20.

Well, these are some examples. You can do exactly the same thing with all those words like 'desire', 'will', 'law' and so on. Just think how different it sounds to say 'I delight in your will, my God, your law is within my heart', if the will and the law in question are those which become manifest starting from that weak presence which alone points up the strong protagonism! If the 'will' has expressed itself to the maximum in that presence of a forgiving victim, and the law consists in reproducing that presence for others, then breezes of delight, of security and of freedom are already to be detected as we find ourselves sailing off the coast of this banquet, beginning to perceive the immensity that is being offered for our exploration.

I would like to note another dimension of the density of this weak presence of a strong protagonism, an element that is very difficult to explain, one which seems to be an element of absence and is difficult to understand as a mode of presence, which is what it is. This is the sense, which is pointed to in differing ways in the Gospels, that Jesus is going before his own. In Mark, the angel at the tomb says to the two Marys and to Salome:

> 'But go, tell his disciples and Peter that he is going before you to Galilee; there you will see him, as he told you.'[8]

In Acts, this sense comes with the Ascension, and in John it comes, among other places, with Jesus' invitation to Thomas to place his finger in the wounds. There are enough verbal equivalences between the Greek of John 20:25-7 and the Septuagint version of the instructions for placing the carrying rods or staves in the rings (lit: 'finger holes') so as to transport the Ark of the Covenant, in Exodus 27:7, for it to be apparent that the risen Christ is in person the new Ark of the new Covenant, who will be borne before his people. This is rather confirmed by Jesus' remark to Thomas that it will be even better for those who believe without having seen[9]. In fact, bearing the Ark of the Presence is going to be less burdensome and easier for those who have not seen Jesus in person.

---

8 Mark 16:7.
9 John 20:29.

Of all these ways of pointing towards this dimension, personally I find the formula 'he is going before you' easiest to digest. It suggests a presence which is *en route*. Only by its being present 'beyond' us, outside our reach, are we being drawn towards entering into new dimensions. That is to say, part of that strong protagonism with a weak presence is exactly this element of opening up virgin territory, which still seems impossible to us. And it is always by virtue of its being a forgiving victim that we are being encouraged to tread on surfaces whose solidity we could never have dared to imagine, terrains which seem terrifying to us, but turn out to be much more spacious and liveable-in than we had imagined.

I hope that, with this, something of the force of that phrase of John's Gospel with which we began can be felt. When all is said and done, what I wanted to do was to do a bit of 'filling in' of what might be meant by 'he gave his only Son so that whoever believes in him might not perish, but have eternal life'. I wanted to point up the way in which this phrase opens up the possibility of a presence which creates criteria, offers a new network, or ecosphere, of associations starting from which the phrase 'God loves the world' can come to be heard in a quite fresh new way. And it is towards that novelty, that freshness, that the word οὕτως, with which we started, points. As I said, it is the little words which always surprise.

Having, then, spent so much time sketching out some elements of the grammar we need in order to identify what is proper to the Presence from which we are working, I am going to set out some of the directions in which I hope to see our conversation develop.

What I think I have just done in the preceding pages is offer you a sketch, doubtless fairly primitive, of what I consider to be central to our faith. I have proposed a way of drawing close to a real, dense, presence, which brings along with it real human associations, and which is, in as far as it is possible for us to speak like this, the way in which the Triune God manifests in our midst. This seems to me to be something absolutely unique. That is to say, this network of associations through which God has projected his self-manifestation in our midst, exercising his strong protagonism in this weak presence, giving himself to be known by means of a completely new criterion, has no parallel, that I know or have ever heard of, in any other part of human knowledge, culture, philosophy or narrative.

The first question which this raises for me is as follows: how should we speak about this quality of absolute 'uniqueness' without that uniqueness being a form, however well-disguised, of human 'exclusivism'? And my first intuition about this, and it is no more than that, is that we have to stop being concerned about being considered exclusivist, as if that which is unique were in some way our property. Instead, we have to refine our understanding of the protagonism of that which is unique, and rediscover our relationality with others as part of what is received from and through that unique protagonism.

The second question, which is the same as the first, but from a different angle, is as follows. This dense presence is not only unique, but also different from all other ways in which religions and forms of worship understand God, and that difference is not something about which we have any reason to be ashamed – quite the reverse. However, and this is important, since in our world, in the world of our protagonisms, every 'difference' is made by contrast with some 'other', sooner or later the fact of making a contrast vitiates the goodness of what we are affirming in the same degree as it has to leave some 'other' in the shade. How, then, can we speak of this criterion-giving presence without falling into the vicious denigration of other religious and cultural realities? And here it is my intuition that it is the notion of gratuity which we have to continue to refine, along with the sensation of 'he goes before you' which I indicated as a dimension of the Presence.

The third and last question that I would like to raise with you is ecclesial. If, as I understand it, that which is central and indispensable to Catholic faith is this strong protagonism of a weak presence, it is evident that everything else, everything ecclesial, and by obvious extension, everything ecclesiastical, revolves around this reality, and is penetrable by and accountable to it. It could not be otherwise, since ecclesial reality, with all its different dimensions of sacred texts, communities, sacramental worship and office holders, only comes to be a sign of this protagonism as it passes through a constant process of losing idols, ceasing to grasp onto securities.

And this means for us, theologians, who form part of this reality, who are, as it were, nudged along by the same cattle prod, that it is becoming clearer and clearer in the modern world how much more flexible and fluid from within is that which from the outside seems pretty sclerotic.

For example, not many years ago, it was common to hear conservative types affirm that 'the Church is not a democracy', and, as I see it, they are quite right. The problem is that neither is it a monarchy, nor an oligarchy, as they seem to suppose, but a pneumarchy, and the pneuma seems to be totally re-structuring the internal life of the Church by fomenting a growing facility in talking about all possible themes and a growing sense of freedom in belonging, a growing sense of the voluntary nature of Church life. And these are tendencies which completely undermine the pretensions of authority of a certain hierarchical style. My question is: how can we contribute to making it possible that these dimensions of voluntary belonging, freedom in speaking and the necessarily hierarchical elements which are' there for our protection' against ourselves, be brought together in such a way that the Sign of God's salvation in our midst becomes properly resplendent?

❖❖❖❖❖❖❖❖❖❖

CHAPTER 9

'He opened up to them everything in the Scriptures concerning himself':

how can we recover Christological and ecclesial habits of Catholic Bible reading?

I propose to do two things with you[1]. The first is to read a passage of Scripture, in the rich sense of 'offering a reading' of it. And the second is to draw out some of the consequences of the method which I shall have used in order to come up with this reading. I am aiming at making a contribution to something which I intuit as being important for the future of our Catholic life: the recovery of the habits necessary for a reading of the Scriptures which is both ecclesial and eucharistic. The route to this recovery winds through the enrichment of our sense of how it is that the Anointed One of God, the Χριστός, makes available for us a fulfilled reading of the texts which we have received.

I am going to begin with a text which is apparently rather unpromising for my purposes: one of the parables, perhaps one of the two or three best-known among them – the one which often gets called the Parable of the Prodigal Son. My reason for saying that it is apparently rather un-promising for my purposes is that it is, at first blush, a parable without any Christological content. There are two brothers, one who is a spendthrift, and the other who is somewhat tediously righteous; there is a father, and there are servants. It is not

---

1 This chapter was born as the Cátedra Kino lecture for the Jesuit University system in Mexico, given in Mexico City and Guadalajara in September 2007. In translated and amplified form, it was given as a lecture for the Voices of Renewal series in the Corpus Christi University Parish in Toledo, Ohio, in October of the same year.

apparent that any of these characters is a *figura Christi*. Nevertheless, I am going to propose a Christological reading for you.

Normally, when Christological readings are in the air, it is because one or other of the New Testament authors refers some incident from the life of Jesus to a text in the Hebrew Scriptures. In some cases, we are talking about an understanding which quite clearly came way later than Jesus' death and resurrection. For instance, Paul sees the Messiah, the Christ, as having been already present in the Rock which followed the Israelites in the desert[2]. On other occasions, we are dealing with a recognition that, in the light of what the authors understand now, they are able to point to an event at which they hadn't been present, and see in it something that one of the prophets of old had been talking about. For example, Matthew states that Jeremiah's oracle about Rachel's weeping was fulfilled when Herod killed the innocents[3]. On yet other occasions, there is indeed some possibility that the author is pointing to an interpretation which was contemporary with the event, at least in embryonic form. For instance, John affirms that a witness was present when Jesus' side was pierced through with a lance, and that this fulfilled what the prophet Zechariah had foretold when he said 'they will look upon the one who they have pierced'[4]. There is no reason, in principle, why someone familiar with a well-known text of Zechariah should not have applied it to the sad spectacle of this public execution either immediately, or within a few days of the event. Perhaps the full density of what that witness was doing, in applying a text which was so close to Jesus' teaching about his own destiny, may only have dawned slowly. However, that does not remove the possibility that the application of the text was contemporary.

Another form of Christological reading is when we glimpse that Jesus himself is doing something deliberately so as to fulfil the Scriptures, as, for example, when he carries out the gesture of 'cleansing' the Temple. This announces the arrival of 'that day',

---

2   1 Cor 10:1-4.
3   Matt 2:17; Jer 31:15.
4   Zech 12:10, quoted at Jn 19:37.

which is foretold by Zechariah[5], and, along with 'that day', the end of the Temple's usefulness. Or in a more wide-ranging form, when we read the whole journey which Jesus makes in Luke's Gospel, from the synagogue at Nazareth to the crucifixion in Jerusalem, as the deliberate trajectory of the One who is fulfilling the coming of the promised prophet, Melchisedek himself, the anointed priest who is to offer the definitive sacrifice for the redemption of Israel. During this journey, allusions are made, in section after section of the Gospel, to the passages and narratives of the Hebrew Scriptures whose fulfilment is being indicated.

A third form of Christological reading is when we find ourselves able to unravel something of Jesus' own teaching concerning himself, not only deducing this from the deeds which he carries out, but working through the texts which we have which give an account of his teaching. In other words, when we get a glimpse of what is proposed, in the passage about the road to Emmaus from which I have taken this chapter's title[6], as the normative ecclesial way of reading the Scriptures, and applying this to the accounts which we have of Jesus' teaching before his death. And here we are in a terrain which is at the same time very interesting indeed and somewhat difficult to traverse, since our texts are not, and do not pretend to be, cinematographic accounts of what went on. They are something both much richer and much more fun than that. Rather than continuing to describe this form of reading from the 'outside', as it were, I would like to invite you to participate with me in having a go at it 'from within'. That is to say, we are going to dare to look for a spark, a hint, of the Master's own Christological teaching from the midst of the Gospel text.

First, let us listen to the parable[7]:

> [Jesus] said, 'There was a man who had two sons; and the younger of them said to his father, "Father, give me the share [μέρος] of property [οὐσίας] that falls to me." And he divided his living [βίον] between them. Not many days later, the younger son gathered all he had and took his journey into a far country, and there he

5   Zech 14:21.
6   Lk 24:13-35.
7   Lk 15:11-32.

squandered his property in loose living. And when he had spent everything, a great famine arose in that country, and he began to be in want. So he went and joined himself to one of the citizens of that country, who sent him into his fields to feed swine. And he would gladly have fed [ἐπεθύμει χορτασθῆναι] on the pods that the swine ate; and no one gave him anything. But when he came to himself he said, "How many of my father's hired servants have bread enough and to spare, but I perish here with hunger! I will arise [ἀναστὰς] and go to my father, and I will say to him, 'Father, I have sinned against heaven and before you; I am no longer worthy to be called your son; treat me as one of your hired servants.'" And he arose and came to his father. But while he was yet at a distance, his father saw him and had compassion, and ran and embraced him and kissed him [ἐπέπεσεν ἐπὶ τὸν τράχηλον αὐτοῦ καὶ κατεφίλησεν αὐτόν]. And the son said to him, "Father, I have sinned against heaven and before you; I am no longer worthy to be called your son." But the father said to his servants [δούλους], "Bring quickly the best robe [στολὴν τὴν πρώτην], and put it on him; and put a ring on his hand, and shoes on his feet; and bring the fatted calf and kill it [θύσατε], and let us eat and make merry; for this my son was dead, and is alive again [ἀνέζησεν]; he was lost, and is found." And they began to make merry. Now his elder son was in the field; and as he came and drew near to the house, he heard music and dancing. And he called one of the servants and asked what this meant. And he said to him, "Your brother has come [ὁ ἀδελφός σου ἥκει], and your father has killed the fatted calf, because he has received him safe and sound." But he was angry [ὠργίσθη] and refused to go in. His father came out and entreated him, but he answered his father, "Lo, these many years I have served you, and I never disobeyed your command [οὐδέποτε ἐντολήν σου παρῆλθον]; yet you never gave me a kid, that I might make merry with my friends. But when this son of yours [ὁ υἱός σου οὗτος] came, who has devoured your living with harlots [ὁ καταφαγών σου τὸν βίον μετὰ πορνῶν], you killed for him the fatted calf!" And he said to him, "Son [τέκνον], you are always with me, and all that is mine is yours. It was fitting to make merry and be glad, for this your brother [ὁ ἀδελφός σου οὗτος] was dead, and is alive [ἔζησεν]; he was lost, and is found.'"

Now for a little bit of context. Please imagine that you are in a synagogue in first-century Palestine. Or, perhaps better, just outside
one, since on this occasion Jesus is teaching people who might find
it painful to go inside a synagogue. Please also imagine that you are a
scribe or a Pharisee, removing from your imagination all the weight
of the modern connotations of those words. That is to say, you do
not consider yourself a hypocrite: rather you are observant, modest
and sober, you have a genuine religious enthusiasm, a sure devotion
to the way of the Torah, a good knowledge of all the narratives and
incidents which are received as Holy Writ, and you are authenti-
cally curious about this Jesus who might perhaps be a prophet.

You are used to there being a lectionary reading cycle in the synagogue. For over a century before Christ, the books of Moses had
been divided into 150 chunks so that the Torah would be read in
its entirety over a three-year cycle. They had been divided according to the convenience of the feasts, and the passages were known
as *sedarim*. Also, more recently, readings of chunks of the prophets
had been added, and these were known as *haftarot*. So, there are
appointed readings for every Sabbath, and the person who was en-
trusted with the reading and the commentary did not pick a text at
random, but expounded the assigned readings. Unfortunately, we
do not have much evidence for the exact distribution of the readings at the time of Jesus, rather in the same way as we do not have an
exact knowledge of all the books which were considered holy by the
diverse groups which made up the Hebrew people in the Palestine
of the time. In both cases, our more exact knowledge begins somewhat after the period of the Apostolic Witnesses. Nevertheless, we
do know that there was such a lectionary cycle and some elements
of it can be glimpsed from the texts of the New Testament.

What would have been normal at the period would have been to
take the appointed texts, and to have used them as a basis for con-
structing something for the edification of those present. And it is
this that we see Jesus doing with the Parable of the Prodigal Son. It
looks as though we are faced with a teaching which has, as its base,
the texts for the Feast of the Dedication of the Temple, where the
appointed passages were Genesis 46:28-47:31 and Ezekiel 37:15-
28. Both texts refer to the difficult fraternal relationship between

two tribes, Judah and Joseph, and to possible measures to overcome their differences and bring them together to form one single flock in celebration of God. At least, those were the texts for the feast in one of the three years of the cycle[8]. There has also been detected, beneath the texts of this central part of Luke's Gospel, a commentary on several sections of the book of Deuteronomy[9]. The Torah passage in question on this occasion would have been Deuteronomy 21:15-23, which instructs as to the distribution of an inheritance between an older and a younger brother, and then as to the appropriate treatment for a rebel son: that is to say, his being stoned to death. It ends with the indication that whoever is hanged from a tree dies under the curse of God. The passage from the prophets would perhaps have been Malachi, either in its entirety (the book is not very long), or certain passages from it, since it begins with recalling an elder brother, whom God did not love, and a younger brother, whom God loved, and it ends with the promise of the return of the prophet Elijah, who will reconcile parents with their children and children with their parents[10].

The context of the parable is not only given by the texts of the feast, but also the feast itself: that of the dedication of the Temple, now called Hanukah, or the Festival of Lights. This feast points, in the first place, to the re-dedication of the Temple in the mid-second-century before Christ, and, secondly, to the original dedication of the First Temple carried out by Solomon in what was already, at the time of Christ, the remote past. Knowing something about this living context will allow us to get a little further 'inside' what Jesus is doing in offering us the parable.

I would also like to comment on the fact that we are dealing with a parable. Please forget the familiarity with which we pronounce this word. We have grown used to listening to Jesus' parables as if

8   According to the well-known work of A. Guilding, *The Fourth Gospel and Jewish Worship* (Oxford, 1960).

9   C.F. Evans, 'Central Section of St Luke's Gospel' in *Studies in the Gospel: Essays in memory of R.H. Lightfoot* (Oxford 1957).

10   I owe my reading of these passages, and many of the intuitions I develop in this paper, to the works of J.D.M. Derrett, *Law in the New Testament* (London: DLT 1970), especially Chapter 5, and *New Resolutions of Old Conundrums: A Fresh Insight into Luke's Gospel* (Shipton-on-Stour: Drinkwater 1986) pp. 105-7.

they were simple and brilliant teachings which Jesus plucked out of thin air to the delight of the simple faithful, and the confusion of the learned. We are so little familiar with the Hebraic resonances of Jesus' world that we jump almost immediately to an allegorical reading of the parable, as if the final version of the story were all that there is to be understood, and as if there were a more or less obvious allegorical application of the text. For example, that the father is God, the prodigal son is the Christians, or sinful and re-pentant Jews, and the elder brother is the Pharisees, or perhaps Old Israel, and thus the bad guy in the story.

Well, I would like to suggest that it was not like that originally. A parable is a much more interesting teaching technique than this. It is rather like launching a toy into the middle of a group of chil-dren who, at first, do not understand what it is, nor what it does, since it confounds their expectations, and everything seems to be the wrong way round. So, bit by bit, they take it apart so as then to be able to put the pieces together again as they begin to understand what it is about. It is in the act of piecing it together that they begin to 'get it', and understand what it is for. This is what is important: with the parabolic method, if there is not first a moment of confu-sion, of having to pull the thing apart, then neither is there a process of learning and discovery.

Let me give you an example of this, taken from our parable. When the prodigal son is homeward bound, the father espies him from a great distance and, running towards him, falls on his neck and kisses him. This has served all of us as a beautiful reminder of how God is a Father who loves us and comes rushing towards us from long before we have reached him. And nothing in what I am going to tell you should dim this memory. However, if we had heard the story in the context of the synagogue, our first confusion would have arisen, because in Genesis, it is Joseph, the son and younger brother, who leaves his palace in Egypt, and goes out to meet his father, Jacob, who is arriving, along with his elder brother, Judah, so as to receive him, from a great way off. When they meet, Joseph falls on his father's neck[11]. Earlier, he has fallen on his brothers'

---

11 Gen 46:29.

necks and covered them with kisses – the phrase is the same[12]. So, the first reference point for the father in the parable is not God, but Joseph, the younger brother, and it is *towards* the far land that Jacob and the elder brothers are journeying for the festive re-encounter.

It is also possible that there is here a word game from which Jesus might have drawn fruit, for Joseph goes out to Goshen to receive Jacob and Judah, and might not someone have noticed that the name of Moses' firstborn son was Gershon? There is enough similarity among the consonants for such a word game. Gershon was born while Moses, himself a younger brother, was living exiled from Egypt, in the land of the Midianites, whose flocks he tended. He was married to a daughter of Midian, Zipporah, and their eldest son's name means 'I am a stranger in a foreign land'.

Well, I hope that you are suitably confused, and that a series of confusions is beginning to open up. The father can equally well be Joseph, or God, or even the Pharaoh from the Joseph story, since he gives the younger son a ring and places him over all that is his. So far, the place where they are living might equally be Israel or Egypt. The younger brother might equally well be Joseph, Moses, Jacob (the younger brother of Esau) or even Abel (Cain's younger brother). He might also be the younger son who appears in the passage of Deuteronomy 21, about dividing a father's inheritance. This younger son receives only a third of the inheritance, since his elder brother receives two-thirds according to the Law. The younger son might also be the rebellious son who is to be taken outside the city to be killed according to the command of Deuteronomy, whether the killing be by stoning or by hanging him from a tree.

In the same vein, the elder brother could be the one from Deuteronomy who receives the two-thirds share of the inheritance; he might also be Aaron, Moses' elder brother, or Cain, Ishmael, Esau or Judah. Which is to say that there is a wide spectrum of possible occupants of each place in the parable, and we should not dismiss the possibility that they are all there, in a sort of kaleidoscope: now one appears, now another, all in different configurations vis-à-vis each other.

---

12 Gen 45:14-15.

In this kaleidoscopic vision, the elder brother who comes back from the fields and complains that his father has not even given him a kid so as to celebrate with his friends, might be Cain the horticulturalist coming back from the fields where he has just killed Abel the shepherd, so as to meet up with Joseph, who is Abel risen from the dead. He might equally be Esau, whose primogeniture had been stolen from him by Jacob through a piece of trickery involving the hide of a goat, and the father might be Isaac, trying to help his elder son overcome his anger and his envy. Or, indeed, the elder brother might represent Joseph's elder brothers who, after having sold Joseph, killed a goat so as to bloody Joseph's coat of many colours, thus convincing their father, Jacob, that Joseph was dead. And, of course, the punch line of the Joseph story, as of our parable, is the reversal of this, when Jacob is able to say 'Joseph my son is still alive'[13].

I hope that you are beginning to suspect that the parable, rather than being a finished story, is rather more like a collection of hooks from which hang many references, allusions and lines of thought which a good storyteller might follow. Only if we grasp something of the richness of those allusions, and of the different ways in which they can be blended, do we have some sense of why they have been so well put together within the schema of the parable which Jesus is casting before his listeners.

Now, let us follow the story, noticing some curiosities as we move forward. First, there is the distribution of the property. On asking for his inheritance, the younger brother receives a third part, which is what would correspond to him on the death of his father, since his elder brother, following Deuteronomy 21, would receive two-thirds. As it happens, that 'third part' turns up again in the book of the prophet Zechariah, whom the New Testament, and apparently Jesus himself in his own teaching, follows very closely. For that 'third part' is the portion of the flock which belongs to the Shepherd who is going to be wounded, and it will be saved, while the two-thirds will perish. Might it not be the case that the parable is alerting us as to how strange it is that the Good Shepherd, the one who is to fulfil

---

13 Gen 45:28 (see also 45:3).

the Scriptures, is going to be like a younger son, whose own family, following both Deuteronomy and Zechariah[14], treat him as a rebellious son and take him outside the city to kill him?

Interpreting Deuteronomy in the light of Zechariah would not be at all impossible for a teacher and an audience accustomed to Midrash, the family of Jewish interpretative techniques. And let us remember that it is just at this point of Deuteronomy that there appears the famous phrase 'the one who is hanged on a tree is under the curse of God'[15], from which St Paul will derive such important conclusions[16]. Let us add to this the referential framework of the Joseph story, where it is the younger brother who is cast out and left to die, but who gets to be the one who forgives his brothers and receives them into the land of plenty, recognising that that was what God had been planning for all of them all along[17]. It looks, indeed, as though this referential framework is at work here as a storyline which allows the rather cruel passage from Deuteronomy to be re-read against the human sacrifice which it apparently commands. It makes of it instead a prophecy of a reconciliation, which is to be brought about by a sacrificed son, considered to be a rebel, and led to his death apparently under the curse of God. In modern terms, we would say that it is the text of the Joseph story which provides the hermeneutic which allows the texts of Deuteronomy to be read in an apparently inverted way. And we need have no doubt as to the presence in the parable of the capacity to make such an inversion: this is demonstrated by the change of roles which we have already observed between the one who comes out to receive the other while the other is yet far off, falling on his neck and covering him with kisses.

Let us get back to the parable. The younger son goes off with his inheritance, and, being in a far-off land, he fritters it away. So, he deserves nothing more. When a serious famine hits that country, the son goes to work for one of the locals, as Moses went to work for a Midianite. The son even longs to eat the food which is given

14 Zech 13:6 - the wounds come from the house of his friends.
15 Deut 21:23.
16 Gal 3:13.
17 Gen 45:7-8; 50:19-21.

to the pigs, a splendid element in the story, for it demonstrates to a Hebrew public the repugnant degree of sordidness to which the son has fallen. It also brings to mind the Maccabees, the heroes of the story of the dedication of the Temple, who preferred to undergo death rather than eat pork, which is what the Greek king was trying to get them to do. Our younger son certainly feels the pangs of longing to eat the pigs' food – and the words ἐπεθύμει χορτασθῆ ναι, 'he desired to satisfy himself', may be an echo of the Israelites in the wilderness, whose desire to return to Egypt and eat the food from there came to be a symbol of the very nature of distorted desire[18].

However, that younger son 'comes to himself', and here we begin to get some very interesting words. He realises that he might be better off living somewhere else, in the house of his father, even if only as a servant. And he says, literally, 'Arising, I will go', but the Greek word is ἀναστὰς, and it is also the technical term for what happened to the High Priest when he was ordained and prepared for the angelic life: he was 'raised', or 'resurrected'[19]. The idea was that the High Priest already lived a life of angelic 'resurrection' while communing with YHWH in the sanctuary, and representing YHWH before the people. So, a priestly element is entering the story. Solomon himself announces, at the beginning of his dedication of the Temple, that he has 'arisen', or 'ascended', to the dwelling of his father[20]. Any doubt about this disappears when we hear the younger son preparing himself for his return to his father's house, for he uses a set phrase which would have been well known: 'Father, I have sinned against heaven and before you'. This may well have been a liturgical phrase from the Atonement rite on Yom Kippur[21], in rather the same way as we recite in the Mass the penitential formula 'I confess before Almighty God and before you my brothers and sisters, that I have sinned ...'. In other words, suddenly the younger son is the High Priest who is going to enter his Father's dwelling,

18 1 Cor 10:6.
19 For more details, see the works of Margaret Barker, especially *The Great High Priest* (London: T&T Clark 2003).
20 2 Chr 6:10
21 See J.D.M. Derrett, New Resolutions, pp. 105-7.

carrying out the rite of Atonement, a rite which was inaugurated by Solomon in his dedication of the Temple[22].

This leads us to some considerations about the presence of Moses in our story. For Moses was a younger brother, he lived in a foreign land, and he began, with the people of Israel, the return to the Promised Land, which was also the land of the Fathers, or Patriarchs. However, after the idolatry of the Israelites, that is, when they allowed themselves to be overcome by their desires, Moses offered to make atonement for his people[23]. Nevertheless, God did not allow him to do this, telling him merely that he (God) would send an angel before him. It would not have been difficult for Jesus to link this angel, a priestly figure, to King Solomon, who did manage to achieve an atonement which was accepted by God when the fire consumed his offerings in the Temple, and to the future prophet whom Moses promised the people of Israel in the book of Deuteronomy[24], just before our passage about sons and inheritance. The link is made even stronger if the younger son is not only the shepherd who is to going to be wounded, but the priest-prophet who is going to carry out the definitive Atonement, and, on his way to the sacrifice, will be considered a rebel son to be killed, and his sacrifice reckoned a curse from God. That is to say, part of what is going on in the parable is the suggestion that 'one greater than Moses is here, one greater than Solomon', and an insinuation as to the manner by which the coming prophet will fulfil what was lived out and promised by Moses himself, and prefigured by Solomon. Thus it will be known that he is a true prophet[25].

So, the son 'rises' in a priestly manner towards the sanctuary of his Father. The Father shows himself viscerally moved – ἐσπλαγχνίσθη – which is rather specially the emotion of God, his 'chesed', by running towards him, falling on his neck and kissing him, just as Joseph, another younger brother, had done with his father and brothers. Please notice that the dynamic of the father who forgives is exactly the same dynamic as the brother, expelled and left for dead, who

---

22 2 Chr 6 and 7.
23 Ex 32:30-4.
24 Deut 18:15-22, commented by Stephen in Acts 7:37.
25 Deut, loc. cit.

forgives his brothers. Divine paternity is cast in a recognisably fraternal form.

At this point, the High Priest pronounces the penitential formula, but the Father does not even speak to him. In fact, once our younger brother has recited his penitential formula, he totally disappears as a protagonist. He neither says nor does anything else at all. It is as though, once he has become a sacrifice of expiation, he no longer has a separate role to play. The Father speaks instead to the servants, and here we have another piece of word play, because the priests were also known as 'servants' while the High Priest, above all at the time of the Atonement rite, when he acted 'in personam' YHWH, was known as 'son'. So, the Father tells the servants to put on his son στολὴν τὴν πρώτην, which might be both 'a very fine tunic' or, indeed, the priestly robe with which the priests dressed the High Priest when he came out of the sanctuary for the sacrifice. He tells them to put a ring on his finger, in just the same way as Pharaoh had placed his ring on Joseph's finger, signalling Joseph's role as Viceroy, that is to say, the one who was to exercise the Pharaoh's royalty before all[26]. And he tells them to put sandals on his feet, for, earlier, Moses had had to take off his sandals before the Presence, but now, since the Atonement has been accomplished, the prophet who fulfils what Moses began, the one who can indeed enter into the Presence, this one can put on sandals. In other words, the Son is being enthroned as Priest, King and Prophet, all together.

Symbolising and inaugurating the feast and the rejoicing, the fatted calf is sacrificed (and the word is θύσατε – the term for sacrificial slaughter) in the same way that Solomon ordered thousands of bulls to be killed, and the feasting begins. It would not be too much to remember that in the book of Leviticus[27], it is the younger brother, Moses, who ordains his elder brother, Aaron, as High Priest. He anoints him with oil, dresses him in a tunic and girds him around with a girdle. And then he sacrifices the calf as a sin offering, following the same order that we find in Luke. Once again, the father figure and that of the younger brother flow into one single role

---

26 Gen 41:42-4.
27 Lev 8:12-14.

in the rite of ordination. Now the father speaks in the same way as Jacob speaks of Joseph: that his son, who he had long thought dead, is in fact alive. But here, the father signals that he is also celebrating the fact that the Son (the High Priest) has 'risen', that is, has made his ἀνάστασις, and that everything which has been achieved by the rite of Atonement can now be celebrated with noisy jubilation.

Meanwhile, the elder brother is in the field, but as he returns and draws near to the house (and τῇ οἰκίᾳ may always refer to the Temple also), he hears the sound of singing and dancing, and so calls one of the servants to find out what is going on. The servant replies with a curious phrase, for he does not say 'your brother has returned'. The word 'return' would have penitential connotations, since the word 'shuv' in Hebrew means 'turn', or 'repent'. Instead, he says 'your brother has come' or 'is present', 'and your father has sacrificed the fatted calf on getting him back safe and sound'. Which is to say, the servant is giving the reason for the joy, and the festivities, of the Presence, which is what is maximally realised in the rite of Atonement.

At this, the elder brother becomes enraged – ὠργίσθη – and refuses to go inside. And indeed, his wrath is not without interest, since at the great feast of the Presence which is fulfilled with the Atonement, it was well understood that wrath – ὀργή – was in the air, and was in fact attributed to God. It was understood that, in the composite person of the Priest and the Lamb, YHWH was offering himself as an expiation to protect his faithful ones. However, it was reckoned that the wrath would fall upon those who were not covered over by the blood of the Lamb. The image was of the wrath emanating from the Holy Place to avenge God's enemies: from this, people needed protection. Here in the parable, however, and in absolute coherence with all his teaching, Jesus inverts the expectation, showing that the only wrath which is present is purely human, purely anthropological. In the feast of the Presence, with Victim, Priest and King enthroned, there is no room for vengeance. The only wrath which is present, and it is very powerful indeed, is the sort of envy which leads one brother to kill another.

Those who know the narrative of the dedication of the Temple will remember at this moment that, when Solomon had carried out the ceremony, the Glory of the Presence came down with such strength that the priests, sons of Aaron, could not enter into the Lord's House[28]. You will also remember how Moses was unable to enter into the tent of the Tabernacle when the Glory was dwelling in it[29]. Yet here, it is the elder brother himself who is keeping himself outside, out of envy of his brother, just like Cain, and Esau, and the brothers and father of Joseph, all of whom were full of envy. It is envy which makes it impossible to perceive the Presence, far less enter into it.

Now the father comes out in person in order to beseech him, with no hint of violence or vengeance – there is no wrath coming out of the sanctuary. Rather, the father speaks to him, as it were, from below, acting as the humble spokesman for the plenitude of that forgiving and non-vengeful Presence. Of course, the father has now allowed himself to be defined by that Presence. He begs the elder brother to come in to the feast of the celebration of the Presence. The elder brother explains that he has been a servant. And indeed he has – he has been the servant to the priesthood, through the order of Levites. And he has never put aside one of the father's commandments – for the phrase in Greek hints at the commandments of the Law οὐδέποτε ἐντολήν σου παρῆλθον. It would seem, in fact, that he is representing an obedient order of Levites, whose ordination had occurred when Moses commanded them to kill their brethren among the people of Israel who had participated in the building of the Golden Calf[30]. The elder brother even says that his father never gave him a kid with which to celebrate with his friends. This may be a reference to the prohibition of the Levites from carrying out the tasks of the priesthood in the matter of sacrificing live animals, which appears in the book of Numbers[31]. And naturally it will call to mind, as I have already mentioned, the fact that Cain, whose sacrifice was not acceptable, practised horticulture, while Abel was a shepherd, and his sacrifice was acceptable. It will also summon up memories of the different pieces of sheep and

---

28 2 Chron 5:14; 7:2.
29 Ex 40: 34-8.
30 Ex 32:26-30 - I'm not making this up you know.
31 Numbers 18:1-23.

goat-related skulduggery which pepper the Hebrew Scriptures[32]. We might even imagine, in the voice of the elder brother, a tone of complaint that, unlike what happened with Abraham and Isaac, God had not provided for sacrifice[33] with a substitute lamb which might teach him not to sacrifice his brother. In his envy, he is unable to recognise that the brother who is present is exactly that lamb who YHWH has provided, providing himself.

Next, the elder brother himself refers to his brother as 'this son of yours', recognising in his envy that the one who he does not even deign to call 'my brother' has been elevated to the rank of 'Son'. And he criticises his father, since he claims that this son 'has devoured your living with harlots', and, even so, the father has sacrificed the fatted calf for him. The phrase is very interesting indeed. In Greek, it reads as follows: ὁ υἱός σου οὗτος ὁ καταφαγών σου τὸν βίον μετὰ πορνῶν. Now, if we read that sentence in priestly idiom, then this Son has not devoured the *living*, so much as eaten up the *life*, of the father, in the same way that the priest eats the body of the lamb which is YHWH once the sacrifice has been offered on the altar. And the High Priest has done this amongst an idolatrous people. In his envy, the Levite does not realise what he himself is saying, for the High Priest is precisely the one who eats and distributes the very life of God, being his Son, as forgiveness in the midst of a people given to fornication, or idolatry – notions which are interchangeable in the prophetic texts. And the fact that the Son is now present, his priestly mission fulfilled, is very justly symbolised by the sacrifice of the fatted calf in the feast of the Presence. Between an accusation of immorality and a recognition of priestly presence, there lies only the blindness which is the fruit of envy, and the irony of the good storyteller.

As if this were not enough, the father who has listened to the bitterness of the elder brother now addresses him as τέκνον – which is to say 'child'. It is, in fact, a tender word, but it is not the same as 'son', which is important, since, as we have seen, both the father and the elder brother reserve the word υἱός, with all of its implications

---

32 See Gen 30:25-43.
33 Gen 22:8-13.

of high priesthood, for the younger brother. 'Child', says the father, 'you are always with me, and all that is mine is yours'. And here, just in case further detail were needed, we are once again plunged into a reference to the Levites, and indeed into the same central section of Deuteronomy which has lain beneath the surface of our parable. For there, it says[34]:

> The Levitical priests, that is, all the tribe of Levi, shall have no portion or inheritance with Israel; they shall eat the offerings by fire to the LORD, and his rightful dues. They shall have no inheritance among their brethren; the LORD is their inheritance, as he promised them.

And so we are at the end, as we were at the beginning, faced with words about inheritance. But it now turns out that the elder brother also has as his inheritance the Lord, who is by definition inexhaustible. So the elder brother should have no envy as to how the Lord distributes what is his and brings it to a good ending. The one who is more than Moses, more than Solomon, younger brothers both, has arrived. The dedication of the New Temple which is himself, more originary than even the temple of Solomon, is being carried out. In the parable, we are given all the elements necessary for an extraordinary recapitulation of the entire story of Israel, starting with Abel, passing through Moses and Solomon, and pointing towards the definitive sacrifice which will overcome all the ambiguities in the previous sacrificial regime. The insinuation is that this sacrifice is indeed about to take place. The parable leaves open the question, or throws down the challenge: will the elder brother overcome the envy which keeps him out of the house, of the Temple, of Paradise? Will he accept receiving his inheritance at the hands of his risen brother? Will he enter in to take part in the Feast of the Presence?

At the beginning, I told you that I would try to offer a glimpse of how we might develop an ecclesial and eucharistic reading of Scripture, and I promised to develop some consequences of this for you. So here, by means of three 'theses', I would like to point up three more or less suggestive directions for your future consideration.

---

34 Deut 18:1–2; cf. also Num 3: 5–13

My first thesis is about the text. The Scriptures – and here I am talking about the Hebrew Scriptures, which we sometimes call the Old Testament, are not and never have been, a book or a unitary text. They have always been a series of texts which rub against each other in a constant process of mutual elucidation. Thus was it before the time of Jesus, at the time of Jesus, and so it is now. Furthermore, the Scriptures were never designed to be a final version for a *reading* public. They were designed as a *base text* for public proclamation and commentary. That is: from the beginning, the liturgical function of explaining and narrating the 'wherefore' of things, of events, of stories and of festivals, preceded the production of texts. The texts are, as it were, manuals for preaching or exposition, helped along by their divergences, their internal references, their allusions, repetitions and contradictions. These allow the person doing the teaching to take advantage of the hooks, the hints and the bifurcations, so as to get more juice from their possibilities, from the various 'How would it be if …?'s, and so on. Which is to say that it is the *performance* which is important, because it is the performance which makes the story come alive and allows it to be applied to the 'today', which is always the moment of challenge in any good liturgy: 'Today this scripture is fulfilled in your presence …'[35], or, 'Today the Lord puts before you this choice …'[36].

The second thesis flows from this: if the responsibility for the life which comes from the texts falls to the preacher, *now, today*, then what is central is not what the text says; rather, it is the hermeneutical starting point of the one who is performing the reading. And this starting point must not only be intellectual, but, to some degree, self-implicatory. Those who make the text alive take on board a great responsibility and their truthfulness will be perceived in the way they are found to be involved in the narrative they are developing, and in the long-term consequences of that involvement. Now it is just this which would seem to be what we have in the New Testament. All the gospel writers point towards a teacher who interpreted the texts by offering a very particular hermeneutical starting

---

35 Luke 4:21.
36 Deut 4:8; 11:26; 30:15.

point and implicating himself very strongly in the interpretation. That the full consequences of this could not be grasped until after Jesus' death take nothing away from – in fact, they rather add to – the originality of Jesus' own teaching; a teaching about a mysterious priestly function – 'anointed' and 'messianic', especially in the priestly sense – which only moved from promise, hint and intuition to reality and Presence after the sacrifice was carried out.

However, there is no *a priori* reason to think that the indications, suggestions, challenges and insinuations of an 'anointed', a 'Christological', fulfilment of the Scriptures could not have originated in Jesus' own teaching. We would have someone who was interpreting the received texts with very great seriousness, and at the same time with a thoroughly disconcerting freedom, pointing to a 'today' which was breaking in. And we would have, in the persons of the Gospel writers, people who were, themselves, producing preaching manuals, with their different versions and angles. These manuals would have been crafted to make available for Christian teachers the memory of what Jesus had done and said, organised by hooks so as to help them to relate what was done and said to the lectionary cycle in use at the time. Thus, they would be able to expound how it was that Jesus was the Anointed One of God, the Χριστός, who had fulfilled the Scriptures, and what sort of 'today' it was and is that, thanks to him, is being inaugurated.

My third thesis flows from all this. The principal context for the reading of Scripture is liturgical, and liturgical space is, at least in the Jewish, the Catholic and the Orthodox traditions, the space of the Presence. We understand that the Presence of God is enthroned on the praises of Israel. The Presence of God is eternal, and does not change, and, in its light, all our diverse 'presents' are contemporary, synchronic. It is this Presence that Jesus is opening up for us by his preaching of the Kingdom, his promise of being among us, and through his own role of being the living hermeneutical principle: the one who opens, and points towards, and is, himself, that Presence. This allows us to be found as contemporaries of all the stories of the Old Testament, including even Deuteronomy. A synchronic reading opens up for us because Jesus causes the internal tension within those texts to be laid bare when the role of the victim, in both the sociological and the liturgical senses of the word, and the role of the priest comes together in his person. This coming together allows us to glimpse itself as *something which was always on the point of breaking through in the world of the texts*. Or in other words: the Son of Man *was always coming into the world*. And his coming always points towards an enriched density of the Presence. Once his coming has been achieved in history, the Presence, which is always contemporary, includes the sacrificed and forgiving victim, who is at the same time the protagonist who interprets the texts. It is exactly with *this* tension, between interpretation and Presence, that we have something very close to a proposal for how we might recover an eucharistic reading of Scripture.

CHAPTER 10

❖❖❖❖❖❖❖❖❖❖

Love your enemy:

within a divided self

I hope you will be surprised that I am going to begin by introducing you to what may be for many of you, as it is for me, something pretty new: a recent scientific discovery[1]. It is one whose importance is creeping up on all the human sciences, and it may turn out to be as important for psychology and related fields as the discovery of DNA has been for biology and everything that flows from it. I also hope to introduce this discovery to you, not so as to run away from my title, which is, on the face of it, to do with moral theology and psychology, but rather in order to approach that title in a slightly unexpected way.

The scientific discovery to which I am referring is that of 'mirror neurons', and here I include a brief list of accessible reading material on this subject, so that you can get a more reliable introduction to this field than the one a complete layman in this sphere, such as myself, is able to offer[2].

---

1   This chapter was born as a lecture given at St Martin-in-the-Fields Church, Trafalgar Square, London, in October 2007. 'Love your enemy' was the overall title for a lecture series, and I was asked to look at the issue of 'The divided self'. Other lectures, given by other presenters, included the titles 'Within a divided Church', 'Within a divided world' and 'Within a divided community'.

2   Scientific American Mind, April/May 2006, 'A Revealing Reflection', by David Dobbs, pp 22-27, with links to other literature including:

'Action Recognition in the Premotor Cortex', by V. Gallese, L. Fadiga, L. Fogassi and G .Rizzolatti, in Brain, Volume 119, No. 2, 1996, pp 593-609, available at http://brain.oxfordjournals.org/cgi/content/abstract/119/2/593;

'How Mimicry Begat Culture', by Beth Azar in Monitor on Psychology, Volume 36, No. 9, October 2005, pp 54-57, available at: www.apa.org/monitor/oct05/mimicry.html.

In addition, for a more fleshed out account of the relation between research on mirror neurons, infant mimicry and the understanding of desire advanced by René Girard, see the groundbreaking article 'Imitation, Mirror Neurons and Mimetic Desire: Convergence between the Mimetic Theory of René Girard and Empirical Research on Imitation', by Scott R. Garrels in Contagion, Volume 12-13, 2006, pp 47-86. This article is available online at www.mimetictheory.org/bios/articles/GarrelsContagion.pdf.

For those who read French, a recent book by the leading Paris-based neuropsychiatrist and psychologist, Jean-Michel Oughourlian, begins to explore the relationship between the discovery of mirror neurons and clinical practice: Genèse du désir (Paris, Carnets Nord, 2007).

Mirror neurons were discovered by a group of Italian scientists working at the University of Parma in 1996. They noticed that when a monkey, whose brain had been wired to a neural electrode, picked up a raisin, certain of the neurons in its brain fired. What astounded them was that when, by chance, one of the scientists himself picked up a raisin while the monkey was watching, the same brain neurons fired in the monkey as had fired when the monkey itself was performing the activity. These results were replicated across many other experiments, and so it was that the neurons which enable mimicry were identified. These neurons literally mirror the activity of another in the brain of the one watching. Thus, they allow actors other than the monkey to be reproduced by, and in, the monkey, and enable its socialisation.

When it comes to humans, who are vastly more accomplished imitators than monkeys, scanners are discovering more and more areas of the brain which demonstrate this mirroring activity, suggesting that we have many more, and more widely distributed, mirror neurons than monkeys, and that these are fired off from birth onwards by the activity of adults towards infants. So, for instance, within half an hour of birth a baby will stick its tongue out at an adult who sticks its tongue out at it. Within a very short time indeed, a baby will be able to defer its imitation of an adult. When an adult makes a face at a baby who has a dummy, or pacifier, in its mouth, and then resumes a neutral face, the baby who is temporarily restrained from responding by the dummy will imitate the facial gesture later, when the dummy is removed.

Even more significantly, from much earlier than had been thought, a baby is able to distinguish between an adult doing something, such as putting a rubber ring on a stick, and an adult failing to get the rubber ring on the stick, so that the baby is able to get right what the adult got 'wrong'. This means that it is not merely adult *activity* that is being imitated, but adult *intention*. And so it is that we learn to desire *according to the desire of the other,* in the phrase at the root of everything which my own principal teacher, René Girard, has taught. And thus it is that we as humans no longer have simple instincts, for food, for sex, for safety. Rather, our very way of being in contact with our instincts is received by us through a pattern of desire which is interiorised within us through our imitation of what is prior to, and other than, the self of each one of us.

A simple, related example might be that, if an infant is perceived as a gift by its principal carer, then it will receive itself as a gift. If it is perceived as something frightening by its principal carer, then it will mirror the fear in the attitude towards it, and learn to hold itself in fear: it is always the eyes of the other who let me know who I am, and, as I detect them perceiving me, so will I find myself to be. And, of course, all of us are used to any number of variations of the mixture of love and fear in the eyes of those before whom we are vulnerable.

Here, I am melding together two fields of enquiry, one concerning mirror neurons and another concerning infant imitation; fields which, according to their own leading exponents, are converging. What is staggering about this convergence is that it brings to an end the assumption that imitation is something 'we learn how to do', starting from something else, and which makes of imitation a secondary, and rather an undervalued, mode of interaction. Instead, we discover that humans are exceptionally finely prepared imitating bodies for whom imitation, at which we can indeed improve, is the normal conduit through which we acquire language, gesture, memory and empathy, and so receive ourselves as ourselves. In other words, it is not the case that we reason about something or someone prior to imitating it or them. Imitation is pre-cognitive and it is as a result of the flowering of our highly developed imitative capacity that we come to know.

Another way of saying this is to point out that it is inaccurate to talk about humans as if we have a 'self' within us which is just born that way, owing to the mixture of genes, chemicals, given personality type and parental circumstance with which we find ourselves, and which then independently, and from out of its own resources, chooses to get in touch with the rest of humanity. What we have instead is an intrinsically relational self, one which is inducted into us by the relationships which surround us as we learn to receive ourselves as the mixture of genes, personality type and parental circumstance which our body is, through our imitation of what is other than us. Mirror neurons are, as it were, the welcoming gateway through which the social other reproduces itself, within, and as the unique body that is becoming constituted as the 'self' of any one of us.

With this, we are well on the way to being able to understand, for the first time rigorously, how it is that what we normally call the 'self' of each one of us is constituted by the desire of another. How it is in fact that the self of each one of us, rather than being something hermetic, locked into itself until we choose to enter into relationship with what is other than us, is in the first instance a real but malleable construct which is a symptom of the way *this body* has been brought into being, and is held in being, by the relationships which preceded it. We are well on the way, in short, to being able to understand the scientific underpinnings which configure the reality seen more often by poets and mystics than by our recent philosophical and psychological tradition – 'Hypocrite lecteur, mon semblable, mon frère'[3] – or the sense we occasionally glimpse that, just beneath the surface of the way 'I' behave consciously, there are others acting, speaking, desiring, through me. Furthermore, 'who I am' is not in a necessary opposition to this social other which precedes me, and to a great extent 'runs' me; 'who I am' is enormously dependent upon a more or less pacific relationship with that other which forms me. In fact, when I say 'I', or express my 'self', it is the symptom of a series of negotiations within a 'we' that is speaking.

The avenues made possible by the discovery of mirror neurons are only now beginning to be opened up, and I do not want to pre-empt anything of what might get revealed as we move beyond the last traces of the heritage of René Descartes in our way of understanding the human mind, the beginnings of language, empathy and culture, and of course pathologies like autism or schizophrenia, to name but two. The results of this discovery are going to be formidable all across the sciences. And, closer to this evening's subject, they are, of course, going to have a profound and benevolent effect on our understanding of group dynamics, psychology and the spiritual life.

---

3   Charles Baudelaire, last line of 'Au Lecteur', from *Les fleurs du mal*.

What I do want to do this evening is begin to show how this discovery feeds into something which I have been attempting to clarify, as a theologian, for some time: namely, that in passages like the Sermon on the Mount, Jesus was not teaching something called 'morals'. He was making available an anthropology of desire, and one that presupposes an understanding of who we are, how our selves are constituted, which seems to have a great deal in common with what we are now learning from the scientists.

You are all familiar with the phrase from St Matthew's Gospel alluded to in my title:

'Love your enemies and pray for those who persecute you.'

Yet comparatively rarely do we give it its full context, as I will do shortly. The result is that it is presented to us as a kind of heroic moral demand, the sort of thing that would make one somehow especially noble, if unworldly. That is, when it is not presented in a more sinister light, as if it could be paraphrased 'Jesus wants you as a doormat' – this is what happens when the phrase is used to urge meekness upon a battered spouse, or passivity upon someone who is genuinely being victimised by someone else. And this, of course, is the danger of reading a phrase which is illustrative of *who we are and how we function*, and thus is *directive,* something which sets us free as it gets along side us and enables our perspective on things to be broadened, as if it were *a moral commandment* spoken straight to our conscious mind which we must therefore struggle to fulfil irrespective of circumstance.

In fact, however, the context of that phrase, as supplied by St Matthew, is rather different. Here are the verses in question[4]:

'You have heard that it was said, "You shall love your neighbour and hate your enemy." But I say to you, Love your enemies and pray for those who persecute you, so that you may be children of your Father who is in heaven; for he makes his sun rise on the evil and on the good, and sends rain on the just and on the unjust. For if you love those who love you, what reward have you? Do not even the tax collectors do the same? And if you salute only your

4   Matt. 5:43-8.

brethren, what more are you doing than others? Do not even the Gentiles do the same? You, therefore, must be perfect, as your heavenly Father is perfect.'

Now, of course, the phrase 'You shall love your neighbour and hate your enemy' appears nowhere in the Hebrew Scriptures. And yet all Scriptures, whatever they actually say, are capable of an interpretation such that those who give voice to them turn them into bulwarks for the cultural creation of identity. Give people a common enemy, and you will give them a common identity. Deprive them of an enemy and you will deprive them of the crutch by which they know who they are. It does not take much acquaintance with popular preaching, whether of a Christian, Jewish or Islamic sort, to see how easily a commandment like 'Thou shalt love thy neighbour as thyself'[5] can become mitigated by the presence of phrases like:

> Do I not hate those who hate you, O LORD?
> And do I not loathe those who rise up against you?
> I hate them with the utmost hatred;
> They have become my enemies.[6]

In fact, it is perfectly normal for the culture in which we live, and not just modern culture, but human culture altogether, to speak through our minds and our texts such that they, minds and texts, wedded together, become guarantors of reciprocity, and we are confirmed in our assumptions that we should do good to those who do good to us, and take revenge on those who do evil to us. It is this normal human cultural way of living out reciprocity that Jesus is pointing to. He knows that we are reciprocally-formed animals; he seems to understand that we are ourselves radically imitative creatures who are very seriously dependent on what others do to us, for what we do.

Jesus is offering a contrast between this way of being, this pattern of desire which runs us, and how God desires. God, he says, causes 'the sun to rise on the evil and on the good, and sends rain on the

---

5   Lev. 19:18.
6   Ps. 139:21-2.

just and on the unjust'. And our typical reading of this is as if Jesus were saying that God is somehow indifferent, in that removed, detached sense which we normally give to the word 'indifferent'. Rather as though God were saying 'Well, they're such a bunch of losers, that I may as well give up hoping they'll get up to anything good, so why don't I just carry on doing the kind of regular, creative thing, causing it to rain or be sunny, which seems to be my lot in life regardless of whether they get anything right'.

Far from it! The sort of 'indifference' about which Jesus is talking could not be more removed from that sort of apathetic detachment. Jesus is making a point about a pattern of desire which is *not in any way at all* run by what the other is doing to it; which is not in reaction in any way at all, but is purely creative, dynamic, outward going, and able to bring things into being and flourishing. If the 'social other' tends to teach us a pattern of desire such that what is normal is reciprocity, which of course includes retaliation, then Jesus presents God as what I call 'the Other other', one who is entirely outside any being moved, pushed, offended or any retaliation of any sort at all. On the contrary, God is able to be *towards* each one of us without ever being *over against* any one of us. God is in no sort of rivalry at all with any one of us; he is not part of the same order of being as us, which is how God can create and move us without displacing us. Whereas we who are on the same level as each other can only move each other by displacing each other.

I hope you now see that the instruction 'But I say to you, Love your enemies and pray for those who persecute you' comes as the mid-point, the point of passage, between these two different patterns of desire: the first pattern of desire, in which our identity is given to us and grasped onto by us imitative creatures as we mirror each other in our reciprocity; and the second pattern of desire, in which our identity is given to us by someone moving us entirely independently of being moved by us. The instruction is not one about being a doormat, it is one about how to be free. 'Love your enemies and pray for those who persecute you' means: 'Do not be towards them as they are towards you, for then you will be run by them, and you and they will become ever more functions of each other, grinding each other down towards destruction. Don't pay them the tribute of giving them that sort of free rental space in your soul. Instead of that, allow your identity to be given to you by your Father who is in heaven, who is not in any sort of reciprocity with them, and is able to be towards them as one holding them in being and loving them, without reacting against them. Given that you can't do this by a simple act of decision, you will require that your whole pattern of desire, formed in reciprocity, be turned around; and the only way to do that is to pray for them. For in praying for them you are beginning to allow the pattern of desire which is God to enter into your life, so allowing you to recognise your similarity with your enemies, rather than your exaggerated differences. This enables you to relativise the way you are towards your enemy, and will eventually empower you to be towards your enemy as God is. Thus you will be free of any contagion from their violence towards you.'

Jesus then goes on to show that it is not only the contagion of *hostile* reciprocity from which we need to be freed, but also that of *friendly* reciprocity:

> For if you love those who love you, what reward have you? Do not even the tax collectors do the same? And if you salute only your brethren, what more are you doing than others? Do not even the Gentiles do the same?[7]

Whether it is a matter of love or hate, reciprocity is the same in both cases: you are run by the social other, and you become a function of that social other. So, you love those who love you, and become more and more dependent on their approval, which means that you allow your behaviour to be shaped by their expectation, and find yourself automatically tied into having shared attitudes of contempt for those whom they despise. But, says Jesus, there is nothing especially good about that: tax collectors do just the same, making good bonds of friendship with the occupying authorities over against the despised 'native population'. Nowadays we might say: arms dealers, or cocaine smugglers, are perfectly capable of building up just such bonds of affection among an in-group, by contrast with the law enforcement agencies which try to make their lives difficult.

---

7   Matt. 5:46-47.

Mafiosi of all backgrounds and nationalities have 'strong family values'. There is nothing especially *good* about this sort of thing, which happens throughout human culture, and is simply the result of the sort of imitative animal that we are.

The same applies when we exchange marks of recognition. Giving recognition to those who recognise you: what is that but a sign that you and they are dependent on each other for a fragile sense of respect? But, of course, that sort of giving of recognition, and seeking of recognition, being greeted, having 'face', always also means by contrast that there are people at whose face you do not look, people you do not recognise because they are of no value to you, people you neither see, nor do you want to see yourself reflected in them, so you look away. They become a blind spot for you. There is nothing particularly good about that: there is not a tribe, a club, a religion or a culture anywhere on the face of the planet that does not work in just the same way. The fact is that friendly reciprocity and hostile reciprocity are part of the same thing, variations on a theme of us being run by what is other than us.

But, Jesus says, this being run by the adulatory other, or the excoriating other, which is the same thing, has nothing to do with God. What God's love looks like is being creatively *for* the other without being defined over against the other in any way at all. That is what is meant by grace and freedom. It is going to involve breaking through the strong-seeming, but ultimately fragile, dichotomies of 'in group' and 'out group', 'pure' and 'impure', 'good guys' and 'bad guys' which are quite simply the ambivalent functions of our cultural identity, and coming to love other people *without any over against at all.* Living this out is going to look remarkably like a loss of identity, a certain form of death. And living it out as a human is what it is to be a child of God, and to be perfect as the heavenly Father is perfect.

I think that we are now in a better position to look at the second half of our title for this evening: the divided self. The main point I want to make is that the divided self is not a particular individual tragedy. It is the normal condition of our being brought into the world. The condition in which we find ourselves is as apes with an extraordinarily well-developed imitative capacity, such that in our process of growing up we take on board, not only the signs, the language, the behavioural norms of our culture, but also the pattern of desires of those who precede us. We absorb such patterns voraciously and without being conscious of what we are doing, and when we react against certain parts of those patterns of desire, we do so from within a huge seedbed of what we have accepted without knowing it. And, of course, the more we react against certain elements, the more we become like the worst caricature of what we are reacting against – though it is usually only others who can see that.

However, one of the things we pick up from our social group with astonishing ease, is enemies: the one who is not like us and, by comparison with whom, we know who we are. What we do not realise, of course, is that the moment there is comparison, the other is already inside me as part of my identity-building kit. In the act of thinking that I am defending myself against becoming such a person, I am already giving free rental space inside me to the person 'whom I am not like'. And the more attention I give to that person or group being wicked, and not like me, the more I allow myself to be fascinated by the evil of that person, the more I give that person or group permission to dance around inside me outside my control. What other people will notice is that I have become the mirror image, the enemy twin, of the evil that I am fighting against. I, however, *cannot recognise this*. And this is not because I am stupid, or have not studied enough, but because my conscious 'I', the one which 'knows' things, is a symptom of the pattern of desire which runs me, and symptoms have no direct access to their causes.

Here we are, back at the image of the mirror. An eye has no direct access to the optic nerve that enables it to see. But it does have an indirect access: either it can look at someone else's optic nerve, or, if we can imagine a particularly delicate piece of brain surgery, it might see its own optic nerve in a mirror. And we are the same. Only by means of a human mirror do we have access to ourselves. One of the things our friends know about us, but we do not know about ourselves, is that the people we find most difficult, the ones who really get on our nerves, are the ones who are most like us. These are the ones about whom we have all sorts of theories and explanations about how awful they are, and why they are like that. And, of course, the more convinced we are of our theories and explanations, which may indeed contain elements of truth, the more blinded we are to our likeness to our pet hate. I say the theories and explanations may contain elements of truth, but it is an entirely useless and redundant truth, since the only thing the truth communicates to the other person is the relationship of hostility I have towards them. This is why taking the speck out of another person's eye is impossible, since the only thing that communicates itself to the other person is our own hatred of our own beam, projected onto them, and why should they learn anything from that?

It is here, I think, that we can start to see the genius of Our Lord's instruction, one which, as I say, completely takes for granted the mimetic, projective nature of humans and of the fact that it is how we are in relation to others which runs our reason, and not our reason which runs the way we are towards others. He makes it clear throughout the Sermon on the Mount that the only path towards having a non-divided self is by loving our enemies, forgiving those who do us harm, and praying for those who persecute and hate us. And this is because it is only in our relationship with others, 'out there', that we have any access at all to what constitutes us 'in here'.

And this seems to be true as a matter of experience as well: as I have prayed for, and tried to learn to look on, certain people in my own experience with whom I have been locked into what seemed at first glance like righteous hatred, I have found that the veriest glimpse of the tiniest iota of affection towards them produced a huge harvest of self-acceptance and peace within me. I could have prayed for years to be able to forgive myself and not got anywhere at all: it was in being able to let *the other* go, forgive the other, that I began to be able to forgive myself. It is for this reason that I think that telling people that they need to forgive themselves is to place a terrible burden on them. It is to direct them to fruitless introspection and breast-beating, since none of us has direct access to what makes us conscious. The only way to forgive yourself is projectively, which is to say, in another person. As you forgive another, so you will find yourself being let go.

Before I end by giving a few examples of the sort of changes of perception and relationship produced by loving our enemies, I would like to pre-empt a question that may have arisen in the minds of some of you. I described as normal, as 'where we start from', a state of hostility, in which the 'self' of each one of us is received by us in such a way that we carry around in ourselves all the ambivalences, loves, and hatreds of our culture. Without that 'self' received from, and largely run from within by, the social other, we would not be human. And yet we receive that self as pre-divided, massively nurturing us and yet also locking us into hostilities and hatreds we do not understand, but which inform our capacity to understand. Is this not, you might say, the state of being human which is described as being 'with Original Sin'?

And to this, I want to give a very careful answer: the doctrine of Original Sin points towards a perception of the condition which we share, simply by virtue of being human, which is in the process of being left behind as we are enabled to become something else. It is a backwards glance at a reality we are being empowered to leave behind. Original Sin is not a matter of an accusatory moral judgment on humanity. It is, curiously, the first fruits of our being able to perceive ourselves in a way that is free of moralism. It says to us: 'Thanks to Christ having loved those who were, without knowing it at all, enemies of God, locked into a failed mind and self-destroying patterns of desire, which is to say, all of us; and thanks to him having been prepared to be towards these enemies as one who was not in any sort of retaliation towards them, but was able to give himself freely into their midst allowing himself to be killed so as to show what being towards them without being over against them meant; thanks to all this, we can begin to see how what we thought was the *natural* state of affairs, this being locked into a divided self, is in fact a *cultural* state of affairs from which we are being set free by being able to become a different sort of imitator, one who receives being from another, without any grasping of it at all by rivalrous comparison with anyone else.'

In this vision, our being baptised is the rite by which we celebrate our decision to accept having the 'I', that was structured from within by elements of hate, fear and crowd, undergo death in advance;

to accept it being, as it were, drowned by a lynch mob, so that our 'I' can start to be restructured from within by the One who forgives, and is towards others as God is. The 'others' who are within my self and are constitutive of it are reconfigured as ones in the process of being forgiven as the new 'self' is born. This is why it is through baptism, whether by sacrament or desire, that we become children of God. Baptism presupposes the possibility of a radical restructuring of the 'self', from within such that we become what humans were always meant to be, but are locked into resisting: bearers in the flesh of the life, freedom and vitality of God.

Well, that parenthesis aside, let me end with a couple of examples of the sort of thing I mean by the way in which loving the enemy restructures the self. Some of you will have followed, with a mixture of amazement and derision, the Larry Craig affair. I am referring to the hard-right Republican senator from Idaho, with a perfect anti-gay voting record, who, in August of 2007, was arrested for, and initially pled guilty to, attempting to solicit sex from a male undercover police officer in a Minneapolis Airport men's room. The police operation had been set up following complaints from the public since this particular bathroom had acquired some notoriety as being a venue used by the intrepid for other than its apparent purpose. When the news of his arrest broke, Senator Craig first resigned from the Senate, then un-resigned, then tried to change his initial guilty plea, and then claimed that his arrest was unconstitutional. Throughout, of course, he has said, loudly and repeatedly, and to a crescendo of increasingly raucous background laughter: 'I am not gay. I am not gay.'

For people like me, Senator Craig has been, in a very obvious sense, an enemy: a solid functionary of the system of hatred which has used people like me as a wedge issue to frighten people into acquiescence with other, and far more serious, forms of evildoing. A system of hatred which is, thank heavens, far less strong in this country now than it is in the United States, and far less strong than it was in this country as recently as fifteen years ago. I say this, since there is an obvious sense in which I, as a child of my culture, am tempted to rejoice in the discomfiture of my enemy, to depict Senator Craig as the 'not me' which gives me a tidy little identity. It was in this context that I was very moved to read a piece by one of the gay-bloggers in the US, fairly shortly after the Craig story broke, which helped remind me of the truth of the Gospel.

This blogger, whose name I cannot now remember, showed me something that enabled me to see *sameness* rather than difference. He pointed out that Senator Craig was born in 1945, in rural Idaho. When he was ten years old, in 1955, there was a scandal in Boise, the Idaho State Capital, not too far from where young Larry lived. It was the big tabloid gay scandal of the 1950s, coming just as America was in the grip of the McCarthy witch hunts, themselves helped along nicely by at least two self-hating gay men, 'killer fruits', as Truman Capote wryly called them: Roy Cohn and J. Edgar Hoover. It was revealed that in Boise, of all unlikely places, there was a network of public officials and influential citizens employing the services of a group of rent boys. Well, you can imagine what sort of impact the news of all this – the sensation of it, the hatred it revealed – might have had on a ten-year-old boy. It might well have taught him that, if he wanted to grow up being good, then the one thing, above all else, that he was not, was gay (or whatever approximation to that word existed in his milieu at that time). A boy like that might well have been taught by his culture, just as he came close to puberty, simultaneously who he was, and who he was not; and, faced with any little boy's desire to grow up to be good, he may have been locked into a form of denial and self-hatred which could then perpetuate itself for many years thereafter.

Now you will notice that I have used the subjunctive form, 'may', and 'might', throughout this description, because I do not know Senator Craig personally, nor, I suspect, did the blogger who pointed out these background dates and events. But as I read the blog, I did remember a ten-year-old boy whom I knew in this country, fifteen or so years later, and so already in a much easier cultural climate, who found himself impossibly riven between the growing knowledge of who he was and the absolute cultural imperative that he not be that thing. Even in the much easier cultural climate of Britain in the early 1970s, that little boy came as close as dammit to opting for public 'goodness' and success, denial and dishonesty, instead of the long route through the mystery of forgiveness and integration which was later offered to him by the Catholic faith.

That little boy is, of course, myself, and what the blogger did for me was open up the possibility of my seeing Senator Craig not as an enemy, but as someone like me, riven by the same things of which I am riven, driven by the same things as those by which I am driven – 'mon semblable, mon frère'. The blogger showed me what mercy, which is equality of heart, looks like. There but for the grace of God go I, and what the grace of God looks like is being empowered to work through what it means to love those who hate you, to pray for those who persecute you, and stumbling towards finding a non-reactive way of being towards those who once thought of people like me as their enemies, but are now my friends. It is this perception of the essential similarity between my enemies and myself which makes me insist on refusing to allow myself the dangerous self-indulgence of regarding the frightened hierarchs of my Church as evil caricatures. They are my trapped brothers and, if I cannot be towards them as Christ is towards me, a presence who longed for my integration and freedom long before I was able to trust that he would be taking me to a new creation, then really, I am no more than a scribe or a Pharisee.

And finally, an example from a totally different field, but one that is also now strongly present in our current cultural mix: I cannot recommend highly enough to those of who haven't read it already, Ed Husain's book *The Islamist*[8]. This is a Londoner's account of how he joined the world of radical Islam in the East End, participated in it, found himself disgusted at what he was becoming, and was able to move away from that world, bringing with him a wonderfully-informed vision of how its groups and ideologies work.

Husain's writing impacted me, but not because he was opening my eyes to something entirely different from anything that I knew. In one sense, he was doing that: the world of Arabic-named groups, the scholars and ideologues of a different cultural world, was fairly new to me. What astounded me, however, and this has been a great grace, is the realisation of how much similarity there is between the world that Husain describes concerning the student Islamist

---

8   London, Penguin, 2007.

religious politics of his East London adolescence, well organised or poorly organised, self-deceived and self-deceiving as he portrays it, and the world of Christian religious politics among hot-headed students familiar to any one of us who has ever attended university. The tensions between the religion of Husain's parents and his own journey of flight in search of something else, and gradual return to a love of much of what he had left behind, and along with it a growth in love for his own country of birth: these are all elements to be found in the biographies of how many of us? I learned from his book because, in it, I saw someone upon whom I might have projected 'difference', and at whom I might have allowed my hate to fester. But I saw him making a journey towards becoming a truth teller, and, in the process, becoming someone who can lead us readers, amply equipped as we are with mirror neurons, into discovering something about who we are. For it is only as part of such a process of discovery that we are able to move out of being trapped in an un-decidable row between enemy twins, and to begin instead to look together at what really is and learn from it, as it is in the process of being gifted to us.

This, finally, is what I would leave you with: unless we learn to relax into our appreciation of our similarity with each other, of how the other already runs me from within, then we will have no access to real knowledge about each other and about the world we live in. The human being is not the sort of animal who can have direct knowledge of what things really are, objectively, except in the de-gree to which we are set free from having our knowledge run by hatred of each other. If we want to come to know what really is true about our world, then we will have to learn to have our knowledge set free from being forged in hatred. That, it seems to me, is the basic framework for what, at the publicly expressed invitation of Pope Benedict, my Church is now proposing to study seriously: how to talk about a natural law which is universal in scope and true independently of those who hold it. I suspect that, as we grow in our discovery of how mirror neurons work, the phrase 'Love your enemies and pray for those who persecute you' may turn out to be closer to the founding principle of that natural law than any of us had any right to expect.

CHAPTER 11

Letter to a young gay Catholic

Carissimo,[1]

What a privilege it is to be given the chance to write to you! So much so, that I would like to savour the word 'you' for a little bit and ask you to consider what a novelty it is, how open-ended a form of address.

How often have you ever been addressed by the word 'you' in a Catholic publication? I don't mean the word 'you' in the weak sense, as when advertisements ask: 'Have you considered a vocation to be a priest or sister?' Because those advertisements don't really mean 'you'. They really mean 'someone who is like you in every way, but happens not to be gay, or at least is good at hiding it'. Normally, whenever there is a discussion about matters gay in Catholic publications, the style very quickly becomes stiff, and a mysterious 'they' appears. This 'they' seems to inhabit another planet from the one you inhabit. Whoever is talking about 'they' is, in fact, on another planet, one where a strange lack of oxygen makes it impossible to use the pronouns 'I', 'you' or 'we'. If someone does start to use those pronouns, you quickly sense that the only thing that gives them the freedom to do so is that they are heterosexual, and are honest enough to say that they don't really understand what it's all about.

You may have tried to talk informally about being a gay Catholic to a priest, or even a bishop, whom your gaydar has picked up as likely to be 'family', and you will have noticed how, with all their desire to be friendly, a hidden check comes into their voice. A kind

---

1   This chapter was written for, and appears in, the International Catholic Theological Review, *Concilium* 2008. The whole issue, which is dedicated to 'Homosexualities', can be ordered in several different languages, via www.concilium.org.

of internal restraining order means that when they say 'you', you can pick up that the 'I' that is speaking has moved into a mode of masking, has become somehow official, and the 'you' who is being spoken to is not being breathed into being, but somehow designated as 'to be handled with extreme caution'. There is a 'but' hovering in the background of the voice which speaks as loud as anything they say, because the 'but' says 'you, but not as you are'.

So here you are, reading a Catholic publication, part of that huge and fantastic worldwide communication network which is one of the joys of being a Catholic, and somehow something new is being allowed to happen. For you, a Catholic who happens to be gay (whatever that means), are being addressed as 'you' by a Catholic who is able to say 'I am a Catholic who happens to be gay, whatever that means'. *I* am being allowed to talk to *you*, who are aware of having the beginnings of a life-story in which being gay plays a part. And I am being offered the chance to speak to you not in an official capacity but as a brother, a brother with something of a life-story which includes being an openly gay man. I am being given the chance of addressing you from the same level as you are, as one who doesn't know better than you about who you are, and doesn't even know very much about who I am. Yet a novelty has occurred. It has become possible in a mainstream Catholic publication for the word 'you' to be pronounced in an open-ended way, one which I hope will resonate creatively in your being, by an 'I' whose tone has been inflected and stretched through living as an openly gay man within the Catholic Church.

Like all cowards, when I was faced with the privilege of taking part in this communication, my first reaction was to run away. For a privilege is a responsibility. And there is something particularly awesome about this privilege, since there is only One who can address you as 'You' in such a way as to call your 'I' into being without displacing you or bullying you. And that is Our Lord himself. And he won that ability by going through death, so as to be able to speak you and me into being and give us both an 'I' not run by death and its fear. There is nothing cheap about being able to talk to another as 'you' in such a way that it calls into being.

When the teaching officials of our Church remember themselves – which is usually when they are on the defensive – they point out that what they call the 'magisterium' can never be a substitute for conscience, but can only be a voice alongside your own, at the same level as your own, as subject to the breath of Our Lord as your own. A voice prompting you, counselling you, helping you to form your conscience, and never one drowning you out so that you take on its voice instead of going through the hard work of allowing yourself to be given your own.

They are quite right in this. And I have no right to be any less careful than the magisterium is when talking to you. You see, the difference between my attempt to address you as 'you' and that of the priest or the bishop with the 'check', the glowering 'but', in the back of his voice, is not that he is a hypocrite and I am not, that he is constrained, and I am not. No, I am just as much a hypocrite as he, and I am just as constrained. There is a 'but' in the back of my voice too, though it is not applied to you. However, it would be dishonest if I were to pretend that loving the Church as a gay man had not left some wear in the back of my voice. The realities which cause the priest or bishop to talk to you in a tense and unnatural way are the same realities as force me to think long and hard about how I am to talk to you. And I dread to think how inadequate you would find me if you could talk to me face to face, rather than encounter me through this mask which I am spinning with words – words which I can correct, and edit and change before they reach you.

If there is a difference between the tone of voice with which I am speaking to you and the one you are accustomed to hearing, it is largely one of accident, or grace, depending on how you interpret it. And yes, *you* will have to interpret it, *you* will have to decide whether I who am addressing you as 'you' am able to do so only because of some slip-up, some crack in the system, or whether there is something of the Shepherd in this unauthorised voice which is speaking to you – something of the Shepherd, whose voice you know, and of which you are not afraid. I can lay no claim to being a channel of that voice myself. None of us can. We can hope to be used, or to be in preparation for being used. However, only those who each of us addresses can perceive who it is, what mixture of voices it is, that comes singing through our airwaves.

If there is a difference, then let me confess, it comes from an act of stubbornness, of defiance, on my part. A refusal to believe something. That is the 'but' in the back of my voice: 'But the God who is revealed to us in Jesus could not possibly treat that small portion of humanity which is gay and lesbian to a double-bind in the way the Church has come to do. He could not possibly say "I love you, but only if you become something else", or "Love your neighbour, but in your case, not as yourself, but as if you were someone else", or "Your love is too dangerous and destructive, find something else to do".' And, for a Catholic, an act of stubbornness or defiance doesn't seem an awfully good place to start. It sounds satanic. Unless, of course, this refusal to believe something is empowered by such a strong sense of someone's goodness that you know that you would be seriously offending them if you were to believe them capable of acting in the way that is imputed to them.

You can imagine, as I can, a wife refusing to believe in the guilt which a duly appointed court, and a jury of his peers, imputes to her husband concerning some financial dishonesty. All the evidence seems to point in the same direction, but still the wife stubbornly and defiantly refuses to believe that her husband could have done this thing, even when he himself sometimes wavers in his own defence, maybe so as to let her off the strain of having to support him. In some stories, this affair will end with new evidence, or a shift in circumstance, completely exonerating the husband, and the wife will be shown to have been right in refusing to allow her faith in her husband's goodness to be contaminated by public calumny. In other stories, there will be no happy resolution, and a generation of bystanders will consider the wife to be a pathetic figure, unhinged from reality, so deep in denial as to be unable to accept that her husband was a crook.

Well, I don't want to pull the wool over your eyes! I am that stubborn and defiant wife, and the story hasn't ended yet. Neither do I know, nor do you know, whether my refusal to believe that God could possibly treat gay and lesbian people in the way that the village elders and the local court say he does, is a refusal born of faith in a love which will turn out to be true, or is simply a sign of my delusional flight into unreality. Those who speak to you with a check in their voice know perfectly well that it is one or the other, and they are taking your safety seriously, not wishing to embark you on such a risky journey.

No, I don't want to pull the wool over your eyes. For to invite you into the place of that defiant wife, and therefore the place of vulnerability and uncertainty until the story is brought to an end, is not something I do easily. It is a frightening place. For I cannot offer you a resolution. I do not know whether it isn't an act of arrogance on my part which says: 'It is better to dare to go through the place of being afraid that being gay may simply be a lie, a form of self-deception leading nowhere, trusting that the Spirit of God will dissipate the fear, reveal the fear as a mirage, enable me to grow childlike as I face down the fear; better that, than to cling to the opinion that the fear is for our safety, protecting us from an abyss of meaninglessness, and so allow ourselves to be guided by the prudent "no" of our Church tradition .'

You see, I don't despise the prudent 'no' any longer. I used to. I used to hate the cowardice, the two-facedness and the lies. But now that I realise the cost of stepping out of that, I also realise how careful I must be when addressing you. For which of us can tell whether some petulant desire for heroism might not be pulling our strings, rather than the breath of the Lord saying *'Duc in altum!'* — 'Put out into the deep!'[2]? There, where the prudent think there are no fish to be caught, no humans worth loving with equality of heart, only a swirling of messy and unrescuable desires. The cost of stepping out of the protective 'no!', of believing that someone might be addressing me as 'You' without that dreaded 'but', is finding myself naked before the Spirit and more vulnerable than ever to my own self-deception. And the only resolution will be when the catch begins to come in, and that may not be in my lifetime, or in yours.

No, I don't want to pretend that being an openly gay Catholic is something easy or obvious. It isn't. For a start, merely the fact of your wanting to read a letter like this at all is a sign of how many

---

2   Luke 5:4.

obstacles you must have overcome already. You may have faced hatred and discrimination in your own country, from family members, at school, at the hands of legislators eager for cheap votes, through shrieking newspaper headlines that sear your soul, and, in the glare of which, you are speechless in your own defence. And you've probably noticed that at the very best, the Church which calls itself, and is, your Holy Mother has kept silent about the hatred and the fear. While all too often its spokesmen will have lowered themselves to the level of second-rate politicians, lending voice to hate while claiming that they are standing up for love. The very fact that, through and in the midst of, and despite, all these hateful voices, you should have heard the voice of the Shepherd calling you into being of his flock, is already a miracle far greater than you know, preparing you for a work more subtle and delicate than those voices could conceive.

You will share in all the contempt which the modern world has for the Catholic Church, by virtue of holding firm to the faith you have been given – you will be considered as having little of worth to offer. And, by virtue of being a Catholic, you will always be on the brink of being considered something of a traitor to whatever project your contemporaries seek to build. No surprise there: that goes with the turf. However, you will face something in addition, for you will be considered something of a traitor within the Church as well. 'Not quite one of us .' And certainly not someone who can publicly represent the Church, be a visible part of the sign which leads to salvation. And how could it be otherwise? For, if being gay is a defect in creation, as is held, then the only sign of grace attaching to being gay would be the removal of being gay from what makes you or I to be.

Do not be surprised, then, that they will be considered loyal and trustworthy who pursue every conceivable psychological false lead with a view to finding scientific backing for the claim that being gay is a pathology. They will receive approval as 'a sign of contradiction', of not yielding to the spirit of the age, while you will be considered a bad Catholic, if a Catholic at all. For, long after the evangelical groups which gave birth to 'reparative therapy' and the 'ex-gay' movement have moved on, and their leaders apologised for leading people astray, such ideas will find Catholic backers and supporters, since they flatter current Church teaching. But don't be afraid of those ideas, and don't hate their propagators. They are our brothers. The very fact that these brothers understand that, if the Church's teaching is true, it must have some basis in the discoverable realm of nature, means that ultimately it is the evidence of what is true in that realm which will set us free. It will be bigger than what either you, or I, or they, can guess right now, and it will set us all free.

But what of the long 'meanwhile'? For you, called by your name, just as for me, who am learning to receive an 'I', being Catholic implies a vocation to some sort of ministry, some sort of creative acting out, some sort of public imitation of the life and death of Our Lord. So I don't want to pretend: you will find yourself developing a ministry, as I find myself developing one, without any public backing from Church authority. It will be as if you did not exist. You will have to learn to live in the silence of being neither approved of, nor even disapproved of. You will fall out of the gaze of men, and, if you are anything like me, desperate for an approving glance, you will experience this as a form of dying. For each of us is given to be who we are through the gaze of others, and we respond to that gaze, allowing it to give us who we are to be, and we behave accordingly. So, to drop through the floor into a space where there is no gaze, no approval, not even any disapproval, is a terrifying and risky business.

For, of course, I may have dropped through the floor into the space where there is no gaze because I have become hermetic in my own pride and self-deception. In which case, I will never find a gaze, but will dance to the rhythm of that deception, thinking myself very holy and special until death comes. Or, if I am being led by the Spirit of God, the place where there is no gaze may turn into the space where I am found in the regard of God. And this will be experienced by me as a 'nada', a nothing, all around, and only others may perceive that there is an 'I' being called into being by One whose eyes I cannot see, but who can see me, a breath I cannot feel, and yet upon which I am being held. And, of course, others will not necessarily understand what they see coming into being any more than I will.

What might you be embarking on? Let me give you an analogy. I don't know whether you are old enough to remember the Cold War? Or indeed whether the Cold War had enough of an incidence in your part of the world to have made much of an impression on you as you grew up. One of the spin-offs of the Cold War was a literary and cinematic genre of spy stories, tales of intrigue and underground life waged (in the worst cases) by goodies against baddies and, in somewhat rarer, better, cases, by morally ambiguous people on both sides of the NATO/Eastern Bloc divide.

Try to imagine yourself an agent for one or the other side – from my perspective it is easiest to imagine myself as a western agent buried deep in communist lands. Now imagine that, long ago, you received your instructions from the head of the agency which is to 'run' you, and were given appointed 'handlers' for your mission. So, confident that you were being backed up by them, you plunged into your work, starting to build up community, small signs of the kingdom you serve, deep in enemy territory. Then imagine that something weird happens, there is something of a coup within the agency that sent you out, a policy shift, and all the people who had 'handled' you, knew you, and prepared you, are quietly retired. So you find yourself with no direct line to anyone back at the agency. You are deep underground, and you are suddenly without cover, without back up, without resources, without even recognition. So much so that the new agents sent out by the agency don't even know of your existence, and would probably heartily disapprove, since if you are who you say you are, then you are part of an older and currently discredited approach to the 'enemy territory' in which you have long gone underground.

And, of course, there are people in the agency who might know about you, but they can no longer afford to say so. For to be seen to have contact with you would put into jeopardy their own standing in the agency. In short, you find yourself having become a non-person. 'Doesn't exist on our books, Madam,' is the answer given to any enquiry at HQ made by someone foolish enough to have claimed to have known you. Plausible deniability is the lubricating oil by which the agency works.

What are you to do? You are still loyally at work, loving the project for which you were originally sent out. But communications have become seriously patchy. You can hear on the radio the official pronouncements of the agency. You can read between the lines the 'real' meaning of what is being said, but you do not exist, you have no line of communication back to HQ, you are a no one. So, do you allow your anger and resentment at your treatment by the agency to cause you to give up working on the project for which you were originally called and trained? Or do you so love the project that you are prepared to love the agency which now hates you, confident that, eventually, things will work out? Loving the agency when it loves you is easy enough, but loving it even through the time when it disowns you? Now there is the finger of God!

This is where I would urge you, as I urge myself, often with a fainting spirit, to see the privilege of what we have. Yes, there is a communication black-out with an HQ which can only talk about a 'they' and never address 'you'; yes, they either don't know of our existence, or need plausible deniability for their own sakes, but meanwhile, here, deep in enemy territory, we can carry on building not just a wee little corner of something defensive, but the Catholic Church itself – the full thing, the whole whack. And curiously, with less interference from busybodies than would be the case if the lines of communication were up. So, do we dare to have our love stretched by building without approval, as we wait longingly for the day when some Berlin Wall comes down, and communication is restored? Can you take responsibility for that? Can you persevere?

'¡Esto va para largo…!' – 'This is going to be a long haul!' That was the sage advice to me of one of my formators, one of my handlers, who, in addition to being a gay man, is an historian. He was telling me, as I am telling you, that the process of adjustment to truth in this sphere is going to take a long, long time. And it will only happen if people like you and me are prepared to love the project and not mind the turmoil in the agency, if we are generous in giving the handlers time to summon up the bravery to seek us out and talk to us as co-workers. One of the things that will keep us going is that we can keep returning to those weird, cold-war meeting places, the drop-boxes of spy communication, where, very quietly, from beneath ancient texts and through bread and wine, our original formator and our first handler, the One who first enlivened the project for us, will whisper courage and strength and perseverance into us, while the current agency boys run distraction, creating senseless noise, but fail finally to quench the ancient code.

Who knows, my friend, whether this opportunity for communication will be repeated? Who knows whether this is just a blip in the ether, whether the blockers of the Catholic radio waves will manage to prevent further open exchange between a Catholic 'I' and a Catholic 'you', both of whom happen to be gay? Or whether there is not some thaw in the ecclesiastical permafrost, and talk will get much, much easier? One way or another, let me tell you what I have discovered in my years underground in enemy territory: you are not alone, and his promises are true.

With a big hug

from your brother,

James

✤✤✤✤✤✤✤✤✤✤

CHAPTER 12

The pain and the endgame:

reflections on a whimper

Dear C,[1]

You wrote to me to say how overwhelmed you were with the various incidents in the public domain relating to being Catholic and gay which piled up over the last few weeks of 2008, and wondered if I had anything to say. I asked you for some time, since I too have found it all somewhat overwhelming, and wanted to avoid immediate commentary, which tends to be reactive and not helpful.

However, I've been trying to work through it all, and have sort of got a handle on it – one which is odder than I had expected.

So let me list the various *incidenti*:

- There was the press surrounding the Vatican document on the use of psychology with regards to the preparation of candidates for the priesthood;

- There was the simultaneous good news of Obama's election and the bad news of the victory of Proposition 8 in California, made worse by the way in which our Church was associated with the Mormons in helping produce that victory, and made weirder by the odd semi-apologies / semi-justifications made by several bishops to gay and lesbian Catholics;

- There was the row over the Vatican's initial refusal to go along with a UN proposal concerning depenalisation of homosexuality, justified with some truly bad arguments by Archbishop

---

1   This chapter is, with scarcely any alteration, a long letter which I wrote to a friend early in 2009.

Migliore, and then rather inelegantly backed-down from by the Vatican spokesman, Fr Lombardi;

- There was the huge kerfuffle surrounding the Holy Father's pre-Christmas remarks to the Curia, surrounding ecology and 'gender';

- And finally, and this has happened since you wrote to me, there has been a minor, but very interesting, flap in the Italian press, surrounding a much more sensible than usual article which appeared in the official newspaper run by the Italian Bishops' Conference.

Before I look at each of these, I'd like to raise something for which I have no empirical evidence, but seems to me to be worth exploring. That is this: I wonder whether our pain threshhold isn't getting much lower, and that, ironically enough, the greater the pain we feel concerning the various blows we receive, the less the actual damage they are doing to us. I'm not sure whether this is a position which I can sustain or not, but I get the sense, at least with relation to my own capacity to put up with the pain and violence that is directed against us, that years ago the levels of hatred and violence directed against people like us were so strong, so effective and so silent that we seemed to be more thick-skinned, or to have large chunks of our capacity to feel anaesthetised (and at that time it didn't even feel as though there was an 'us' – much more like multiple, scarcely bridgeable solitudes). It was automatic to go into a sort of 'Stockholm Syndrome' of siding with our haters, at least with large parts of our psyche, simply because the pain of being what they hated was so great that we abandoned our feeling selves in order to survive.

And, indeed, how could we 'feel' what was so unavailable to language that we could scarcely dare to say that we wanted it for ourselves, let alone imagine that it was a healthy and normal thing to want or to feel? I'm thinking of those 'little boy' feelings – the love, the passion, the knowing that you wanted to be with someone forever – that I first encountered aged eight or nine. And then I'm thinking of the sheer panic that engulfed me thereafter. My awareness, as a nine-year old, that I was completely lost and alone in a dangerous and hostile world, in which the thing which I most wanted – the love of another boy, and to be with him forever – was not only impossible, but utterly reprobate and an abomination. Agreeing that my love was dangerous, and should be controlled and hidden, seemed at the time far less painful than the realisation of the reality of the love, and the terror of the abyss, which was opening up before me.

It seems ridiculous to think that a small child can really be vulnerable to such huge feelings. Yet my sense is that I picked up, quite clearly at that age, the hugeness and dangerousness of the abyss over which I was about to be unmoored. That, from then on, I sensed that I was really and truly alone, would never really 'make it' as a person, with a career, a partner and any stability. And, in a way that is only now seeming to come to an end, I have lived that out since then, with a sense of my life being on hold until the basic issue of the impossibility and unacceptability of my love is resolved. But no one can live with such terror and such pain close to the surface for long. How easy it is for the adult world to kidnap a small child in his own soul, and take him into a country that is toxic to him and get him to agree that it is good, all for the best, normal!

Part of the shame to do with talking about such things is, for me, at least, a fear around using words like 'torture' or 'child abuse', even when I know that people who have studied the growth patterns of gay kids brought up in strongly religious environments do find striking evidence of patterns of behaviour which are similar to those of abused children – an internal wedding to self-destruction. And even when I heard that Commissioner Fleury, the most notorious torturer of the military regime that ruled Brazil from 1964 to 1985, had commented in an interview how surprised he had been to discover that it was much more difficult to break gay men under torture than straight men.

Yet, even now, when I can put words to these things, I feel ambivalent about doing so, partly from shame, and partly from a belief that this is making too much of a fuss – it's self-indulgent, that one oughtn't to talk about pain, and, in any case, since everyone has such pain, then it's really nothing special. The reason for the ambivalence is that, to this day, I'm not sure whether this is right. I'm not sure whether that pain, which only now begins to seem talkable about, is just what everybody has, or whether there was something akin to torture in being a gay kid who learned that his feelings were an abomination. There don't seem to be any sure points of comparison from which to triangulate my position on the 'normal human feeling' charts.

If you are told your feelings are wrong, and you cannot trust them, then you are indeed radically unmoored. For who is to guarantee that any point of comparison you find is the right point of comparison? If it seems to validate your feeling, might it not be just some evil influence? And yet, in the absence of your own feelings, it is not as though you have any other feelings, other than a shame at the growing realisation that you are not able to respond appropriately to all the markers which prompt the feelings that you are supposed to have. So there is a sort of shutdown, and a lostness, which seems even to be prior to any ability to feel and verbalise pain.

In any case, please excuse my long background build-up to my point: the pain seems much closer to the surface now, much more able to be talked about. Which means it can be felt. Whereas I had imagined that one 'felt' things and then could talk about them, it actually seems to me to be closer to the mark, closer to a fact of observation, that it's when they start to be talked about, that then they can be felt. Socialised talking makes the feeling possible. And, as they can be felt, so they can be sympathised with easily by healthy people of all walks and stripes.

And that's what I've noticed over these last months: how the fact that the pain not only can be talked about, but that it seems obvious to talk about it, and other people, who aren't gay at all, clearly regard it as normal and sane to talk about it. All that feels like something of a seismic shift, a quantum leap into a field of ordinariness, of being part of ordinary human discourse, that I wasn't used to before. A sense of being recognised into the normal human world.

I guess that this was one of the things that became more obvious in the aftermath of Proposition 8's victory in California. An awful lot of straight people were clearly as shocked and upset as we were. It was amazing to me to behold it being so obviously right and straightforward to many of them that people like us have lives, hearts and emotions, like others, and that of course we must be treated the same way under law. That this is even clearer the lower you go by age down the demographic lists, is even more encouraging.

So, in answering you, I wanted to start with this impressionist sketch of the plateau on which we find ourselves – one where the increased sense of pain is actually the fruit of a major cultural shift which is bearing us up.

In this new place, unsurprisingly, we run the risk of being blown off course by our anger and pain at the constantly grudging nature of our Church's movement toward getting used to this new sense of shared humanity. Especially as part of the shift in the plateau also involves a shift in the way we relate to our own Church. Since, and again this is an impression, it seems that what used to be genuinely, mortally-wounding coming from Church authority is increasingly just irritating and silly.

So I'd like to offer some hints for 'reading' the various *incidenti* which I referred to above, really for the purpose of maintaining our mental hygiene as we move into the new space which is opening up for us. And then, later, make some more substantive points about how I see us living what seems pretty clearly to me to be the 'endgame' of this whole issue.

First, the document of the Congregation for Catholic Education on the use of psychology with regards to the preparation of candidates for the priesthood. I've actually read this, at the urging of a gay seminarian friend of mine who was thrown by it, and it is, for the most part, a perfectly straightforward and sensible document concerning formation. My take on it is that it is transitional, as though a new team at the Dicastery for Catholic Education were trying to move on from the hole into which Cardinal Grochelewski, and the 2005 document forbidding gay people to enter the priesthood, had got them. It was really very curious that *Avvenire*, the daily newspaper belonging to the Italian Bishops' Conference, wrote about this new document under the headline: 'Homosexuality precludes admission to the priesthood'. It then went on to quote Cardinal Grochelewski as saying: 'If a candidate for the priesthood manifests deep-seated homosexual tendencies, even though living a perfect chastity and thus not committing any sexual sins, even so he cannot be admitted to the priesthood. This is because the deep nature of the priestly vocation contains a sense of human and spiritual paternity which a homosexual doesn't possess.' Well, Cardinal Grochelewski may well have said such a thing (and he does have form – he told a North American vocations conference in 2002, at the time when every day yielded a new headline concerning the US hierarchy's cover-up of child abuse, with Boston as the lead story, that the vocations crisis would be solved if only priests were to spend more time with their altar boys), but, nevertheless, this little gem appears nowhere at all in the document.

The document only mentions homosexuality once, as a reference to those with 'deep-seated homosexual tendencies', along with a list of other things like 'affective immaturity' and so on. And that mention is highly ambiguous, since no one knows for certain what the entirely un-professional term 'deep-seated homosexual tendencies' means. It is not a term that appears in psychological literature with any fixed meaning. So it will be interpreted by religious authorities, as is usual in matters vocational, according to what they want it to mean. Some will interpret it to mean 'all gay men', some will interpret it to mean 'any gay men who seem to have a strong sex drive', some will interpret it to mean 'the sort of gay men who I don't like having around'. In short, it will make little difference to the arbitrariness with which gay men are treated by the formational structures of the Church, so often at the behest of other gay men.

However, the key thing about this reference, and the quick nod in note 25 of the document to the 2005 Instruction, which banned such people, is the way in which those references are put in as things to be taken for granted. Obligatory nods, as it were. As though these things have to be said in deference to the previous document and the fuss surrounding it, but the real weight of this document is elsewhere, and nothing to do with gay people. One might be forgiven for thinking that this is a classic piece of the Vatican 'moving on' from an unworkable previous position: make a nod to the previous position as though taking it for granted, while in fact heading somewhere else. If you want further evidence that this document is the Vatican 'moving on', then sense the way that *Avvenire* and Grocholewski tried to make sure that the document, which did not contain their hardline and unworkable positions, became publicly associated with those positions. It was as though they sensed that someone was gently pulling the rug from under them, and they needed to fight back. In any case, it's worth remembering as a general rule that people in and around the Vatican are as likely to want to torpedo an initiative, or seriously to alter public perception of what it means, for their own political purposes, as any agency of the 'liberal media'.

The next incident to register was the the row over the Vatican's initial refusal to go along with a UN proposal concerning depenalisation of homosexuality, a refusal which was later walked back from by Fr Lombardi, the Vatican spokesman. More than anything else, this whole fuss seemed to me a sign of institutional incompetence and lack of savoir-faire in publicity. My guess, and this is only a guess, is that it revealed how closely the Vatican United Nations desk in New York was in league with the Bush administration's own handling of this issue – the bad reasons given by both for not supporting France's proposal seemed remarkably similar: ideological disapproval dressed up in concern about things which would allegedly follow if homosexuality were depenalised. Not for the first time, Catholic gay people were left with the uncomfortable knowledge that our own Church authorities' first reaction is to prefer the positions of theocratic Islamic states to our own freedom. Happily, the outcry was such that even Church authority realised that they had scandalised people, and so there was an attempt to backtrack.

All of this had scarcely quietened down when there emerged a huge row about the Pope's pre-Christmas address to the Roman Curia. His remarks, which were in Italian, and not translated into English for several days, percolated into the English-speaking world through two principal sources: Reuters and Zenit. Both, in their own way, interpreted the Pope's remarks as having something to do with homosexuality. Neither was forced to by what Jozef Ratzinger actually said. Reuters, and with it the liberal press, played the remarks as another shocking papal insult to gay people, suggesting that his observation about ecology and gender were a coded attack on gay people (as if, one supposes, being gay were a form of deforestation or environmental pollution, while being straight and married were a form of much-to-be-prized-and-cared-for, surviving virgin rainforest). And Zenit, from the more conservative and Catholic side of things, also interpreted the papal remarks as to do with homosexuality, explicitly interpolating the word into their press report, where it didn't appear in Benedict's actual allocution. Their aim seemed to be to give comfort to those who like it when the Pope attacks homosexuality.

Now, I have read Benedict's entire speech given on that occasion, concentrating with particular attention on the last four points about the Holy Spirit (the controversial paragraph is in the second half of the first of these four points). I found what he had to say concerning the link between Creation and salvation good and helpful (and, if I may say so, just the sort of point that helps us understand how we must proceed as gay Catholics – for it is in the understanding the link between Creation and salvation that the 'gay issue' will be properly and creatively worked out in the Church). Furthermore, he seemed to me to be doing something good and proper in giving, as a context for his references to gender and marriage, not questions of law, or of biblical or magisterial interpretation, but the overall picture of the Spirit of the Creator who loves us, brings us into being and wants us to be more than we know we are. If the Roman Curia, which he was addressing, regularly understood its task as responding to the Spirit, we would certainly be a better Church. However, I must say that I quite simply do not know what Benedict was referring to in his remarks about gender and the self-emancipation of humans from the Creator. It is conceivable that these were indeed a sort of donnish sideswipe at gay people, a 'clever' criticism, all the more clever for being a sort of collective calumny which, because it never focuses on anything specifically identifiable, can't be refuted or defended against.

However, it may be that these remarks had nothing to do with gay people at all. It is quite conceivable that they referred to particular understandings of human self-construction in academic discussions about gender, of the sort which have been of concern to the dicastery that was, until recently, headed by the late Cardinal Lopez Trujillo. These would have far more relevance to discussions concerning transexual or transgendered persons than anything to do with the comparatively stable field of those whose gender identity is in no way complicated by their attraction to people of the same sex. But, in the end, I don't know what he was referring to. Not for the first time, his style tends to leave hostages to fortune.

My point here, for our sanity, is that it is not very important that we excavate exhaustively and find out exactly what he was referring to. It is very important that we learn a little mental hygiene, acquire a little immunity, when faced with these kinds of incident where a remark which might, or might not, have had something to do with gay people, becomes a huge source of offence, of scandal. Part of that mental hygiene involves being able to stand back with certain awarenesses. The first awareness is that of a distinction between what any given text says and how it is reported. In almost all the cases quoted above, there was a time lag between what was reported and the text that was being referred to becoming available in English.

The second awareness is that of a distinction between the figure of Peter and the particular personal and cultural opinions of his current vicar. It is easy enough for any of us to enter into a sort of personal mimetic rivalry with the Pope, such that he becomes far too important to us, and we are far too easily inclined to imagine that we know what he actually thinks about any given thing, and usually far too quick to 'read' some reported remark as hostile to us, and so to interpret him in a relentlessly negative way. If we are all only political animals, and the Church merely yet another player in the field of human culture wars, then this appears to be a perfectly reasonable attitude to take: the Pope can be assimilated into our particular political and cultural struggle, and be adopted as a useful cultural marker against which we can react when what he says appears to be, or genuinely is, against us, or occasionally he can be used as a positive banner, when he happens to stand up for something with which we agree.

However, for our mental hygiene as gay Catholics, it is worth remembering that this is not how either Jozef Ratzinger, or the Church, sees the Pope. Jozef Ratzinger may be a somewhat culturally conservative Bavarian theologian of a certain age and generation. He may have many of the social and political richnesses of view, and prejudices, proper to those of his time and place. He may or may not have ignorant or well-informed views about matters gay. He may or may not be a self-hating gay man who has a blind spot in this area, as a certain press suggests. We can't know, and I don't suppose we ever will: the papal 'persona' makes of its occupant's biography too much of an interpretative minefield during his life, and for too long after his death, for us really to 'know' the man. And, in the sphere of matters gay, he long ago gave up the possibility of expressing his personal opinions in any sort of public forum. But what he certainly is, and knows he is, is called to act as Peter, whose role and function is one of strong, mistaken and penitent service to us as the Body of Christ. Someone in fact, whose mistaken-ness and penitence make him the only sort of leader with whom we can't really be tied into a mimetic rivalry.

Here it seems, to me, that we need to spend more time thinking about the figure of Peter if we are not to be scandalised by who-ever the current office-holder is. What I would expect of Peter is someone who had strong views concerning religious rightness and sanctity. When faced with the mounting evidence that, in matters gay, the teaching of the Church has been based on a taboo, that is, a sacred idol, a series of violent lies which seemed to be holy but were not, I expect Peter at first to hold firm. Then, as it becomes clearer that what seemed to be from God was not from God, and that God is revealing something new and fresh about God's Cre-ation, God's impartial love for all of Creation and how no human is profane or unclean[2], I expect him gradually to get it, to recognise that what had seemed 'outside' has been brought in by a power not his own, for God's holiness is shown in Creation made fully alive. I then expect him to help this change of heart concerning what *is* to percolate through the Church, by removing such obstacles to it as he can, while doing his very best not to scandalise those of weak faith who feel lost and threatened by the change of world which is coming upon us; nevertheless, I expect him ultimately to ratify the change. I would expect him to be very keen to be trying to formu-late other ways of making clear God's holiness and power, given the collapse in vision which seemed to accompany the realisation

---

2   cf. Acts 10.

that what seemed holy was not. I expect this to take place over time, over several pontificates (and so relatively independently of the personalities of the different occupants of Peter's Chair), and to be a thoroughly messy business, an endgame full of flailing around in which the Gospel truth only emerges slowly, but does emerge surely.

Given this, it seems to me that we can allow ourselves a far more healthy reading of recent developments. And here I'd like to bring into evidence something which I had expected to emerge as part of this endgame, though nothing like so soon: the article I referred to from the 7 January 2009 edition of *Avvenire*, by Vittorino Andreoli. The article, one in a long series about priesthood, is about priests and homosexuality, and its author is a respected mainstream doctor and psychiatrist. While making the usual appropriate acts of reverence to the teaching authority of the Church in moral matters, and the right of the Church to choose whomsoever it wants for its presbyterate, what is striking about the article is that its author is perfectly clear and straightforward that he does not consider it to be scientifically acceptable to regard homosexuality as a form of sickness.

This would not be a striking opinion in, say, the *Guardian*, or even a much more conservative English-language newspaper. However, it is a sign of something having moved out of the sphere of the taboo and into the sphere of the rational that it appears in the official newspaper of the Italian Bishops Conference. Let us remember that the first two documents in Church history to try to say something professional about homosexuality – in 1975 and 1986 respectively – both sought to define homosexuality in such a way that it could not be regarded as something neutral. The latter document insisted that it be regarded as an objective disorder, as the necessary basis from which an absolute prohibition of homosexual acts could be sustained. And yet now, quietly, and without much fanfare, it rather looks as though it is perfectly possible publicly to maintain the opposite position in a properly Catholic context, without fear of immediate retribution. Proper discussion has broken out.

Now here, I would say, Jozef Ratzinger has been Petrine. Whatever you make of the occasional donnish sideswipes, culturally
conservative positions, affinity for the trappings of papal liturgical
kitsch and signs of having lived too long in the small curial world
which the press bring to our attention, he has, in ways which are
much more difficult to make a story out of, quietly enabled this
kind of breakthrough to go ahead. And not just permitted them:
provided the kind of background and context which makes these
moves possible. After all, he has been resolute and firm in standing
up for the way in which scientific learning is ultimately not going to
be found to be in contradiction to the truths about humans revealed
by God. He has been a strong champion of the traditional Catholic
view that it is not because God has prohibited something that it is
bad for us, but that God prohibits only what is bad for us. The cor-
ollary of this is that if we come to discover, through the opening up
of the world which faith makes possible, that something which we
thought was a disorder isn't, it is a normal part of Creation, then
what we thought was a prohibition from God, wasn't. It is a sacral
projection of our sinfulness and violence.

Naturally, Benedict XVI has been subtle in his presentation of
these things, and, some may say, timid in drawing out logical conclusions from them. However, to interpret him as correctly applying
something to Islam (in his Regensburg address) while deliberately
excluding the possibility of applying the same Christian principle to
Christian teaching, would be to accuse him of major hypocrisy. And
the fact that he made almost exactly the same point several months
later, in an address to the Congregation for the Doctrine of Faith,
opening up that self-critical possibility for them, would make that
accusation an innaccurate one. I have no reason to doubt that, in his
Petrine role, he's anything other than serious about maintaining the
proper Catholic way in which truth about being human becomes
available to us, however embarrassingly or inconveniently for traditional Church understandings the chips may fall.

The third awareness is that concerning the role of the media, or
press, during this period of the endgame. I want to suggest that we
have to stand back from some of our immediacy regarding the relationship between Church authority and the media. To be caught up

in the kind of knee-jerk reactions which that relationship produces is not at all healthy, regardless of one's view of the matter at hand. It is tremendously easy for the more liberal media to use whatever comes out of the Vatican as fodder for a view of the world in which the Vatican has a place as a kind of permanent irritant that needs to be scratched. And, of course, it is tremendously easy for Church persons, especially Church office holders, to go into victim-mode, seeing themselves as being somehow heroic in standing up against the secular, liberalising horde. It is one of the easiest identities in the modern media market for them to plump for, and it is, of course, a straightforward betrayal of Christianity. However, by no means all the press is liberal. The conservative press (especially as it works in the majority Catholic countries) is as capable of traducing whatever the issue is, but doing so in a way which plays to a quite different gallery in cultural wars in different places. This was much in evidence in the coverage of the *incidenti* which I walked through above. And, of course, the same Church persons who are so quick to present the Church as the victim of liberal conspiracies, are very rarely brave enough to stand up and forcibly challenge the conservative worldviews which are being reinforced by a mendacious media reading of the sometimes quite moderate, subtle and sensible things which different bits of the Vatican bureaucracy can come up with from time to time. Not least because those conservative worldviews are far too often their own.

Now, with relation to matters gay in this endgame period, the need to be aware of all this is even clearer. Here's the problem: the liberal and anglophone media world understands quite clearly that it can keep alive the gay question as a permanent irritant in its dealing with the Church. It can always make the Church look bad in this sphere, and thus reinforce its way of fitting the Church into its own concerns and worldview. The trouble is that here, and this is by no means true of all the spheres where the media deals with the Church, they know that they've got the beast by the throat.

There are two quite objective issues which are going to play in this media's favour in the foreseeable future. The first is that it is, by now, abundantly clear that the basic characterisation – the whole 'objective disorder' package – which underlies current Church attempts to deal with matters gay, is untenable. And yet no one in a public position of authority in the Church dares to speak reasonably or truthfully about this. What starts as a mistake does eventually turn into a lie when it is held onto deliberately while the evidence grows against it, and it is more and more obvious that those charged with defending it know that it is indefensible. In this sphere, the media know they've got the Church in a lie, and they enjoy making the Church squirm.

The second, and linked, objective issue is that the media knows perfectly well that it is dealing, in a significant number of cases, with closeted gay men. Those who live in the press village in Rome know a great deal concerning who is gay, and who is who's boyfriend. This is nothing new. What is new is that what, in generations gone by, was agreed by everyone to be a subject not fit to be talked about, is now increasingly normal and non-scandalous conversational fare. So when Church authority starts to talk about matters gay, it is talking out of a 'don't ask, don't tell' culture, which is increasingly not shared by anyone else. In short, the media knows not only that it has the Church in a lie, but it also knows that very frequently in this sphere it is dealing with liars. This is what dwelling in a field of mendacity has done to us all.

And the liars have absolutely no idea how to cope with this. The office holders are entrapped liars, living in a sphere in which they appear to suffer from a moral impossibility of truthtelling, and are constantly vulnerable. The good reasons for silence and discretion (not scandalising those of little faith, enabling slow and gentle change) and the bad reasons (self-preservation, convenience, job security) are impossibly closely intertwined. So they retreat into implausible, dry and defensive positions which only make the Church more ridiculous. And, of course, they can never draw attention to the small, sensible shifts which they are longing to bring about, and *are* actually bringing about, since that would be to reveal themselves. The sensible ones don't dare to say anything except in the most oblique of codes, while the less bright shoot their mouths off at the slightest provocation.

All of this is far too good news for the media to be able to be resolved easily. Closet cases can be relied upon to be excessively hardline in backing up right-wing causes, knee-jerked by the tacit blackmail of the more conservative press, which at least is trying to keep alive the 'don't ask, don't tell' world so vital for the survival of the closet, while the liberal press can constantly titillate, rile and scandalise, with its subtle hints of the hypocrisy of the whole operation.

Now it seems to me quite important, again, for our own mental hygiene, that we be able to stand back sufficiently from all this, not to be too quickly and easily drawn into the scandalous world of the scandalised, which is what is promoted by the current link between matters gay, Church authority, media and cultural shift. The Holy Spirit is not part of the scandal, and is quietly, gently, undoing its knots from within, so as to set us free.

So I would like, in my final section to see if I can make some more substantive points for us, as gay Catholics, about this period of living the endgame.

1) The first point is that the taboo has fallen. I want to bring attention to this, since it is a much bigger issue than it at first seems. There is an obvious sense in which the appearance of a sensible article in an official Catholic publication, like Dr Andreoli's in *Avvenire*, doesn't sound like much of a deal. But it really is. It is a sign that Church authority has realised that the opinion that there is no physiologically or psychologically recognisable objective disorder that is intrinsic to an orientation towards those of the same sex is, at the very least, an opinion which it is possible for Catholics to hold in good faith, alongside the older opinion that being gay is some sort of defect in an intrinsically heterosexual human being.

It must also be apparent at this stage, in more and more countries and cultures, that the newer opinion is by far the more probably true of the two opinions, which means that it is, by far, more likely that moral and spiritual life-projects and decisions made in the light of its truth will be good ones, while those made in the light of the older opinion, since it appears not to be true, will be bad life-projects and decisions.

Now, my guess is that we, in the Church, will be fairly slow to work out what the consequences of the tiny shift in anthropological understanding, to which Dr Andreoli's article is but one small witness, will look like. Yet they will be huge. Because a huge amount of the life of the Church and its culture has depended on a vision of humans of which the old opinion appeared to be an absolutely necessary part. And it appears that the Holy Spirit, which is of course the principal motor behind the emergence of anything that is true, is not letting that old vision stand.

This means that we are in a new place. It is not a question of 'How can gay people fit in by becoming like people they aren't?', but rather 'What does it mean to be Church where, as part of what we can see to be a genuinely Christian pattern of salvation, God has manifested that gay and lesbian people are sons and daughters even though the shape of their flourishing doesn't seem to fit into the schemas of goodness which we thought to be definitive of who we are?' This is a huge question, not least because it flows both ways: a mistake about being gay is also a mistake about being straight. For being normative and being a large majority are two very different things, and the shifts in self-understanding which will flow from this are only just starting.

However, please let us be clear, and honour the logic which comes from the Holy Spirit: the moment it is conceded that gay and lesbian people 'just are that way', it is conceded that they are part of God's project of Creation and salvation *as* gay and lesbian people, and not in spite of it. Enforcing understandings of goodness on them that are derived from the previous vision of them as defective heterosexuals, makes no more sense than enforcing the rules of soccer on rugby players, as though rugby players were defective soccer players who were forever disobeying the cardinal rule of soccer – that only the goalie may handle the ball on the pitch. Instead, we are going to have to trust that the same Holy Spirit which has opened up the truth of our *just being* this sort of thing, is also going to show us over time what is the best and richest shape for our *living out of our just being* this sort of thing, giving us the human, social and ecclesial tools to create whatever signs of God's love we are asked to birth.

Now I don't know about you, but I would have loved the fall of the taboo to be greeted with a mighty trumpet blast, the logic of it immediately to have become clear, and the deadwood of the old world to be tidied away as quickly as the new American administration is trying to tidy up the world of criminal lawlessness and unconstitutionality bequeathed to it by its predecessor. However, my guess is that it won't work like that. The logic of the truth will only impress itself upon us gradually, and it will have to undo a good number of our presuppositions and apparent certainties on the way. The taboo is going out, not with a bang, as I had hoped, but with the whimper to which I referred in my title.

2) So, my second point is that I suspect we are in for a time in which Church authority will be flailing around, illogically trying to hold onto bits of the old world. We can already see some of the flailing in those Church authorities who attempt to say something like this: 'Of course we don't think that gay people are defective straight people. The Church merely says they mustn't do certain things'. So, they try to hold on to the prohibition, even though the basic premise of the 'defective heterosexual', which was necessary for its maintenance, has fallen through. This is of course easier, and more loyal and traditional-sounding than the, in fact much more loyal and traditional, view that, given a new basic premise, the Gospel law of freedom obliges us to find out, together as Church, what the new shape of flourishing is going to be.

Another example of flailing will be the shift from attacking gay people head on ('The sort of thing you are involved in is a mortal sin, and not capable of receiving any sort of recognition as rights'), which becomes impossible to defend when it becomes clear that people *just are* that way. Instead, the new watchwords will be 'Defend marriage': 'We're sorry, but marriage between one man and one woman, as it has come to be understood by the Church over the course of the last millennium, just is an unalterable, anthropological human data, so we mean no disrespect to gay people by saying that the current civil institution known as marriage can't include them. Indeed, we ask Catholic gay and lesbian people not to support political movements to alter the civil law in their countries, since they would be doing irreparable harm to something against whose introduction in the civil sphere we fought with great vehemence in many countries when it was first introduced, but which we now declare to be essential to the order of the universe.'

Now there is nothing wrong with working to strengthen, and make more happy and fruitful, that wonderful human institution which is freely chosen marriage between opposite-sex couples. However, that the campaign is, in this case, an example of 'gay-troubled flailing', will be understood perfectly clearly by gay catholics, since the only way in which it might be a reasonable tack to take is if it were arrived at *after* the following steps had been worked through: 1) a clear, public recognition that the official Church teaching about gay and lesbian people had been wrong, and part of a deeply damaging world of mendacity which the Church was now committed to helping overcome; 2) sufficient time had gone by for it to be clear what the shape of healthy gay and lesbian partnered lives looked like, a process in which gay and lesbian people are by definition protagonists and speak with authority; 3) it had become clear to large numbers of those concerned that the shape of God's sponsal love for the world is better reflected, in the case of gay and lesbian partners, in a different institution than that by which it seeks to show itself through the love of opposite-sex partners and their offspring.

However, in fact, step one hasn't taken place formally, neither has sufficient time elapsed since it became clear that the truth is different than what it was thought to be, nor has Church authority shown any sign of regarding gay and lesbian couples themselves as protagonists in developing a true understanding of their lives, people whose opinion should actually be taken into account when discussing political measures taken in their name. And, of course, we haven't even begun to have an ecclesial discussion of the appropriate ways by which same-sex partnerships between baptised Catholics bear witness to God's sponsality. So, instead, we have a typical bit of ecclesiastical flailing – moral opportunism disguised as loyalty to tradition. It is just another mode of scandalised thinking: trying to keep a prohibition, or at least its cultural effects, alive, even though it has become clear that the fundamental premise for the prohibition is untrue, and thus that it will take time to work out which cultural effects should simply wither away.

Something similar is starting to happen as bishops' conferences face up to the pressure for same-sex legal arrangements in different countries. Many of them want to say something like this: 'Oh, anything but marriage'. The more conservative ones would say: 'Well, gay and lesbian people can make individual legal arrangements to protect their partners in any sphere where it is just that they be protected'. Several Italian bishops have talked like this. The more liberal ones would say: 'Well, they can have civil unions, with all the rights and responsibilities of marriage, if they want to, but the word marriage itself must be reserved to opposite-sex couples'. The secretary of the Portuguese bishops' conference said just this in early 2009, giving, as an example, the UK Civil Partnership legislation (which was not, of course, backed enthusiastically by the bishops of England and Wales when it was introduced).

These bishops' conferences are clearly quite unable to obey the perfectly straightforward and entirely wrong-headed 2003 Vatican instruction on the matter. That instruction insisted that they oppose not only any attempt to introduce gay marriage, but also anything even remotely analogous to it. Perfectly logical, if being gay is a defective form of heterosexuality, and any form of same-sex coupling is a form of mortal sin. The bishops can't obey this, because its fundamental premise is untenable, but the dog-less tail still wags them mightily, and so they end up making the Church ridiculous by maximising their unpleasantness to gay people without the benefit of any real logic in their position.

So, unless we are blessed with some extraordinarily wise leadership in the next years, this flailing around is going to go on. I used to hope that part of the Catholicity of the Church was that lessons learned in one cultural sphere would be able to be applied relatively easily in another. So, for instance, the Church in the English-speaking world has had to deal with the emergence of matters gay within the parameters of our own cultural world, religious history, military culture and political wars. I had hoped that, these lessons having been learned, some of their fruit could be applied to other cultures where the change was starting later. I was wrong. It really does look as though each culture has to work through having its demons of misogyny and homophobia cast out for itself, without any shortcuts.

3) And this brings me to my third point: I suspect that the pain, about which I was talking at the beginning, is going to increase. Or, at least, the awareness of the pain. Because, for anyone who loves the Church, the realisation that we have been subjected to a lie, our lives hugely affected by a lie, is a big deal; a really huge deal. I don't want to go on about this much at this stage, having already touched on it, but I suspect that it is going to be more and more common for us to find ourselves, while loyal and loving Catholics, thrilled to be in the Church, and clearly delighted by the way that Jesus reveals himself to us through the Church, able to talk about ways in which we are coming up, spluttering and coughing, as if emerging from an acute dose of poison gas, or from being held underwater for a long time. The fact is that lies are not innocent, nor is mendacity a trivial matter. Lies poison and kill. And, without being in any way victimary in our self-understanding, we need to be able to identify and cast off those lies which have affected us very greatly and very gravely. All the more so for having been so closely enmeshed with so much that was, and is, true and good and loving[3].

What is new and interesting about this, is that this is going to be part of a new, self-critical understanding of what it is to be Church, one which earlier, more authority-based and more polemically forged accounts of being the Church were unable to contemplate. For we will have been witnesses to the Church, God's vehicle of salvation for us, having been terribly caught up in, and marked by, something wrong which was antithetical to what God wanted for us, and for it to have been terribly difficult and painful for us to be released from the lie and the damage. Traditional apologetics, concerning the rightness of the particular pronouncements of Church authority, will look seriously shallow in the light of this lived,

---

3   As I am writing this, the news of the confirmation, by the authorities of the Legionaries of Christ, of the double life lived by their founder, Fr Marcial Maciel Degollado, is percolating through the airwaves. My heart goes out to the many good-hearted members of the Legion and of Regnum Christi, its lay branch, who are having to work through this same nausea of discovering that they have been severely misled by people they trusted.

written about, historically researchable and demonstrable change in self-understanding.

4) To the relief of both of us, my final point. Because we are talking about a work of the Holy Spirit, leading us into truth, and because we are talking not about a culture clash, nor a political struggle, but the birthing of the new Creation through the sacrament of salvation which is the Church, there is a quite specific dynamic which has been given us to live out creatively in the midst of this time of flailing. The nausea-inducing lies, poor arguments, moral opportunism and cowardice will flourish as sideshows while the Spirit gradually brings its work into being. But the Spirit's work will not be achieved by clever victories, or putting bad people down. One of the key things I have learned as a theologian is that, in our world, forgiveness is prior to creation. It is through being forgiven that we are created. This means that there is a quite specific shape by which the New Creation is brought into being. The Son of Man has power on earth to forgive sins, and we are invited into living out this priestly forgiving of sins kenotically. In so far as we score victories over our enemies, we join them in helping hold back the New Creation. In so far as we allow ourselves to be forgiven for our own grasping onto being constituted in the violent lie, and present ourselves towards those who are still run by it as forgiving them, emptying out any grasping at identity or need for security. In so far as we are involved in this, then we are part of the priestly shape of the bringing in of the new creation.

I want to suggest something, particularly for those of us who are gay and who are ordained presbyters, And, thus, particularly for those of us who have been living out the lie in one of its most nausea-inducing and violent forms, as both heirs to and enablers of these lies (but also, of course, for all those who share in Jesus' High Priesthood by baptism): this apparently weak form of truth, which is the kenotic living out of an unbreakable forgiveness in the face of all the lies and all the violence, is the strongest sign there could be of the inbreaking of this tiny corner of the kingdom, in whose harvest it is turning out to be our unspeakable pleasure to labour.

I'd like to conclude with a couple of quotations I found in the most recent book of the thinker I follow, René Girard, called

Achever Clausewitz. The first is from Pascal[4], and says incomparably well what I have been trying to flesh out above:

> C'est une étrange et longue guerre que celle où la violence essaie d'opprimer la vérité. Tous les efforts de la violence ne peuvent affaiblir la vérité, et ne servent qu'à la relever davantage. Toutes les lumières de la vérité ne peuvent rien pour arrêter la violence, et ne font que l'irriter encore plus. Quand la force combat la force, la plus puissante détruit la moindre; quand l'on oppose les discours aux discours, ceux qui sont véritables et convaincants confondent et dissipent ceux qui n'ont que la vanité et le mensonge: mais la violence et la vérité ne peuvent rien l'une sur l'autre. Qu'on ne prétende pas de là néanmoins que les choses soient égales: car il y a cette extrême différence, que la violence n'a qu'un cours borné par l'ordre de Dieu, qui en conduit les effets à la gloire de la vérité qu'elle attaque, au lieu que la vérité subsiste éternellement, et triomphe en fin de ses ennemis; parce qu'elle est éternelle et puissante comme Dieu même.[5]

What a long and strange war it is where violence tries to crush truth! Hard as it may struggle, violence cannot weaken truth, and its efforts only make truth stand out more clearly. Truth, however brightly it may shine, can do nothing to stop violence, and its light only irritates violence even more. When might is ranged against might, the stronger defeats the weaker. When discourse is ranged against discourse, what is true and convincing confounds and dissipates what is based only on vanity and lies. But violence and truth can do nothing, the one against the other. Nevertheless, don't be fooled by that into thinking that they are at the same level as each other. For there is this extreme difference between them: that violence only has a course marked out for it by God's command, such that its effects redound to the glory of the truth which it is attacking, while truth subsists eternally, and triumphs in the end over its enemies. Because it is as eternal and powerful as God himself.

---

4   In the English-language edition of this book, published under the title *Battling to the End* (East Lansing, Michigan State University Press, 2010) the Preface from Pascal has not been included.

5   *Achever Clausewitz* (Carnets Nord, Paris 2007), p. 7. My translation.

The second is from Girard himself, commenting on Charles Péguy, a French Catholic writer, who had stood up for the falsely-accused Jewish officer in the French army, Dreyfus, against all the lies and inertia of an anti-semitic and reactionary Catholic culture in his country:

> *On ne peut d'ailleurs avoir défendu Dreyfus comme il l'a fait et être belliciste, sinon dans le bon sens: ce qu'il appelait 'le combat pour la vérité'.* Comme si c'était la défense acharnée d'un bouc émissaire qui lui avait donné ce goût du réel![6]

> Besides, no one could have defended Dreyfus as he did, and still be a warmonger, except in the good sense: what he referred to as 'the struggle for the truth'. *It's as if it had been his whole-hearted defence of a scapegoat which had given him this taste for what is real!*[7]

May we be given to drink deep from this 'goût du réel'!

Your brother,

James

---

6   *Achever Clausewitz*, p. 42. My italics and my translation. (cf. Battling to the End, p. 74.)

CHAPTER 13

The priestly pattern of Creation and a fraudulent reading of St Paul:

a Catholic reads some Pauline texts in the light of Mimetic Theory

It is one of the best known of René Girard's principles for reading certain texts – those of myths, those of Scripture and some early modern texts – that he asks how the text in question relates to an incident of persecution[1]. Girard posits a real incident of persecution, a murder, a lynching, a mass expulsion of some sort which has structured the context within which the texts have come to be written. He then asks what the relationship between the real incident and the text is. His claim is that the relationship is of one of two kinds. In the vast majority of cases the texts are structured by the scapegoat mechanism, which is to say that the ganging-up of all against one is either completely hidden in the text or is presented in such a justified way as to make it impossible to imagine that the 'one ganged-up against' could conceivably have been anything other than guilty of terrible misdeeds. So, for instance, in the myth of Oedipus, the King agrees with the crowd that he is guilty of the crimes which have produced a significant social disturbance in Thebes, and is expelled from the city. This is tributary of the same mechanism whereby an anti-semitic, mediaeval French poet could blame an epidemic (in fact the Black Death) on Jews secretly poisoning the wells, thus justifying their murder.

The whole point of such texts is that they do *not* highlight the scapegoat mechanism. In fact, they are unaware of it and it runs

---

1   This chapter was born as a contribution to the colloquium entitled 'Saint Paul: Apocalypse et révélation', held at the Villa Bonaparte and the Villa Medici, Rome, in March 2009.

them successfully. This is because they genuinely take it that they have got it right: the accused really was guilty, and they are right to go along with the unanimous account which saw the balance of nature, or the Universe, restored when the evil one was done away with. The notion that the one they hold to be the guilty party is a *scapegoat* – that strange and complex modern term, meaning 'someone who is not guilty of whatever they are being blamed for, but *we can clearly see* as being made to carry the blame in the interests of the cohesiveness of the group as defined by those who have the power to do so' – is unavailable to them. They are blind to that possibility. The story that they are telling is a certain sort of hiding, a certain sort of lie. In fact, a quite regular sort of lie, since, as Girard points out exhaustively[2], there is a regular menu of ingredients which go into the structuring of such texts: stereotypical accusations and depictions of various forms of monstrosity attached to the one who is soon to be thrown out.

Then there are the other sort of texts, which are much rarer. Isolated examples can be found in ancient and classical texts, but the only place where there is a regular stream of these texts is in the Hebrew Scriptures, culminating in the texts of the Apostolic Witness, known as the New Testament. These were seen by the authors and compilers of the Witness as pointing up what had been achieved by the One who had always been coming into existence through the Hebrew Scriptures, and had at last given to their generation the key to those Scriptures.

These other, and rarer, kinds of texts are structurally no different from the texts we saw previously: there are significant and real incidents of persecution in their hinterground. The difference lies in that these texts appear to know something which the others do not. These texts know that the one-ganged-up-on was either innocent, or no more guilty than anybody else, and that they who have lived to tell the story do so from the position of people who are being uncovered in a lie. In other words, these texts are not tributary of the scapegoat mechanism, but are able to reveal it. Their knowledge is uncomfortable, destabilising, not very flattering, and the

---

2   Especially in *The Scapegoat* (Baltimore, Johns Hopkins U.P., 1989).

result is texts which look much more violent than those where the unknowingly guilty victor is able to tidy away the violence. These unflattering texts know something real in knowing that the victim is innocent, and their knowledge is sure, and has real consequences for human living.

I hope that those of you who are familiar with René Girard's writing will recognise my brief summary as being accurate, and that you will allow me to develop something from it with relation to St Paul, in whose honour we are meeting together these days. For St Paul provides, as was pointed out by Robert Hamerton-Kelly in a pioneering article from 1985[3], a particularly good test case for Girard's thought. Paul combines a strong awareness that his world was turned upside down through his having learned from God what he had really been doing as a persecutor, with an equally strong awareness of the way mimetic desire structures the reality of our living together.

I would like to follow the logic of Girard's thought a little further, and explore two questions with you. The first is this. Girard teaches us to detect certain stereotypical accusations embedded in texts written from the perspective of persecutors. The 'lie', as he points out, has quite a regular, recurring pattern. My question is: can we find a regularly occurring structure to the reverse of this pattern, to the exposing of the lie? Are there regularly detectable features of the emergence of the truth in our midst, of the way God communicates himself to us, such that in their presence we know we are in the presence of the Real Thing? Can St Paul help us in this? I hope at least to get a hint of a certain 'regularity' in the Real Thing, by striving for a glimpse of the significance of the identification between YHWH and Jesus in Paul's writing.

The second question is this. It is easy enough to stand outside texts and make judgements concerning who wrote them, when, with what in mind, against whom, and so on. We are applying our criteria, our judgment to them. The spirit with which we are reading them is our own, and we project, as we cannot fail to do, our

---

3   Robert G. Hamerton-Kelly, 'A Girardian Interpretation of *Paul: Rivalry, Mimesis, and Victimage* in the Corinthian Correspondence', *Semeia* 33 (1985), pp 65-81.

sense of 'goodies and baddies' into the texts, and convince ourselves that Paul is on our side, or that, had we been there, we would have been on his side. However, if Girard is right about certain texts bearing witness to the scapegoat mechanism, that is to say, being written by people who are undergoing a certain sort of 'being undone' by the knowledge that comes from an innocent victim who is not themselves, then the logical conclusion is that they can only really be read by people who are themselves undergoing that discovery of their own involvement in the lie. That is to say that they can only really be understood by people who *find themselves being 'read'* by the text in question.

This for me is, if you like, at the heart of how we engage in a Catholic, ecclesial reading of the texts of St Paul. The question of how we may pick up 'the Real Thing', which is at the centre of Paul's witness, is absolutely interwoven with the question of the degree to which we are willing to allow ourselves to be uncovered as frauds. So what I am proposing is, if you will excuse the term, a relaxed, fraudulent reading of St Paul. A reading which presupposes that I, and other readers of St Paul, are frauds, that being a fraud and being 'the Real Thing' look very similar under a certain light, but wildly different under another light; and that the Real Thing, as it shows itself to us, will take us in our fraudulence and turn us somewhat uncomfortably into something else. It will do so regularly, generously, inexorably, but also precariously, dangerously, in a way fraught with fragility.

For this purpose, of keeping alive my own fraudulence while reading St Paul, and doing so ecclesially, I am going to do something rather risky: to read the text alongside, and in the company of, a brother priest of mine, now dead, who, it has now been widely and definitively recognised, was a fraud. You see, I do not want the words 'fraudulent reading' to become a fashionable post-modern label. I want us to remember what a terrible, terrible thing it is to be a fraud. What damage it causes, and quite how gratuitous it is that we fellow frauds can sometimes be sucked up into something bigger and more real than ourselves.

I hope the Catholics present will not mind if I explain to the non-Catholics who are among us how, over the last sixty years or so, a person who passed himself off as a holy man, founding a hugely rich, religious congregation, publishing interminable tracts of righteousness, fitting in in every perfect way with my Church authorities' understanding of what goodness is all about, turned out to have been a serial paedophile, to have sired several children by women to whom he was not married, and to have been financially devious. Yet, throughout, he presented himself as a model of sanctity to his many followers, convincing them that accusations levelled against him were so many persecutions, which he was bearing in a Christ-like manner. In pursuing the perfection of his deception, he was, in fact, a masterly quoter of St Paul.

To be honest, this, the case of the late Fr Marcial Maciel Degollado, is far, far worse than the typical televangelist-busted-with-hooker scenario to which we have become accustomed, and for reasons which cannot be laid squarely at the door of the poor, tortured soul at its centre. For the affair brings to light something upon which we Catholics scarcely dare to comment: the major failure of discernment, judgment of character, and ability to tell 'the Real Thing' from a fraud, of at least one Pope, John Paul II, and of a large number of very high-ranking cardinals – 'pillars of the Church', in New Testament language – who were either knowingly or unknowingly duped, or, in some cases, effectively suborned, by Fr Maciel[4]. Thank Heavens (and this is no mere rhetorical aside), Jozef Ratzinger, first as Cardinal, and then as Pope, seems, however slowly and timidly[5], to have smelt what the threat of an unfortunate alliteration obliges me to refer to as 'a small, toothy rodent', and pushed for a serious investigation. Even though this has meant facing down the ire, and the inertia, of Maciel's very highly-placed enablers and boosters within the Roman Curia.

One advantage of reading St Paul alongside Fr Maciel is that any tendency to an anti-semitic reading is immediately relativised by the evidence that the counter-examples Paul talks about while

---

4   'Fool me once, shame on you; fool me continuously over 60 years, shame on me!'
5   There is a famous documentary film shot of him, as Cardinal, irritatedly slapping the wrist of an insistent reporter who was asking him about some of the Maciel allegations, and saying 'Not yet.' This at least shows he was aware that the problem was real, and was going to be difficult to deal with.

bearing witness to the Real Thing are perfectly able to be actualised by apparent insiders of one's own religious group, and thus perhaps even by oneself, with only minimal reference to our varying current reconstructions of the schism within the Hebrew world, from which Christianity and Rabbinical Judaism emerged.

Indeed, Fr Maciel sounds like just the sort of 'super-apostle' who Paul refers to in his Corinthian correspondence[6], one who turned out to be one of the

> false apostles, deceitful workers, disguising themselves as apostles of Christ. And no wonder! Even Satan disguises himself as an angel of light. So it is not strange if his ministers also disguise themselves as ministers of righteousness. Their end will match their deeds.[7]

In other words, whoever Paul meant by the sort of apostles who were in rivalry with him, or who were 'preaching another Gospel', the matter suddenly becomes rather contemporary when we consider that it is at least conceivable that the same people who went along with Fr Maciel's fraud, convinced that he was the 'real deal', might have been just the sort of people who would have found it difficult or impossible to discern that Paul *was* the Real Deal, someone who genuinely *was* undergoing the Real Thing[8]. The past reaction of Maciel's boosters and followers to those whistleblowers who turned out to be truthtellers (which included stonewalling, persecuting, sueing and defaming them), suggests exactly this.

Thus, by standing alongside Fr Maciel (for he sorely needs our prayer, and we sorely need not to judge our fellow-fraud), and by standing in the company of the thoroughly contemporary brothers and sisters, both highly-placed and much less highly-placed, for whom the revealing of Maciel's fraudulence is also the revelation of their poverty of judgment, I hope that we will get a somewhat fuller

---

6   2 Cor. 11:5 and 12:11.

7   2 Cor. 11:13b-15.

8   In the interests of transparency, I should say that I never met Fr Maciel in person, and have no reason at all to think that, had I met him, I would have been immune to the charisma which he evidently possessed.

sense of the dangerous earthquake which the Real Thing provokes in the midst of all our perceptions of goodness.

In order to get a sense of the Real Thing, I propose trying to hold together two elements of Paul's witness: what I would call a 'foreground' element – something that he tells us about, where he is excitable and pointing something out; and what I would call a 'background' element – where he appears to be quite serenely taking something for granted as part of whatever he is talking about. The 'background' element is, in a sense, more difficult to bring into evidence, because it is not immediately obvious what in the background 'is just there', and what, if interrogated intelligently, is pointing towards the foreground. At a crime scene, the victim's body, the blood spatter and the bullet marks are very much in the foreground. While the questions of the temperature of the room, whether the window was open, whether the chairs are arranged in a particular way, whether the famous dog in the Sherlock Holmes story barked in the night, are all 'background' questions. They may be things that 'just were that way'. Or, if properly interpreted, they may give a quite different reading of 'what went down' in the foreground than the one which appears obvious at first sight.

So I have chosen to take two passages from the same text – in this case, the Epistle to the Philippians, to see if, by aligning something that Paul is bearing witness to in an explicit, foreground way, with something that is closer to being taken for granted by him, we can get a better sense of the shape of the happening which had come upon him, and which he was both relating, bearing witness to and allowing to be seen, merely by being who he was, when he was. The two passages in question are, for an example of excited, foreground Paul, Philippians 3:1-11, and, for an example of serene, something-apparently-taken-for-granted Paul, the text often referred to as the pre-Pauline hymn, Philippians 2:5-11. In the former, with that awareness of the dangerousness of what he is doing that is his hallmark, Paul is using his own case to point out the depth of the upset to anyone's former belonging which is caused by Jesus. In the latter, he is using something he had received from others who shared, at least in part, and maybe to a very great extent, elements of his former belonging. This seemed to him to be such a paradigmatically good way of describing what Jesus had been about, that he is able to use it wholeheartedly as shared background to a particular understanding of what living together in the midst of conflict might look like.

Let me start with the background material, and in particular with the pre-Pauline hymn, to see if we can get from it a sense of the shape of the happening which then aligns with the excited Paul of Chapter 3. So, verse 5:

> Let the same mind be in you that was in Christ Jesus,

Paul is urging something on his listeners that depends on their recognising, and accepting as valid, something which he shares with them, to wit: a particular account of who Christ Jesus was.

> ...(W)ho, though he was in the form of God, did not regard equality with God as something to be exploited, but emptied himself, taking the form of a slave, being born in human likeness. And being found in human form, he humbled himself and became obedient to the point of death – even death on a cross. Therefore God also highly exalted him and gave him the name that is above every name, so that at the name of Jesus every knee should bend, in heaven and on earth and under the earth, and every tongue should confess that Jesus Christ is Lord, to the glory of God the Father.[9]

Here, we are plunged straight into background elements from the 'crime scene' which might benefit from a certain sort of reconstruction, one I will attempt to provide by reference to the ancient rite of the Atonement, whose structure seems to be at work in this hymn.

---

9   Phil. 2:5-11.

Let me attempt to provide a 'working model' of this ancient priestly rite, whose presence is available, but downplayed, in the Scriptures[10]. The rite depended on there being both an absolute unity, and yet a distinction between El Elyon, the Almighty, the Invisible, the One God of whom no image could be made, and YHWH, referred to as the Lord. YHWH did have a form, could turn up in the Garden of Eden, or appear as three angels to Abraham, or in a multiplicity of shapes, genders, and forms in Ezekiel. Central to the annual rite of Atonement was the notion that when, after the appropriate sacrifices of purification, the High Priest entered the Holy of Holies, all clad in white, he would become one with the visible form of YHWH. Then he would come out through the veil to offer the sacrifice. In the symbolism of the Temple, the Holy of Holies represented where God dwelt, outside all material things. Moving outwards from this centre, then, the veil of the Temple was the beginning of created matter, whose different elements were symbolised outside the veil. So, the High Priest coming out through the veil was the sign that the Creator of all things was coming into Creation to bless and renew it and atone for the sins of the people. This 'coming into Creation' was symbolised by the High Priest being immediately clothed by the other priests in a robe made of the same material as the Temple veil, when he came out of the Holy of Holies, through the veil, into the sanctuary. The point was that the in-principle Immaterial and Invisible One had become visible and material, and was making the whole of Creation glorious from within, as it were.

The High Priest would then go up to the Altar of Sacrifice, where the portions of the lamb which had been slaughtered as YHWH, and whose blood had been sprinkled on the Mercy Seat in the Holy of Holies, had been divided. The other priests would solemnly gnaw the entrails, 'the Lord's portion', sprinkled with vinegar. They would also sprinkle further blood over the Temple and possibly the people. At some stage another, identical, goat or lamb (this is the

---

10 Here, and over the next pages, I am greatly indebted to Margaret Barker, and particularly her books *The Great High Priest* (London, T. & T. Clark, 2003) and *Temple Themes in Christian Worship* (London, T. & T. Clark, 2007), pp. 136-7, 150-2.

animal which, since Tyndale's translation of the Bible, the English language has referred to as the scapegoat, the one that got to play the role of Azazel) would have the transgressions of the people laid on it by the High Priest, and it would be driven outside the city. At the conclusion of the rite, the High Priest, resplendent in the Tiara bearing the Name, his white tunic (indicating the angelic status of one who had become a localised instantiation of YHWH) covered by the priestly robe (indicating YHWH's emergence into Creation), would pronounce or ululate the Name as a blessing over the people. He was the only person who could pronounce the Name, on this one occasion in the year, while the people bowed down and worshipped The Name who was temporarily im-personated in their midst by the High Priest.

Apart from very many, usually rather subtle, references to this rite in the Gospels, there are two quite striking New Testament passages which show how central this rite was to understanding what Jesus was really all about. One is the passage at which we are looking, the pre-Pauline hymn found in Philippians, and the other, which has the advantage for us of also not being by St Paul, is to be found in the Epistle to the Hebrews 5:5-10.

I have put the passages together, side by side on the same sheet, as an appendix[11], so that you can see for yourselves how similar their structure is.

In both cases, first there is the non-appropriative nature of what Christ was about in his relationship with God; then there is the human life story of how he acted that out – in other words, how God's project became a historical achievement in his person; then there is the result for all of us of this historical acting out. Whereas, at first glance, the Philippians passage seems to have no priestly language, the Hebrews passage provides the priestly elements which makes the flow of the story comprehensible, and enables us to supply the allusions in the Philippians passage with more confidence. So now I would like to turn to a detailed reading of Philippians 2:5-11. This is my 'background passage', and my examination of it is the forensic equivalent of asking: are certain features of a crime scene – muddy

---

11 cf. Appendix III.

shoes, a closed window – just things that happen to be there, and of no real significance? Or are they things whose 'being taken for granted' points us towards a richer sense of what is going on in the 'foreground passage', Philippians 3:1-17, where Paul puts himself into evidence?

Let us start with the strange word 'form', which seems to be significant, since it is repeated. But let us be aware that our English translation misleads, for we get 'form of God', 'form of a slave', 'human likeness' and 'human form', where the Greek only has the same word for the first two, and a significantly different word for the fourth. I wonder whether these words concerning 'form' might not have had fairly technical meanings.

How about if the first word, 'form', corresponds to the Hebrew word תְּמוּנָה, – temunah – a rather rare and contested word when it came to God? For there were some parts of the Scriptures which attest to God having a תְּמוּנָה, while others insist that God does not. To make a long story short, the Deuteronomistic tradition is keen to emphasise that God could only be heard on Sinai, no form could be perceived, where other traditions in the Scriptures have no problem referring to God as having a form that can be perceived. Within this contested world, Christianity makes a quite specific option: God has a temunah, and the temunah can in principle be seen, and the historical person Jesus of Nazareth was that temunah[12]. This is why, in St Luke's Gospel, at the scene of the Transfiguration[13], the text tells us that Peter and those with him were heavy with sleep, 'and when they wakened they saw his glory and the two men who stood with him'. St Luke is alluding to Psalm 17:15, which says 'In righteousness I will behold your visage and when I awake I will behold the vision of your glory', where the Hebrew word here translated as 'vision of your glory' is תְּמוּנָתֶךָ – our friend temunah again. This is Luke's way of indicating that it was YHWH that the disciples were seeing alongside Moses and Elijah.

So El-Elyon is invisible but YHWH is the 'form' of El, and YHWH does not grasp on to the fact that YHWH is equal to El, but empties

12 Cf. John 1:14.
13 Luke 9:32.

himself into the form of a servant. 'Servant' was an often-used term
to refer to a priest, or high priest, a reading which is legitimised by
the way in which the parallel Hebrews passage makes this quite explicit: it names Melchizedek, the definitive High Priest. For 'form'
of a servant, my guess is that the underlying Hebrew would have
been דְּמוּת – demut (the modern Hebrew New Testament translates
it as such, both here and, alas, in the previous instance, where I have
posited temunah). Demut means 'form' understood in the dynamic
sense of the 'plan of action', the 'reality that "in-forms" something
that is going to be unfolded'.

This priestly-servantlike plan of action began to enter the material realm by Jesus being born in 'human likeness'. Here, my guess
at the underlying Hebrew is that it would have been מַרְאֶה – mareh
– likeness, appearance, but not in the way we often take appearance
as meaning some sort of disguise or deception: 'The Comtesse de
Folleville attended the Ball *in the likeness* of the Marquise de Main-
tenant, fooling all present, but of course the real Marquise was in
Nevers, robbing the safe of the Duc d'Ailleurs.' No, here, the word
'likeness' means something much closer to 'real instantiation of a
project'.

The next phrase, which once again is monotonously rendered
in English as 'form', is the much more beautiful word σχήματι in
Greek. That this word means 'outward appearance', and its allusion
is to being decked out in clothes, appears much better in the Latin
Vulgate, where St Jerome translates 'habitu inventus ut homo'. The
word 'habitu' gives us our English word 'habit' meaning 'religious
form of clothing'. The underlying allusion seems to be to the moment that the High Priest came through the veil from the Holy of
Holies into the material world, and was decked out in the 'glorious robe of superb perfection'[14], so that from then on it would be
YHWH, in the person of the High Priest, made visible in materiality, who would go up to the Altar of Sacrifice to make the offering
of the lamb before pronouncing the Name.

The hymn in Philippians, is, of course, relating all of this to Jesus'
life: especially his road from the Mount of Transfiguration to the

---

14 See the account of this in Sirach 50.

Garden of Gethsemani and then to Calvary. Thus, the death on the Cross is seen as being in reality that for which the Temple rite had been a mere dress rehearsal. And, entirely in line with this imagery, Jesus' Resurrection and Ascension, his 'anastasis', is read in this hymn as the successful conclusion of the rite, where, in the setting of the Temple Court, the High Priest 'became' the Name, and was worshipped as such by all present. Only here, it is not a rite, but the real thing, and the power of the allusion is that God, El Elyon, is giving to Jesus the Name that is above every other name – in other words, YHWH. So, from now on, the artist formerly known as YHWH is to be known by the name Jesus, because Jesus has successfully and completely instantiated YHWH in materiality and history, such that Creation has now been definitively altered from within. The result is that, whereas in the rite of Atonement every knee would bow down in worship at the pronouncing of the Name, and whereas in the Prophet Isaiah it is to YHWH that every knee shall bow and every tongue shall swear[15], it is now established that Jesus the Anointed One is YHWH to the glory of El Elyon, or 'Jesus Christ is Lord, to the glory of God the Father', as our accustomed translation reads.

It appears, then, that Paul is urging the recipients of his letter, who find themselves in conflict with those who frighten them, those who do not accept that Jesus is the Christ, that, in the midst of the conflict, they are to act out the same priestly pattern which we have just seen illustrated, and with which they would have been familiar, giving themselves without fear or self-aggrandisement towards the altar of sacrifice just as Jesus did on his way to being given the Name.

That this is a fair reading is suggested by the verse following this hymn, in which Paul draws the conclusion he wants to bring out of it:

> Therefore, my beloved, just as you have always obeyed, not only in my presence, but much more now in my absence, work out your own salvation with fear and trembling;[16]

---

15 Isa. 45:23.
16 Phil 2:12.

In other words, he is *not* asking them to obey *him*. He is urging them to continue in that kind of arduous listening to the Father which characterised Jesus' path to Jerusalem, since that is what the Spirit produces in them, regardless of who is around to tell them what to do.

When he urges them to work out their salvation 'with fear and trembling', I wonder whether this is not a reference to Psalm 2:11, which was clearly of enormous importance to the early Christians, since in it 'The Lord and his Anointed' appear. The Lord sets his King on Zion, his holy hill, and the decree of the Lord is announced 'You are my son, today I have begotten you', exactly the quote we saw in the Hebrews passage concerning Melchisedek, which I hope to have shown to be parallel to our hymn. When the kingdom of this son has been established, the kings and rulers of the earth are urged to '*serve the Lord with fear and trembling*', lest they be destroyed. Paul has just explained to his listeners that those who are ranged against them will be destroyed, so it is natural that he points to his listeners as being those who job it is to serve the Lord with fear and trembling. In other words, he is taking for granted that Jesus fulfilled this psalm – instantiated it and filled out its full meaning – and therefore that this psalm is useful evidence for the consequences of what Jesus' fulfilment meant.

This priestly language continues when Paul urges his listeners to be 'blameless and innocent, children of God without blemish'[17], where the words involved often had a liturgical sense, especially the word ἄμωμά which referred to the sort of animals proper to sacrifice, and how the priests should be in order to be fit for sacrifice. The irony is that these words, laden with considerable cultic weight, are henceforth going to be bereft of cultic meaning, since the real sacrifice by the real High Priest turned out to have taken place firmly outside cultic bounds, and the Real Temple turns out to be one made out of living human bodies which are learning to relate together and be mutually sustaining in an entirely new way.

Just in case further evidence is needed that this priestly, liturgical thinking underlies what Paul is talking about here, then note how

---

17 Phil. 2:15.

he ends this phase of his letter with a reference to his own circumstance, runnning the risk of execution, and the tribulations of his
listeners, in the following phrase:

> But even if I am being poured out as a libation over the sacrifice
> and the offering of your faith, I am glad and rejoice with all of
> you.[18]

There is something quite casual about this way in which he refers
to his possible execution as just one of the liturgical elements of the
'rite' which consists in the celebratory, self-giving, kenotic, priestly
living out of faith in the midst of conflict, which is how he sees the
Philippians as being called to live.

Well, I ask you now to stand back a little from this. What I have
offered is a hypothetical reconstruction of why the apparently ordinary furniture in the room of the crime scene might matter more
than it seems. Whether the window was open or closed – or what
is going on with the word 'form' – does make a difference to how
we perceive the body and the bullets. And the muddy shoes, or the
fact that 'being decked out' and 'receiving the Name' have quite
technical resonances, may give us a better picture of what St Paul
is bearing witness to as the Real Thing. My suggestion is that Paul
takes for granted, and peppers his writing with allusions to, a fairly
specific understanding of how Jesus was YHWH, an understanding
which presupposed a rigorous, and no doubt a contested, reading of
the Hebrew Scriptures, one he expected his listeners to have heard
before and to have accepted in broad outline. My further suggestion
is that if we do not take on board this background element in which
Jesus *fulfilled* something, we are not going to get an accurate picture
of the foreground in which Jesus upsets, or *disturbs* something.

So to the foreground, and Chapter 3:

> Finally, my brothers and sisters, rejoice in the Lord. To write
> the same things to you is not troublesome to me, and for you it
> is a safeguard. Beware of the dogs, beware of the evil workers,
> beware of those who mutilate the flesh[19]!

---

18 Phil 2:17.
19 Phil 3:1-2

Paul begins by urging his audience to rejoice – to continue this celebratory living out of their sacrificial role. He then tells them that, for the sake of their safety, he is going to repeat something he has told them before, and gives them a triple warning: watch out for the dogs, the workers of evil and the mutilators. In other words, Paul is well aware of the dangerous, contested nature of goodness and he takes very seriously his task of allowing his listeners to be established in something trustworthy.

Now, and here is where I would ask us to remember that we are frauds listening to the Real Thing, who are these dogs, workers of evil and mutilators? The mutilators are comparatively easy to identify, since Paul then talks about 'the true circumcision' which needs no fleshly mark. So, the 'mutilators' probably do not include all those who perform some cutting operation on someone's body – for instance, a surgeon amputating a gangrenous limb. Rather they are those who insist that goodness needs the particular fleshly mark, 'circumcision', to make one an insider. But who are the dogs? Clearly a literalist reading is wrong: it can scarcely be the four-legged, tail-wagging *canis lupus familiaris* that Paul is warning against. So we are left with some sort of slang, one with which Paul's first listeners would be familiar, for he is repeating something they have heard from him before. And the problem with any sort of slang is that it is very difficult to translate, very context-dependent, and has very slippery resonances. Think of how many meanings the modern word 'bitch' has, and what sort of sensitivity you need to work out the resonances of what is being said, by whom, about whom. Might these 'dogs' be 'male temple prostitutes', which would pick up the slang term used in Deuteronomy 23:18 for that profession? If so, it would be odd, since why, in the conflict in which the Philippians found themselves, would they need a repeated warning against such an obvious and easily identifiable 'they'? Might the term, thinking laterally, refer to gay priests like myself, whose way of being could be seen to be making a mockery of any sort of goodness we might teach? I would certainly be failing to stand in the presence of the Real Thing with fear and trembling if I were not to allow myself to be interrogated by a possibility that has recently been emphasised by some of the 'pillars' of my Church. I am, after all, standing alongside Fr Maciel as part of the 'we' who are being warned about something.

Might these 'dogs' refer to something that Paul has already taught the Philippians about, conceivably those who have become the contemporary moral equivalent of temple prostitutes, people who make a living from religious exchange, or are the 'kept boys' of the religious establishment, keeping alive a fake goodness and receiving well for it? In other words, is his warning not about something 'obviously bad' but about a false sort of goodness? And how are 'we' implicated in that? How is the warning to be heard by us contemporary frauds? The same question arises with his phrase 'workers of evil'. Does this mean literally, and quite simply, those who do evil things, another rather contentless, scattershot 'they'? In which case, again, why alone should this phrase be literal, when the first one cannot be, and the third clearly has a particular association? Might 'workers of evil' not be an 'insider's' allusion to a Pauline teaching about those whose insistent good works mask a rapacious pattern of desire, a denigration of others and a flattering self-regard? In other words, a different sort of 'false goodness'.

However we read 'workers of evil', the warning about 'mutilators' is clearly one about false goodness, since Paul goes on to say:

> For it is we who are the circumcision, who worship in the Spirit of God and glory in Christ Jesus and have no confidence in the flesh.[20]

In other words: there is a real form of goodness to which this circumcision business pointed. This goodness is found in a new sort of worship of God which is given to flow in people by the Spirit, which glories in 'the Name' – Anointed Priestly Jesus – and which is utterly aware that once you have perceived the love which is shown by YHWH's presence as forgiving victim (Anointed Priestly Jesus as Crucified) in our midst, it is your growing confidence in that love for you, and not in anything you do, or have been, or have belonged to, which is what matters.

20 Phil. 3:3.

even though I, too, have reason for confidence in the flesh. If
anyone else has reason to be confident in the flesh, I have more:
circumcised on the eighth day, a member of the people of Israel, of
the tribe of Benjamin, a Hebrew born of Hebrews; as to the law, a
Pharisee; as to zeal, a persecutor of the church; as to righteousness
under the law, blameless.[21]

So here is what Paul is pointing towards as the Real Thing: one of
the signs of the Real Thing being present is that *none* of the usual
forms of religious or moral safety apply. He, Paul, had every reason to think that he was safely involved in the worship of the Real
Thing – he was a circumcised Hebrew with a genuine lineage, a
devout practitioner of Torah according to one of the highly regarded schools, blameless in his observance of the mitzvot and fully
involved from his heart in the struggle against those who were misleading his people.

Yet, when YHWH who he thought he had been worshipping
revealed himself to him as 'YHWH Jesus, whom you are persecuting'[22], he came to see that, in the eyes of the Anointed One, all
of these safe forms of goodness had actually been a hindrance to
him. In the light of the discovery that his system of goodness had
killed Jesus, counting God as a transgressor, he came to see that his
wholehearted complicity in the system of goodness was something
much more like being a fraud than it was like being a good person, and that, in order to receive the goodness to which the system
pointed, he had to let go of the system completely.

> Yet whatever gains I had, these I have come to regard as loss
> because of Christ. More than that, I regard everything as loss
> because of the surpassing value of knowing Christ Jesus my Lord.
> For his sake I have suffered the loss of all things, and I regard them
> as rubbish, in order that I may gain Christ and be found in him,
> not having a righteousness of my own that comes from the law,
> but one that comes through faith in Christ, the righteousness from
> God based on faith. [23]

21 Phil. 3:4-6.
22 Phil 3:4-6.
23 Phil. 3:7-9.

Paul does not say that he was a fraud like Fr Maciel was a fraud – someone who engaged in a form of deception for so long that it is quite possible that, by the end, he no longer knew that he was being deceptive. Paul's false goodness was in a sense even more dangerous through being completely whole-hearted, hence the depth and drama of the drastic nature of the change-around which the Real Thing produced in him.

He had to lose 'goodness', belonging, worth, reputation, everything which was something he had held; in order, as he says in the next verses, to find himself *being held* by someone: trusting someone else to do something that includes you, taking you somewhere else. Identity, belonging, goodness or safety are not things we can hold onto from our past. They are all things that come down to us and draw us on from a future which has already started to manifest in us – it is already something we have attained through our being held, but attained as something towards which we are marching in our creative living out:

> I want to know Christ and the power of his resurrection and the sharing of his sufferings by becoming like him in his death, if somehow I may attain the resurrection from the dead. Not that I have already obtained this or have already reached the goal; but I press on to make it my own, because Christ Jesus has made me his own. Beloved, I do not consider that I have made it my own; but this one thing I do: forgetting what lies behind and straining forward to what lies ahead, I press on toward the goal for the prize of the heavenly call of God in Christ Jesus. Let those of us then who are mature be of the same mind; and if you think differently about anything, this too God will reveal to you. Only let us hold fast to what we have attained.[24]

Our human lives in history are becoming the priestly robe of flesh that Jesus is putting on as he fulfils Creation.

This involves sharing Jesus' kenotic living out, being prepared for a death like his, so as to share its result. So Paul goes back over the same material for his listeners as he had set out in the hymn, but in a

---

24 Phil. 3:10-16.

dangerous first-person narrative. And here, I would like to hypoth-esise something which seems to me to be central to its dangerous, precarious contingent nature, which I can mention here, but will have to develop at greater length elsewhere. That is the extent to which the dangerous, precarious, contingent nature of what Paul is pointing to is related to the Creator. He had discovered not merely that his co-religionists had contributed to the execution of an inno-cent man, not merely that he had now discovered that this innocent man had had a higher teaching whose disciple he had now become, but that this falsely-executed, innocent man with a higher teaching had, in fact, been the culmination of YHWH's self-instantiation in our midst, making of a human lynch death the ultimate priestly sacrifice of God towards us, by which Creation could be opened up for ever, no longer bowed down to vanity and futility.

This for me is part of the excitement of re-discovering Paul in a Catholic, ecclesial reading. The word 'God' for too long has been a cold word describing a powerful object. 'Creation' has for too long been a serious, stable, safe background on which a heavy human morality can be erected, and against which self-regarding approval can be granted. What Jesus did has for too long been described in emotionally blackmailing terms, pushing people into contorted forms of asceticism and fake goodness. But now we can begin to get a sense, absolutely in line with the most authentic Hebrew ex-citement about God, that it is about the Creator, and the joy of the worship of the Creator, that we are talking. And that when Paul talks about what Jesus did, he is talking about the impact of the Creator coming into creation and opening it up definitively.

The dangerousness, the precariousness and the contingency are the signs of the ultimate safety – the Creator bringing people out of fraudulent attachment to fake and vain being, and into a sure and imperishable goodness. When, in First Corinthians,[25] Paul refers to the Crucified Anointed one as 'the Power of God and the Wisdom of God', he is not in the first place engaging in irony or paradox. He is referring quite literally to the power of the Creator and to the Creator's deliberate way of orchestrating Creation into being.

---

25   1 Cor. 1:24.

It is from that fulfilment, that stability and that security that all forms of goodness, wisdom, and belonging appear ironic. Anything less adventurous than the contingency and precariousness of Creation is a fake form of goodness, a trying to close things down, an involvement in futility and vanity. I wonder whether what we now call 'apocalyptic' is not the tribute paid by wrath to the emergence amidst us frightened frauds of the safety and solidity of the 'Τετέλεσται', 'it is accomplished',[26] of Creation.

So, how do we recidivist dogs, evil doers and mutilators plan to hear Paul's warning words? By making ourselves judges over others we consider more fraudulent than ourselves, or by sitting alongside our brother frauds and working out, with their help, and with fear and trembling, what it looks like to be hoiked off into the new Creation?

---

26 John 19:30.

✦✦✦✦✦✦✦✦✦✦

CHAPTER 14

What sorts of difference does René Girard make to how we read the Bible?

I would like to take us[1] into this question by way of John 5[2]. So imagine the scene, please. We are close by the Sheep Gate in Jerusalem. There is a pool called 'House of Mercy', and over it there are five porticoes. Beneath these lie a multitude of the ailing. One of them has been ill for thirty-eight years. Now, with what eyes do we look at what is going on here? If we are so inclined, we can see merely a place that has a name, an architectural structure and some water. We can observe, furthermore, that there is something slightly pathetic about the spot, a gathering point for the long-term infirm; something that makes the name 'House of Mercy' seem ironic, or slightly cheesy, like calling a cemetery 'Happy Fields'. But each one of the details can set a different scene, if we allow it. For instance, it will escape no one's attention that a passage which ends with a discussion of Moses' writings, begins with a scene set under five porticoes. Then again, in Psalm 23, we are told that 'The Lord is my Shepherd', so it is appropriate enough that, near a Sheep Gate, 'he maketh me to lie down beside still waters', for such are to be found in the pool. Too still, in fact, since everyone is waiting for the waters to be 'troubled' by an angel, heralding a lucky cure for the first one in after the 'troubling'. There are many lying there. And they would have known that the one who makes them lie down does so for the purpose of restoring their soul, and that the Goodness and Mercy of

---

1   This chapter was born as a presentation for the Theology and Peace Conference, a gathering of
lay people and clergy from different denominations who are interested in furthering the impact
of Girard's thought through their preaching, teaching and pastoral practice, held near Chicago in
May 2009.
2   The NRSV text is provided in Appendix IV.

the Lord will allow them to dwell in his House for ever. Yet somehow, one gets the impression that the crowd at the House of Mercy by the Sheep Gate was not quite what the Psalmist had in mind.

Does the man who has been ill for thirty-eight years know his Scriptures? If he did, he would know that, in the wake of an act of disobedience by a set of warriors, who had presumed to wage an un-called for war on the Amalekites and Canaanites, in strict disobedience both to God and to Moses, God had forbidden the people of Israel from advancing further, and they had been stuck for thirty eight-years[3]. It was only after thirty-eight years of wandering in the wilderness of Moab, when the entire generation of the men of war had died out, that God gave Moses permission to stop going round in circles, and told him to advance once more, by crossing the brook Zered and entering a new territory. Nothing as dramatic as crossing the Red Sea. Just crossing a wadi. Even if the sick man did not know his Scripture well, he would have known that forty years is a full generation, and that thirty-eight is a good way to symbolise something falling just short of a generation, a hint of 'those who didn't quite make it'.

Jesus has come up to Jerusalem for an unspecified feast. He comes to our pool. Seeing this particular sick man, and learning that he has been lying there a long time, Jesus engages him in one of those strangely asymmetrical dialogues to which St John often treats us. He asks him whether he wants to be healed. Something about Jesus' tone must have suggested that he was wondering why someone who had been there that long had not made it to the front of the queue to be cured. Did he really want to be cured? Hence the sick man's reply is not simply 'yes', but rather an explanation of why he never manages to get to the front of the queue in time. He *wants* for someone to help him in, unlike the sheep in the Psalm, who, having the Lord as his shepherd, *shall not want.* Jesus neither discusses, disputes or sympathises with this. He gives the man an order to rise, pick up his pallet, and walk. Rather as the Lord ordered Moses and the people to rise and cross the wadi Zered. The One who 'maketh me down to lie' has made the place of lying down mobile, and enabled

---

3   Deut. 2:14.

the one who had lain so long in one place to move and lie down, move and lie down, in a more profitable rhythm. The trek to the Promised Land can start up again.

Only now are we told that it was the Sabbath, for a group of the Observant question why this man is carrying a pallet. Presumably, they did not know he had just been cured. All they saw was someone performing a 'work' on the sabbath, thus infringing the Law of Moses. The man enlightens them: the reason he is carrying his pallet is that he was told to do so by the man who cured him. Maybe his thought process worked as follows: 'This is the first day of the rest of my life. I've been stuck with enforced rest for long enough. If someone can cure me on the Sabbath, and in addition gives a minor instruction to carry my pallet and walk, surely it is not unreasonable to obey him?' The Observant, however, look upon him not in the first place as a person who has just been brought to health and mobility, but merely as one who was infringing the Law. Now hearing that it is someone else who has induced him to this law-breaking, they turn their attention to that person. They do not ask 'Who healed you?'. Instead, their question 'Who told you to take up your pallet and walk?' clearly means 'Who induced you to break the law?' The Sabbath Law provides for them a complete lens through which to perceive the reality of what has gone on.

The healed man does not know who it was who cured him, since Jesus has withdrawn, owing to there being a crowd in the place. The dynamic of a crowd, the mutual draw and fascination which lead people to think and move as one, is always hostile to whatever Jesus is about. Where there is a crowd he will always be invisible, until his 'lifting up', which will allow crowds to see him, and some to learn what they have been about. So the healed man owes the Observant an answer as to who turned him into a law-breaker. But later, in the Temple, with enough going on of different sorts to prevent too much sudden group cohesion, Jesus finds the healed man. We do not know whether the man had come to the Temple to give thanks for his cure, or merely to take part in the Feast that was on at the time. But there he is. And Jesus seeks him out and tells him 'See, you are well! Sin no more that nothing worse befall you'. In other words, following Psalm 23, the Lord who is his shepherd, having led him beside still waters, and having restored his soul, now leads him in paths of righteousness. Or, following Moses, this Israelite who has been permitted to cross the wadi is warned against the murmuring and backsliding that would have kept him in Egypt, or in the wilderness of Moab.

The dynamic of 'Rise, take up your pallet and walk' is 'Be mobile – keep going'. The five books of Moses were not supposed to be five porticoes giving shelter to paralysis, when not actively promoting helplessness, leaving people stuck beside a still water waiting for some superstitious passing of an angel. Those books are supposed to be a dynamic path to be trodden by an Israel under orders from an active Lord who opens up a way in the sea, or, at the very least, commands people to cross a wadi. The pathos of the difference between the helplessness of the Israel that the Lord finds on his visitation of the pool, and the power and strength of the Israel that the Lord intended to bring into being, and is witnessed to in Moses' writings, provides the context for the sign which Jesus performs here.

It is also the basis for the discussion which follows on from this sign, at which we will now look. The healed man goes back and tells the Observant who it was who had healed him. They once again read the healing through the lens of the Sabbath Law. For them, this is a make-or-break issue. If the healing, and the minor instruction to carry the pallet which ensued from it, had taken place on the Sabbath, then it could not be from God, since God rested on the Sabbath. So, a healing on the Sabbath must come from some other source. It is at this point that Jesus gives one of those lapidary answers which was so important that St John thought it worthwhile explaining it in some detail. 'My Father is working still, and I am working.' Formally speaking this sounds like a denial of Genesis 2:1-3, where it says that the heavens and the earth were finished, and God rested. In fact, it is more interesting than that. It is part of a quite different relationship to the sacred text than one that had become 'normal' among the Observant group, having developed since

the return of the 'Judahites' from Babylon[4]. This different relationship might be referred to as 'synchronous' and 'liturgical', rather
than 'historical' and 'legal'. One where the Sabbath rest is not a
fence against continuing creation, but a gift that is a prophetic sign
of God's rest into which people are invited to enter.

And Jesus personally instantiates this synchronous, liturgical
reading. The Father, the Creator, El Elyon, is still working; we are
still not yet at the seventh day. And I AM is working. That is to say,
YHWH, incarnated in the priestly figure who was God's Son, is
working. Creation is not a background affair, but a permanently
contemporary affair involving us now, and YHWH is opening it up
for us in the person of Jesus. In such a reading, you would expect
YHWH to be doing the same thing now as he is described as doing
alongside Moses, not because God is tied to some historical drama, but because the scriptural drama is itself a good, permanently
contemporary guide to what YHWH is now doing. Moses points to
this activity in much the same way as a particularly perfect, conical
volcano, thrown up at some stage in the distant past, points to the
permanently contemporary power which throws up perfect conical
volcanoes, and might do so at any moment.

Hence the significance of the 'sign' given in the person of the man
healed by the pool. 'You want to know what YHWH and Moses is
all about? *This* is what YHWH and Moses is all about: setting someone free so that he can walk to worship the Lord on his mountain
and rejoice at the feast in his House. So don't be tempted to pit
Moses against Moses by making your reading of the Sabbath Law
the enemy of YHWH's dynamic project.' Now the Observant knew
perfectly well what this meant. When Jesus called God his Father,
he was not engaging in some nice, friendly talk of the sort which
we might indulge in by saying something like 'We're all children of
God'. He was doing something much more specific. He was indicating that he was the priestly incarnation of YHWH. This notion

---

4   It is these 'Judahites' – that is an Observant religious party, that gives its name to the subsection
    of the Hebrew people known as the 'Ιουδαιοι' to whom St John refers, and which we typically
    translate as 'the Jews'. We thus confuse a modern ethnic term with an ancient term closer to a
    partisan ideological grouping, one that was originally a subsection of the ethnic group of the
    'Εβραιοι'.

was available to the Observant, since they had no difficulty in referring to the consecrated High Priest, who came through the Temple
veil into the Court, as the Son of God[5]. But, along with that liturgical notion of the Son of God, went the strict understanding that the
Son of God was in fact God himself, YHWH, equal with El-Elyon.
For the Observant, 'Son of God' was not a term indicating a subordinate reality, but a term indicating the liturgically incarnate form
of an equal reality with God. You can see the problem: to break the
sabbath is one thing, and can easily be sorted out. But to treat the
Creator in such a way as to indicate that you consider yourself to be
his contemporary emanation and instantiation, thus making of the
Sabbath a function of your own activity, rather than allowing your
activity to be curtailed, or at least judged, in the light of the Sabbath, this is something at a different level of magnitude.

From this point on, until the end of Chapter 5, St John gives us a
discourse from Jesus, and I will return to that soon, since it raises
huge questions about reading Scripture. But first, I would like to
pause, since I hope you have been saying to yourselves 'He promised
us a talk about the sorts of difference which Girard makes to how
we read the Bible; yet so far, he hasn't mentioned Girard, nor has
he performed what we might call a 'Girardian reading' of a text,
since there's not much about either a moment of persecution or
the mimetic nature of desire in anything he's said. Just some more
or less fanciful Old Testament references which anyone could have
dug up.' If you have been saying that, I want to say 'Hooray! I'm
halfway to getting my main point across.' Because my main point is
to try to get across to you something of the sheer *freedom* in reading texts which is, for me, one of the principal legacies of learning
from Girard.

I guess that many of you shared the sort of excitement I felt when
I first read 'The woes against the Pharisees' in *Things Hidden from the
Foundation of the World*[6] or any of the chapters in the second half of
The Scapegoat[7]. Or when I heard René explain 'The woman taken in

---

5   cf. John 10:36.
6   Palo Alto, Stanford University Press, 1987; London, Continuum/Athlone, 2003, pp 208ff.
7   Baltimore, Johns Hopkins University Press, 1989.

adultery', even before he had written it up in *I Saw Satan Fall Like Lightning*[8]. It was, and is, the excitement of experiencing someone handling Scripture in a way that none of us had ever seen or heard it handled before. It was not like the massively erudite deliverences of our Scripture professionals, which so often leave us impressed, or depressed, by their knowledge, but no more enflamed by, or loving of, the sacred pages themselves. On the contrary, Girard's readings do not tell you much about Girard, nor stun you with his erudition. Rather he seems to be reading Scripture from within a logic that is proper to Scripture itself, as though the same spirit which had enabled Scripture to be written was enabling it to be read, so that you, the reader, end up seeing more and more in Scripture than what Girard points out himself, and you find yourself loving and treasuring the Scriptures even more. You get the sense that you are, at last, beginning to understand the text 'from the inside'.

It is because of this that I wanted to start with something which seemingly has little to do with any 'Girardian themes' in Scripture. And yet which is vital, if we are to avoid bibliolatry. That is, to recall the sense, from which I hope we all learn, of someone who simultaneously takes texts extremely seriously, and yet not seriously at all. Girard really looks in a very detailed way at what particular texts say, and then appears to throw them all up in the air so that the textual elements come down any which way, but 'any which way' turns out to be extraordinarily powerful, coherent and whole. It is having seen Girard do this, time after time, that I have begun to get a sense of Jesus doing the same thing, time after time in the Gospels. In other words, what Girard does with texts is in itself an education in the art of 'doing things with texts' which is what we see Jesus do in the New Testament. When we glimpse this going on, so many of the apparently arcane arguments set in an ancient world suddenly become alive and contemporary.

Now there is something consistent which has enabled Girard to read texts in this way. It is not simply an adorable personal quirk of his. And it is something which can consistently help us avoid bibliolatry. It is the realisation that the centre of meaning is not to be

8   Maryknoll, Orbis, 2001: Leominster, Gracewing, 2001, pp 49ff.

found in the texts themselves. The centre of meaning is real, historical, non-textual, or not primarily textual, and the texts themselves
are certain sorts of monuments to this real, historical, pre-textual
reality. At Hiroshima and Nagasaki, so intense were the explosions
that the light from them etched what look like photographs of
buildings and protrusions on the walls of other buildings. Each one
of those light-etched walls is a monument to the unimaginable, and
unsurviveable reality of the explosion, some hints of whose force
can be read off from its monuments. And, for Girard, the centre of
meaning, the unimaginable explosion, is a highly agile and dynamic
centre in which two apparently opposed things are happening at the
same time.

   The first of these is entirely offstage and entirely beyond any sort
of direct knowledge of ours, only detectable in the traces thrown up
against some textual walls (and just conceivably, some cave walls,
as at Çatalhöyük). This is the postulate of the founding murder, a
dynamic postulate which suggests that, however it happened, over
whatever huge length of time, the central building block which has
enabled our human cultures to come to be and to survive at all is
the all-against-one of collective lynching. All human cultural forms
flow from this. Ancient mythical texts do not point to this in a simple affirmative way. On the contrary, they dance round it, mostly
hiding it, occasionally glimpsing it, sometimes horrified by what
they see, sometimes complacently satisfied with the order which
has resulted. The point is not: 'If you read ancient texts, you will
see that Girard is right'. Because, of course, if you want, you can
read anything at all into ancient texts. The point is this: if you accept
Girard's postulate, you will find that the ancient texts make much
more sense than they have before, in a way which is much more
worthy of respect than we are inclined to acknowledge, and that
there was and is a certain rationale in what we call the 'primitive'
mind which, while we cannot go along with it, is not at all stupid.
Rather, it is a serious part of what has enabled our own ways of being and living together to survive, and thus of what has allowed us
to exist as we do now.

   The second part of this unimaginable explosion is also prior to
any text, but it has been reaching into our foreground and into

our texts in a strange and unique way through the adventure of the Hebrew people, culminating in the making explicit, public, evident and frontstage, of something which had been structuring and running people without their being aware of it up until then. The apparently necessary lie by which we bring into being and maintain order, culture, language and memory, thus finding ourselves established as humans, is shown to be exactly that – a lie. So the offstage structuring reality is gradually, over time, brought closer and closer to the surface, less and less dishonestly, in the interpretations which we glimpse in the Hebrew Scriptures, until, finally, that offstage structuring reality is brought centre-stage and made completely visible and obvious in the Passion. Thus, the lie is undone, and we find ourselves embarked on the possibility of humanity becoming something much better, more interesting, more responsible than we had imagined, and, simultaneously, we start to discover how very much more dangerous to each other we can be than we had thought, and how much more precarious is our stability, given that the comfort of 'the old lie' only reassures for as long as we do not know that it is a lie.

I hope that what I have sketched out here is the formidable act of communication which Girard postulates as both a botched but comprehensible 'emerging foundation', and its overcoming in our midst. This, which I call the 'centre of meaning', is prior to any texts. And this means that, before we even pick up the pages of the Scriptures to read them, we have already agreed to approach the text in an entirely different way than would be the case if, for instance, we were to start by assuming that texts offer clear windows or mirrors into the realities which they are describing, or that we are upstream of the texts, and that real meaning flows from us to them. Instead, we find ourselves downstream from the texts, and both we and the texts are way, way downstream from the very, very subtle and dynamic centre of meaning. So we begin to become aware of texts as being themselves always very unstable realities, which can be read this way and that. However, we also become aware that there is an historical reality which is an act of communication towards us by someone else, who is not simply one of the authors of the texts, an act of communication that is completely contemporary, stable and coherent, and to which our texts do bear witness if we read them in the same spirit as that which allowed them to be written.

Now what I want to say is this: whether or not you agree with what Girard says, with this or that detail of the mimetic hypothesis, what seems to me to be undeniable is that anyone who understands what Girard is about does find themselves thrown into the deep end of all the central contemporary questions concerning Revelation, Hermeneutics, textual origins and so forth, and in a way which illuminates all of them at once. Part of the freedom which I have received and learned from reading Girard is that, once in that deep end, there seems to be no limit to the doors which are currently being opened up by modern scholarship, and which start to make sense and can be put together by us. I guess this is why I was rather annoyed recently to hear an ancient cardinal refer to Girard's thought, somewhat dismissively, as a 'système', because he meant by that something which tended to circumscribe and limit scholarship. I have found Girard's thought to be something much closer to a 'centring insight', because it has opened up for me ways of synthesising the possibilities inherent in so many approaches which owe nothing to Girard at all. I think of what I have learned from Margaret Barker and other Old Testament scholars, like Mark S. Smith, who are helping us break out of the straightjacket which nineteenth century German biblical scholars put upon the sacred page, or what I have learned from Duncan Derrett, about the sheer subtlety, sophistication and playfulness of the network of allusions to the Hebrew Scriptures which pulsate just beneath the surface of the texts of the Apostolic Witness. And many of you have found just such doors opened up by other thinkers, like Walter Wink or Walter Brueggeman, and the list goes on.

So, before returning to John 5, let me just point to a few of the ways in which Girard sets us free to handle the sacred page in a manner that is appropriately reverential, but not at all idolatrous. The first, which I have already commented on, is that the event is prior to the text, so what we have in the text is evidence of interpretation flowing from that event. From the basic distinction between interpretations which tend to cover up the event, and interpretations which are part of the allowing the event to be seen for what it is, a huge freedom in reading the texts flows. We do not need to be at all frightened of this freedom in interpretation. In fact, we are anchored in our relaxedness about it by the knowledge of the truth behind the distinction between texts which cover up persecution and texts which reveal it. Once you know that, the texts can be about a huge variety of things, so many things that it does not matter, so long as you are yourself aware of the danger that *you* might use the texts to cover up, rather than reveal complicity in, the human reality of persecution.

A second freedom brought to us by Girard's handling of the text derives from the realisation that the basic scenario – a murder complacently accomplished, or revealed with fear and trembling – is also the basic liturgical scenario for acts of worship. And this feeds in with the realisation that, somewhat contrary to what we imagine, liturgy is prior to text. It is not the case that we have the Bible, and the Bible says we ought to have acts of worship, so we must devise acts of worship, and borrow some of the texts from the Bible to fill up the time during our gatherings. Quite the reverse: once you become aware that not only the murderous scenario, but also the liturgical scenario, is prior to the texts, then you begin to get a sense of quite how many of the texts of the Hebrew Scriptures were born for liturgical purposes, in order to explain and interpret particular gatherings, only gradually becoming what we refer to, deeply misleadingly, as 'a book'. Deuteronomy, for instance, really does sound entirely different depending on whether it is read as a book of legislation, or as a long sermon, full of recapitulations, and reminders of a permanent 'today', when all that is being said is to be embraced and put into action. Mary Douglas has an astounding reading of Leviticus[9] as being a detailed textual walk around the different topographical parts of the Desert Tabernacle, an extraordinary act of textual liturgical mnemonics to take the place of something which had ceased to exist.

---

9   *Leviticus as Literature* (Oxford, OUP, 2001).

Once this liturgical priority is perceived, then the many repetitions, slightly different versions of the same story, word play across long chunks of text and allusions within stories, all start to make sense: we are not dealing with texts which were written as 'completed books' for people to buy, take home and read, as we might do with the latest Grisham or Scarpetta. What we have instead is, often enough, something much more like a mixture between preacher's manuals and orchestral scores: the former in the sense that what is being provided is a series of paths, guides and stories by which a master expositor is to make alive the event that is being celebrated, the feast that is being rehearsed; and the latter in the sense that each performance is unique, that there is real skill, accomplishment, practise and judgment required in rendering the silent annotations into the audible form that is their realisation, and that the meaning of the score is only to be sensed in the performance. This was even more evidently the case in the distant past, when the system of pointing which provides the vowels for the entirely consonantal Hebrew text had not been fixed, so living performers genuinely provided, as their own highly responsible act of interpretation, the succession of vowels which could yield vastly different meanings.

Now, it seems to me that Girard enables us to be very relaxed in accompanying our growing sensitivity to this perception of our texts, because he is giving us the tools to make sense of storytelling surrounding key scenarios. If there is always a danger, in any human gathering, that whatever the positive benefits of that togetherness, some veiled act or movement of exclusion is afoot, then the capacity to highlight the contemporary presence of some amazingly violent and awful stories, and show their being overcome, is always going to be a source of enlightenment. I think Girard accomplishes this by always attending to the physical interactions described in the scenario, as well as by giving such a rich account of the pattern of desire that is at work.

To give an example: in Girard's reading of the woman taken in adultery, the fact that Jesus is defusing a potential lynch mob is, once one has a tiny hold on Girard's thought, perfectly obvious. Yet it is the little details which, once grasped, can never be forgotten. An ordinary scripture scholar could have pointed out that while no one knows what Jesus was writing in the dust, the fact that he was doing so, in the context of a discussion about what Moses commanded, is an enactment of YHWH writing the original tablets which Moses, in his anger, had cast to the ground, thus turning them to dust. It means that the Law of Moses as it stands is always a secondary version, and YHWH's intention is always prior to it and at some distance from it. But Girard's observation that when Jesus, in the face of the questioning of the potential lynch mob, bent down and wrote on the ground, it was by the physical movement of his arm that he was distracting attention both from the woman who was being so horribly shamed, and from himself, using his fingers to draw people's eyes towards a different centre of fascination, thereby defusing the anger and immediacy of the lynch mob: that observation, blending the physical description in the text with an intelligence of the working of desire, and how these two highlight what YHWH is doing, is in a different category of genius.

My penultimate point, before returning to the text of John 5, is to emphasise how, because Girard provides us with the workings of an extra-textual, but permanently contemporary source of meaning for our texts, he also teaches us how responsible we must be in our handling of those texts. It is very much more difficult for us to use the texts as a shield against our own responsibility. It is not, ever, 'what the Bible says' that is the straightforward justification for this or that source of action. But always the question: 'How do you read?' And we know about everyone else, but rarely about ourselves, that 'How does somebody read?', as evidenced in texts, can always be answered in one of two ways: 'They read for self-justification, and, in their reading, cover up their own and their friends' complicity in violence'; or, 'They read as people who are being exposed as frauds and liars who are becoming aware of the unpalatable nature of their involvement in violence.' Whatever the subject at hand, one or other of these is underway (and often, of course, a subtle and self-deceiving mixture of the two).

But this means that part of our responsibility, as perpetual makers- contemporary of the centre of meaning which is witnessed to in our texts, is to be found undergoing the same discovery as enabled the sacred texts to be written, to wit: that of our own fraudulence, flakiness, lack of 'having got it' and of our being taken for an adventure by someone much weightier and more consistent than ourselves. A Girardian reading of Scripture, as you would expect, given the Girardian understanding of the Spirit that brought the Scriptures to be, is one which is both relaxing as to its own fraudulence which is being uncovered, and yet appropriately scared of the potential for damage which our own self-righteousness and blindness can cause. I do not think that you can really be a Girardian reader of Scripture except as someone who is undergoing the experience of being forgiven. Which is merely to say that Girard has highlighted for us, and filled out for us, something which should be perfectly obvious: reading Scripture is only a truthful discipline if it is a penitential discipline, and being ready to be found to be a sinner is a precondition for being a speaker of the Christian word.

The final point at which I would like to look before returning to John is this: because Girard offers us a centre of meaning that is both prior to history, yet historical, liturgical and contemporary, it means that the whole question of the relation between the texts of the Hebrew Scriptures and those of the Apostolic Witness (or New Testament) comes into a much fresher light. Rather than seeing two juxtaposed histories, of which one is newer and the other older, it makes much more sense to see the Hebrew Scriptures as being a permanently contemporary vision of who we are, and the Apostolic Witness being the permanently actual interpretative key, revealing what has really been going on all along as the Word comes into the world. In this sense, what Girard has given us is an extraordinary tool for breaking free of the twin temptations which have beset Christian reading of the Scriptures: the Marcionite temptation of attributing to some other god all the really unpleasant and violent passages of the Old Testament, and the Fundamentalist temptation of applying the words 'God' and 'Lord' univocally across both Testaments. Nor is this a Christian temptation alone: the prophets Jeremiah and Ezekiel were wrestling with the same temptations close to six centuries before Christ, as are shown in their differing justifications for moving beyond the child sacrifice apparently enjoined in the book of Exodus[10].

Back to John 5, so that we can see some of this in action. Let me be quite clear that I am not attempting a complete 'reading' of Jesus' discourse here. What I am doing is pointing to ways in which John, who is, ironically enough, writing a text, shows Jesus both as prior to texts and meaning and as reading texts, and how John's presentation of Jesus is illuminated by the mimetic understanding of desire. In other words, I want to point out what a sophisticated discussion of hermeneutics is at work in this discourse.

First of all, there is Jesus' complete awareness that we are who we are given to be by another. As humans, we have no grasp of ourselves. We are run by the social other. It is only other people who point to who we are, and, as we see or hear them pointing and take on board what their pointing says about us, so we learn who we are and act accordingly. Jesus indicates very clearly that he has no grasp of himself. He is who he is entirely thanks to his doing what he sees the Father doing. And he, Jesus, finds himself to be who he is, as he becomes what he sees the Father doing. This is why he does not bear witness to himself: he is well aware of the psychological danger that, by bearing witness to oneself, one is allowing oneself to be defined by an argument within one's social grouping. This, too, is why he does not pay attention to the witness of other human beings, even John the Baptist. Instead, he relies for his identity on the works that his Father is bringing into being. These works are the works of the Creator, and, since his Father is bringing these works into being through him, he is able to rest in the knowledge that he is the One

---

10 cf. Ezek. 20:25-6: *Moreover I gave them statutes that were not good and ordinances by which they could not live. I defiled them through their very gifts, in their offering up all their firstborn, in order that I might horrify them, so that they might know that I am the LORD;* and Jer. 19:3-6: *You shall say: Hear the word of the LORD, O kings of Judah and inhabitants of Jerusalem. Thus says the LORD of hosts, the God of Israel: I am going to bring such disaster upon this place that the ears of everyone who hears of it will tingle. Because the people have forsaken me, and have profaned this place by making offerings in it to other gods whom neither they nor their ancestors nor the kings of Judah have known; and because they have filled this place with the blood of the innocent, and gone on building the high places of Baal to burn their children in the fire as burnt offerings to Baal, which I did not command or decree, nor did it enter my mind;* both interpreting Exod. 22:29-30: *You shall not delay to make offerings from the fullness of your harvest and from the outflow of your presses. The firstborn of your sons you shall give to me. You shall do the same with your oxen and with your sheep: seven days it shall remain with its mother; on the eighth day you shall give it to me.*

who the Scriptures point to. Please think of the sheer psychological daring and yet relaxedness of this!

Then there is Jesus' complete understanding that, flowing from his awareness of being involved on the inside of the act of Creation as YHWH, he is also the living fulcrum, the living criteria of judgment. He is not in the business of trying to judge people, yet judged they will be, by their attitude towards him. And this means, by their attitude towards the living victim, which he is in the process of instantiating. So he is the criteria for judgment in both real life and scriptural text. In both our stories, and the lives which enflesh them, we expel, kill, drive out and justify ourselves over against, victims, convinced that we are right. And here we learn that the real criteria are not ours, but those enfleshed by Jesus. And it is these criteria, those of the crucified and living victim, which will tell the real story, and are starting to do so already, uncovering the buried dead who had no one to tell their story, because they died so that others could keep alive a lie.

Finally there is Jesus' awareness, as John indicates it, of how this alters the reading of Scripture. For there is a rigorous reading going on here; Jesus says something very strong indeed to his listeners:

> You have never heard his voice or seen his form, and you do not have his word abiding in you, because you do not believe him whom he has sent.[11]

This refers back to Deuteronomy, where Moses says to the people of Israel:

> Then the LORD spoke to you out of the fire. You heard the sound of words but saw no form; there was only a voice.[12]

But even this was only what that generation heard, since so terrified were they that they did not want to hear any more, but besought Moses to go and himself hear the words which they could not bear, and they would listen to him:

---

11 John 5:37b-38.
12 Deut. 4:12.

'Go near, you yourself, and hear all that the LORD our God will
say. Then tell us everything that the LORD our God tells you, and
we will listen and do it.'[13]

In other words, Jesus is engaged in a strictly hermeneutical discussion: those to whom he is talking are, according to their own
texts, those who neither saw the form nor heard the words. Their
only access to the words are by 'listening to Moses'. This means
that the key question they face is 'Whose word is abiding in you?',
which means 'What is your hermeneutical key?', or 'Who is speaking through you when you read these texts?' Because it is the one
who is speaking through you whose voice will be heard in your
interpretation of the words.

Jesus points out that the only access any of them have to what is
really going on in the texts, is their ability to discern who is bearing
witness to him in what he is doing contemporaneously – in other
words, it is if they can perceive the Creator at work in what Jesus
is doing now, that they will be able to read the Scriptures, not vice
versa.

'You search the scriptures because you think that in them you have
eternal life; and it is they that testify on my behalf. Yet you refuse
to come to me to have life. I do not accept glory from human
beings. But I know that you do not have the love of God in you.
I have come in my Father's name, and you do not accept me; if
another comes in his own name, you will accept him. How can
you believe when you accept glory from one another and do not
seek the glory that comes from the one who alone is God?'[14]

Once again, Jesus' understanding of the mimetic issues at play in
reading the Scriptures are completely evident: if we get our reputation, that is to say our glory, from one another, then we will always
be ground down in the hermeneutical circle, only able to reflect
each other, and only able to tell truths of convenience rather than
undergoing the possibility of being told the inconvenient truth by
Another, one who is not part of the social other. The One, in fact,

13 Deut. 5:27.
14 John 5:39-44.

to whom the Scriptures point. The love of God would be found in us if we were able to bring together YHWH's self-revelation and the victims in Scripture, and, in real life, who YHWH brings to life and holds in being. And it is this One who is speaking, who is YHWH and the victim finally revealed as the same person, this one is the criteria for the love of God and knowledge of Scripture.

Jesus ends this discourse with further reference to Moses, who has, of course, been present as the one whom Jesus is making contemporary ever since the miracle under the five porticoes with which we began:

> 'Do not think that I will accuse you before the Father; your
> accuser is Moses, on whom you have set your hope. If you believed
> Moses, you would believe me, for he wrote about me. But if you
> do not believe what he wrote, how will you believe what I say?'[15]

Once again, this is part of a rigorous reading of Deuteronomy. Jesus is the One about whom Moses was writing, so naturally, to refuse to believe Jesus is to reject Moses, and thus to be under his judgment. Jesus is also, however, reminding his listeners that Moses himself, at God's behest, wrote the book of Deuteronomy, and sang the song which is its conclusion *as an act of witness against the people of Israel.* The notion of Moses as witness against his people is not an anti-semitic one: it is very exactly what Moses himself said:

> 'Take this book of the law and put it beside the ark of the covenant
> of the LORD your God; let it remain there as a witness against
> you. For I know well how rebellious and stubborn you are. If you
> already have been so rebellious toward the LORD while I am still
> alive among you, how much more after my death! Assemble to me
> all the elders of your tribes and your officials, so that I may recite
> these words in their hearing and call heaven and earth to witness
> against them.[16]

To sum up, in John 5 we have a text in which Jesus performs a rich and complex sign – a real, non-textual event – against a backdrop of a set of references to the Mosaic project. From there, he moves on

---

15 John 5:45-47.
16 Deut. 31:26-28.

to a rich reading of Deuteronomy in which that text becomes alive, seen as a real pointer to YHWH's project and what it is all about, one in which Moses' role is respected but relativised according to Moses' own criterion. And during all of this, Jesus illustrates how he is the real instantiation of the hermeneutical principle at work in the giving and reading of the Scripture.

What I hope to have shown is that here, it is not so much that traditional Girardian 'themes' are explicitly at work, but that Girard's approach to texts, and his opening up of mimetic psychology give us an enormous freedom to read a text like this from within. Thus, we are left in even greater awe at John's achievement. For John shows Jesus as being the living, active hermeneutical principle who is the Creator, contemporary with and prior to the texts of Scripture. These only come alive when YHWH, who is our victim, is heard by us, and his interpretation is spoken through us, as words which abide in us. Only thus do we break out of going round and round in circles, fooling ourselves, rather than allowing ourselves to be broken open and spoken to by the same One who spoke to Moses and gives us the living criteria by which to recognise his living dwelling places.

❖❖❖❖❖❖❖❖❖❖

CHAPTER 15

Befriending the vacuum:

receiving responsibility for an ecclesial spirituality

One of the things which fascinates me, as a systematic theologian, and which I have a long-term yearning to understand better, is what is meant by the 'giving' of the Holy Spirit[1]. In John's Gospel we are solemnly assured, at a certain point in Jesus' ministry:

> as yet the Spirit had not been given, because Jesus was not glorified.[2]

In other words, rather contrary to any notions of the Spirit as some-how ethereal, insubstantial, a-historical and so on, what we have is a notion of the Spirit as entering into the human realm in a quite specific historical circumstance and, therefore, being constantly and ever-after shaped by that circumstance. Later in John's Gospel, Jesus takes this further when he says that the Spirit:

> 'will glorify me, for he will take what is mine and declare it to you.'[3]

What I would like to do with you today, if I may, is to attempt to understand something of what is going on here, and to do so with some help from St Luke.

My hunch is this: that Luke portrays Jesus, in between Gethse-mani and the Cross, as deliberately retracing in historical form the route back from created reality, to being outside of and thus prior

---

1 This chapter was born as a presentation for the conference 'Sources of Transformation: Revitalising Traditions of Christian Spirituality for Today', held at St Mary's University College, Twickenham, London, in July 2009.

2 John 7:39b.

3 John 16:14.

to Creation. From his prayer of obedience and sweat 'like clots of blood', in which he is fulfilling Genesis 3:19[4], so that the New Adam is able to get right what the old Adam had fouled up, he moves to the formless and dark void which is described at the beginning of Genesis, and once again in the darkness and failed sun that accompanied the Crucifixion[5]. Then, in breathing out his Spirit to the Father on the Cross, he is entrusting to the Father the concrete historical and human form of the bringing into being of the New Creation which he has opened up by going to his death[6]. It is from then, until it is breathed upon us, that the Spirit hovers over the vacuum.

Now, I am no believer in being able to make easy deductions about Jesus' subjectivity from the texts of Scripture. Those texts do not work like modern fiction, giving us glimpses of psychology. Nevertheless, there was a fully human psychological subject there, someone about whom a text like that in Hebrews could say:

> For the joy that was set before him, he endured the Cross,
> despising the shame[7]

So I would like to consider something of what this picture of Jesus going to his death means: it means that Jesus gave himself up to death, facing a vacuum, a 'without form, and void', not knowing what the shape of what he was dying for would look like.

If I can explain what I mean at all, it is something like this: empowered by a joy at what he was bringing into being, but without any control at all over what that would be, Jesus was actively giving himself up to being a dead man, who would become the condition of possibility of other people being able to live as if death were not. And thus that he would be held in being, through what other people make of him.

---

4   Luke 22:42-44. The Genesis verse reads: 'In the sweat of your face you shall eat bread till you return to the ground, for out of it you were taken; for you are dust and to dust you shall return.' There are a series of word games hinted at here, around the words for Adam, ground and blood, the Hebrew of all of which have 'dam' at their root.

5   Luke 23:44-45.

6   Luke 23:46.

7   Heb. 12:2.

I can scarcely say how much difference it makes to our understanding of the Eucharist if, rather than see Jesus giving us a goodness-pill, even an eternal goodness-pill, in the form of a host, we see him giving away his body into the hands of sinful humans so that we may become that body, allowing himself to become *what we make of him* and yet trusting that the Spirit which his self-giving has unleashed in his dying, and therefore which bears his form without being under his prior control, will make of him something that will give glory to his Father.

What I want to emphasise here, for reasons which I hope will become plain later on, is the enormity of this giving himself away into occupying the space of death. It is a fully human act. And, of course, humans cannot fully give themselves away into occupying the space of death with any certainty at all as to what the results of this will be. Or, indeed, even as to whether it is a worthwhile thing to do at all. No surrender of control could be greater.

I would like to look at how this impacts our understanding of Creation. In one sense, if we follow the imagery of the book of Genesis, it is easy to imagine God creating: he creates formless matter and then, little by little, orders it, and adds things here and there until he rests. We can imagine doing something like that ourselves with respect to clay. The one who does the ordering has, one assumes, a clear idea of what he would like to make, and moves towards making it.

But the Christian account of creation is somewhat different from this. In the Christian creation story, the Defining Adam, the first giver-of-self-away-in sacrifice, the first priest, but also the first victim and the first sacrifice, appears in the middle of the story and, with enormous difficulty, gets right what the also-ran Adams, Eves, Cains and Abels, who are all of us, have been getting wrong since the inception of our race, so that Creation really starts with and through the Defining Adam as a human story. And in the Christian account of creation, the Defining Adam is not a passive recipient of YHWH's breath, as the also-ran Adam of Genesis is[8]. The Defining Adam is YHWH as human, and it is YHWH's breath having become

---

8   cf. 1 Cor. 15:45.

a human life story that is breathed into our nostrils so that Creation is in fact a human life story.

What on earth, then, was Jesus thinking? In this account, the relationship between the Spirit and Creation is subtly different from the previous account. Order is not something that comes from without, applied to a formless void. The creative act of both breaching the vacuum into existence and orchestrating its formless void is present simultaneously. If you like, all the energy and emotional push of bringing this project into being, not knowing what it is going to end up like, knowing only that it will zing with joy, has, as its analogy, not an outside agent moulding clay, but a human, offering himself to stand in a place of shameful death so that thoroughly unsatisfactory, as yet incomplete, and often evil, humans can ourselves become the agents of Creation, and can become the physical, historical body of which this human has agreed to despoil himself. It is through this that historical bodies can become the bearers of meaning and purpose pointing to a glory beyond ourselves, rather than being vain vessels of flux, devouring our way from one sort of dust to another.

At the centre of this self-giving up to death is, naturally, the relationship between Creation and death. And again, what must Jesus have been thinking? We have only the benefit of hindsight here. How could a human have created the possibility of living as if death were not, thereby relativising the completely totalitarian grip which death has on our race? How could a human being transform a 'destiny', and an implacably inimical force which runs us far more deeply than we realise, into being merely the outward parameter of the condition of possibility of this sort of material, bodily thing, becoming able to take part in and rejoice in, God's adventure? Well the answer is: if conceivably at all, only conceivably by a self-giving living-into that non-space which is death, such that he occupied it, without being run by it.

So, we have Jesus solemnly going backwards through history and culture, occupying the space of each of the victims, the lambs of Atonement and Passover, Isaac on Mt Moriah, Job, the Psalmist, David as he was betrayed on the hillside outside Jerusalem, Joseph and finally Abel, so as to achieve the status of being the real Adam.

And this, of course, means going backwards to occupy the space where, before there is culture, and therefore sacrifice, there is murder. So it is not death in some abstract sense that Jesus is giving himself over into, but the full cultural human reality of death – murder, shame, being a loser, violence, mob-rule, false accusation, sacrifice, incompetence, mock innocence at the expense of another, apparent legality, political expediency, putative curse-by-God; he occupies the space of all these, and, in the midst of them, his innocence as a victim is not primarily a technical legal matter, but the enfleshed, self-giving harmlessness (which is what *in-nocens* means) symbolised by the lamb. Because of his harmlessness, he is able to occupy the space of each one of those realities without being run by them. That is what the self-giving power of the Spirit, that he is in the process of giving, does: it detoxifies the apparent reality of death with all its out-runners by being in their space and not being run by them.

This, I think, is one of the great pivots of the cosmic change which has come upon us with the giving of the Holy Spirit: the non-rivalry between the self-giving of Jesus and all the panoply of the forces of death. Because the only conceivable thing (and it is to us scarcely conceivable) that could not be moved by the panoply of the forces of death, is something that is prior to life as we know it, and able to hold it in being. In other words, the Spirit which in-formed Jesus' enacted bodily life, and to which Jesus' enacted bodily life gave form, is the Spirit of the Creator, finally detached in our perception from any sort of mistaken identification with death.

Please hold onto this link between the Spirit being 'given', and the deliberate and non-rivalrous occupation by Jesus of the space of death, for a little: we will be coming back to it.

However, now I would like to move from my necessarily impressionistic meditation on what Jesus was doing in the 'giving' of the Spirit, to looking at the Lukan account of how that 'giving' of the Spirit was received.

We all know the account in Acts 2; nevertheless I would like to give a brief run through part of it to see what Luke is pointing towards:

> When the day of Pentecost had come, they were all together in
> one place. And suddenly from heaven there came a sound like the
> rush of a violent wind, and it filled the entire house where they
> were sitting. Divided tongues, as of fire, appeared among them,
> and a tongue rested on each of them. All of them were filled with
> the Holy Spirit and began to speak in other languages, as the
> Spirit gave them ability. Now there were devout Jews from every
> nation under heaven living in Jerusalem. And at this sound the
> crowd gathered and was bewildered, because each one heard them
> speaking in the native language of each.[9]

First of all, the event is linked to the Passover by occurring on Pentecost, the feast celebrated fifty days after Passover, so, whatever
happens, it can be seen as in some way completing Passover, with
its liberation from Egypt. The Apostolic Witnesses are all gathered
together, and there comes a sound like the rush of a violent breath
– πνωη rather than πνευμα – the more personal form 'breath',
as in: that which God breathed into Adam in Genesis 2 (and the
risen Jesus into the disciples in John 20), rather than the yet-to-be-
made, personal form which hovered over the abyss in Genesis 1.

This breath is described as βιαιος – violent or vehement – which
takes us back to the strong east wind which God blew, opening up
the sea before Moses and the people of Israel in Exodus 14:21. It
also points us to the 'rushing stream, which the wind of the LORD
drives,' of Isaiah 59:19, about which more anon. This sound *filled*
the entire *house*, and, of course, those with scriptural ears will have
been intrigued that these are the same words which occur in Isaiah
6:1:

> In the year that King Uzziah died I saw the Lord sitting upon a
> throne, high and lifted up, and his glory (or train) filled the house
> (or Temple)

What makes this verse particularly significant here, is that, apart
from the perfectly ordinary words for 'fill' and 'house' being the
same in both Luke's text and the Greek version of Isaiah, the same
word for 'lifted up' has just been used, in the previous chapter of

9   Acts 2:1-6.

Acts (1:9) to describe what we refer to as Jesus' Ascension. In other words, the Apostolic Witnesses are those who are undergoing, over time, the fulfilment of Isaiah's Temple theophany, seeing the Lifting Up of the Lord to his throne and undergoing his glory filling them, who are becoming the Temple.

Next we have the *divided tongues as of fire*. Apart from the fact that this seems to fulfil the promise that the new fire would be found in the restored Temple, the word translated by *divided* – διαμερ–ιζομεναι – is interesting, since it is more accurately the word for distributing portions, as in the portions of a spoil, or the portions of a sacrifice. And it is the word which appears in a key prophecy in Zechariah 14:1:

> Behold a day of the Lord is coming when the spoil taken from you will be apportioned out – διαμερισθησεται – in the midst of you.

This follows on from a series of prophesies which were enormously important in Jesus' own description to his disciples of what he thought he was doing, concerning the shepherd who would be struck and the sheep scattered and other passages, amply referred to in the Passion narratives. Immediately preceding this passage is the notion of 'a third' who will be left alive, leading to 'I will put this third into the fire and refine them as one refines silver, and assay them as gold is assayed'.

So we have an extraordinary concatenation of images at work here: the spoil who had been taken from the apostolic group is being apportioned out to them. This is, of course, what Jesus had acted out prior to his death, in sharing the portions of himself with his disciples in the Last Supper, just as the High Priest gave portions of the lamb of Atonement to the priests in the Temple. But simultaneously, with the fire resting on the heads of those who are receiving the portions, it is clear that they are not only priests in the New TempleTemple, but also living burning offerings.

It is now, I think, that it would make sense to go back and look at Isaiah 59:15-21:

Truth is lacking, and he who departs from evil causes himself to be despoiled. The LORD saw it, and it displeased him that there was no justice. He saw that there was no man, and wondered that there was no one to intervene; then his own arm brought him victory, and his righteousness upheld him. He put on righteousness as a breastplate, and a helmet of salvation upon his head; he put on garments of vengeance for clothing, and wrapped himself in fury as a mantle. According to their deeds, so will he repay, wrath to his adversaries, requital to his enemies; to the coastlands he will render requital. So they shall fear the name of the LORD from the west, and his glory from the rising of the sun; for he will come like a rushing stream, which the wind of the LORD drives. 'And he will come to Zion as Redeemer, to those in Jacob who turn from transgression, says the LORD. 'And as for me, this is my covenant with them, says the LORD: my spirit which is upon you, and my words which I have put in your mouth, shall not depart out of your mouth, or out of the mouth of your children, or out of the mouth of your children's children, says the LORD, from this time forth and for evermore.'

This is, evidently, a prophesy of redemption, though it has been fulfilled in a way that no one could have expected: it describes the Lord doing himself what no human seemed to be able to do: avenging, which was always one half of redeeming and atoning. And he is going to come to Zion as Redeemer, like a *vehement* (our old friend βιαιος) stream driven by the wind of the Lord. This is linked with making a covenant and putting a spirit upon people which will issue forth in all speaking the words of the Lord.

What is striking, of course, is the contrast between this image of redemption with its language of vengeance, and the reality of the despoiled redeemer, who was entirely without vengeance, much more in the line of the 'suffering servant' prophecies earlier in Isaiah. But it is this despoiled redeemer who has become the *requital* for his enemies, which is also to be understood as 'the one who has made peace'[10], this one who is coming to Zion as Redeemer in a rushing wind.

Finally (and I neither aspire to exhaust, nor have exhausted, the possibilities which St Luke is pointing to), this Spirit, flowing from the self-giving despoliated victim which is giving words to people, fulfils what the Genesis story of Babel was about and undoes what happened there, but again in a surprisingly gracious way. For, at Babel, people had only one language until God confused them and scattered them. The Greek word for Babel in Genesis 11 is Σύγχυσις, which means confusion, or bewilderment. It is clear, then, what is going on when, at the sound from the room where the apostolic witnesses were, devout Jews from every nation under heaven became a crowd that *gathered* (so becoming one) and was *bewildered* (or confused), where the Greek of Acts 2:6 is συνεχύθη – the same derivation as Babel. Astoundingly a new sort of unity is being made available, which is the reverse of the totalitarian gathering together into one which had made Babel. The collapse of that unity had led to a world in which people could not understand their neighbour's speech. But here, the reverse is going on – a unity which is completely respectful of the native language of each: neighbour could at last speak to neighbour.

To recapitulate a little: Luke gives us criteria for what the giving of the Spirit is about. It is the glory of the ascended Lord in a lived-out, three dimensional Temple vision, which is simultaneously the inauguration of Creation, the definitive Passover where it is not the Red Sea, but Death that is passed over, the self-despoiling presence of the Redeemer, the transformation of ordinary people into the New Temple where they will all be self-giving priests, and the first signs of a gracious new human unity not achieved over against someone, but flowing from the self-giving victim whose words are able to reach the hearts of each.

---

10   The Hebrew word here translated 'requital', has as its consonants ש ל ם and is linked to the word for peace, completion, settlement by sacrifice: it is one of those genuinely polysemic words surrounding the notion of sacrifice which should by no means always be interpreted as vengeful. My guess is that the τετέλεσται – 'it is completed' – of John 19:30, is the Greek version of a verbal form of this Hebrew word.

Thus, and I cannot emphasise this enough, Luke is pointing towards, bearing witness to, a huge and genuinely anthropological earthquake being promoted by a Spirit which had not been available before, and which Jesus had made available. This huge, genuinely anthropological earthquake has quite specific features: a completely new form of unity for humans is being made available at the instigation of a forgiving human victim who lived as if death were not. This completely new form of unity is universal, it is able to be entered into by people of any nation under the sun, and is in principle not over against any race at all (the final step to this is taken after Peter's interaction with Cornelius in Acts 10). From this Spirit, a new form of holiness emerges which is nothing to do with the sacred structures of old, but in which what is truly central is the kenotic, self-despoiling living-out of being a priest in the New Temple. This Temple is understood as a new corporate being-together of human bodies. It is human living out of this which is what enables Creation to be fulfilled and to zing with a lasting joy. All of this has happened in the midst of, and through, a quite specific, historical bunch of people, the Apostolic Witnesses, in a normal, non-magnificent, non-liturgical house and is made available through their spoken words.

Now, why have I gone on for so long to get to something as simple as saying that the Church is One, Holy, Catholic and Apostolic, which you all know anyhow? And the answer is, because I am afraid that we are so used to hearing those words with an ecclesiastical tinge, that we forget the anthropological earthquake which produces ecclesiality, and of which the ecclesiastical is the necessary, but sometimes severely dysfunctional, carapace. And it is easy for the word 'spirituality' to become a more or less Gnostic way of abstracting from the corporate, anthropological, historical bringing into being of a new humanity in the face of death, which is the indispensibly ecclesial dimension of the protagonism of the Spirit.

It is just here, I think, that it is going to be increasingly important for us to think in terms of the creative protagonism of the self-giving dead person. And I mean this somewhat literally. If the picture I have begun to sketch out for you is true, then the gift of the Spirit is already the gift of a certain peaceful, unshaken, unmoved, un-driven being able to occupy the space of death creatively. I am afraid that I think in silly pictures, but the picture I have which corresponds to my own occasional sense of dwelling in this space, is that of walking chest-deep in water, with my awareness that the part of me underwater is quite untroubled by what goes on above, and is therefore able both to lose without fear, and also, occasionally, be able to make tiny, creative, non-reactive movements above the surface.

Now, this sense of being held and empowered by a very great peacefulness (the pre-dead, held-in-life quality which I am assuming is co-terminous with what belief in God and life in the Spirit are about) is what enables my heart and my head, above the surface, as it were, to be becoming unravelled from the ways in which they are driven by life above the surface. So, little by little, I can find myself given spiritual longings. And by this, I do not mean ethereal gasps, I mean the stirrings of heartfelt desire for imperishable good to be born in the midst of so much violence and inchoate futility. And maybe even the courage and the imagination to be able to make a first few steps towards bringing such as-yet-unimagined good into being.

Here is where I think it very, very important that we not be in rivalry with the ecclesiastical. The guardians of the edges are by no means always the enemies of the Kingdom, though the temptations for them to identify the edges with the Kingdom are often very great indeed. But, the lovers of that anthropological project in ecclesial form which is the Kingdom, do not receive their identity from the guardians of the edges, and they certainly do not receive their identity over against the guardians of the edges, by rivalrous or contemptuous contrast with them. They receive their identity alongside the guardians of the edges from the unique protagonist of the project.

It is, in my experience, very, very difficult indeed, at least for someone as temperamentally conservative and frightened as myself, to do without human approval. There would be something marvellously irresponsible about being able to forego the hard work of discovering oneself approved by God as a son or daughter upon whom his fondness rests, by delegating that need for approval to someone else, from whom it might be more easily grabbed. And, in as far as such things school us in avoiding rivalry, they may indeed be helpful for a time. However, ultimately, the delegation of approval, or disapproval to others, who, in the last resort usually cannot give an approval that they do not themselves have, is a failure to accept the fullness of responsible involvement for bringing into being the project.

In other words, it is a failure to be dead enough to receive the creative longing of Christ.

However, if we are dead enough, and are thus unconcerned about success, reputation, able not to resist our being despoiled of these apparently life-giving things, then it is conceivable that we will be able to think big enough, think long-term enough, to glimpse the ecclesial form of how the Spirit is befriending the vacuum and bringing Creation into being, and so become the fingertips of its protagonism.

I would like to conclude with a contemporary example of what I mean, corresponding to elements from two of the 'notes' of the ecclesial project which I mentioned before – its apostolicity and its holiness. Central to the notion of apostolicity, following on the imagery of Acts 2 which I developed with you, is the link between word and witness. A certain way of speaking is described, which bore witness to something having been experienced over time, and was picked up by the listeners as something inside them, such that they were able to relate to it, and to its authority from within, from their own starting place. This speaking and listening *of itself*, as a sign of the Spirit which empowers it, both separates the listeners out from being a crowd, and freshly individuates them by making them symptoms of a new sort of unity. We are talking here about a certain sort of anthropology of communication.

Now, one of the things which the last five hundred years have seen, and has advanced dizzyingly in the last few decades, has been an astonishing series of changes in the public use of the word. From typesetting to twitter, from Papal bulls to popular blogs. And, of course, the guardians of the edges (whether secular or religious) are accustomed in this sphere, as in all others, to conserving the forms of the old, long after the new wine has burst out and run away. If we just think of the Holy See's communication mishaps over the last few years, then it should become clear how a certain ex-abrupto teaching style, which always included canonical consequences for public disagreement, has become unviable. For myself, I should say that I far prefer the Ratzinger-Lombardi low key style, in which the human frailties, bureaucratic incompetence and sometimes nutty presuppositions of those involved, become clear. This seems far more genuine than the Wojtyla-Navarro Valls PR smoke and mirror show. Nevertheless, where, thanks to the Internet, people can read things for themselves, disagree with them publicly, find out how others are reacting to them, mock them (often being right to do so) and get an interactive audience, then what it means to speak with authority – from the place of the '*Auctor*' – the one who brings things into being and increase – has changed out of all recognition.

And this means, regardless of how conservative or liberal, ultramontane, orthodox or protestant you are, the anthropological shape of being given the words to bear witness to God has shifted, and is shifting enormously. A consequence of this is that how we take ecclesial responsibility for the apostolicity of the Word, the relation between word and witness, is going to be of huge importance in the future.

I want to make it quite clear that I am attempting to make an anthropological point here, one concerning a sphere in which our current ecclesiastical set up is but a single symptom among many. Think what life in an ancient city was like: no newspaper, no radio. Everywhere gossip, rumour and reputation up for grabs; objective facts very hard to come by, opinions circulating from royal heralds, priestly spokesmen and licensed thugs, whom it is often difficult to tell apart; often, a swirling mass of misinformation abounds, seething conspiracy theories and so forth[11]. Then think what an extraordinary eruption into this world the advent of the written word

---

11 I am very grateful to my friend Andrew McKenna for this quote from *A Woman in Berlin: Eight weeks in the Conquered City,* Anon, trans. Philip Boehm (New York, Picador, 2005), pp110-111:
'So the bookseller stitches away and recounts what she knows. Rumor – the goddess Fama. I've always pictured her as an old woman all shrouded up and murmuring away. Gossip. We feed on it. In the old days people got all their news through hearsay and word of mouth. It's impossible to overestimate how this affected ancient cultures, how unclear and uncertain their view of the world must have been – spooky, nightmarish, a swamp of murmured horrors and fears, of malicious men and resentful gods.'

must have been, and, with it, little by little, an apparent objectivity of learning, of truth. Then think of the importance of designated interpreters of the word, and the changing shape of their link with what we now call political and religious power as cities, sanctuaries and empires rose and fell. All this, in a world in which the vast majority of the people could not read.

Perhaps it makes more sense to imagine why people should have fled to the desert for holiness in such times, for how else could you begin to step outside the seething spirit of the mob which could so easily run you? In the midst of the flux of words and opinions, so violent and so meaningless, so detached from truth, the time of detox spent in silence, the ability to receive an identity from One who was not part of the seething mass must have seemed an extraordinary freedom.

Then consider how, after a long, very long, period of attempting some form of publicly available objective truth, through philosophers, academies, libraries, monasteries, cathedrals, eventually universities and ultimately the printing press, the written word started to become hugely widely available, and literacy a basic requirement for adult participation in life. Then consider that town criers and royal proclamations yielded to newspapers, and once again the appearance of objective truth in the public sphere seemed to grow. Even more with radio, and then television.

However, I wonder whether we have not entered a new sphere in which the easy interactivity of the published word and the viral spread of information has severely undercut all the pretensions (for that is all they were – though often enough decent, protective pretensions) of the objectivity of the truth proclaimed by the public holders of the word. I am not sure whether this is merely a subjective and partisan perception, but I can scarcely begin to fathom the depth of the shock to the possibility of public truthfulness wrought, in the English-speaking world at least, by the eight years between the Florida election of 2000 and the end of the Bush era. I do not merely mean the objective evil wrought by particular individuals within or around the Bush administration, and the other governments infected by their lies, or indeed the farcical nature of newspaper and television reporting surrounding these events, or even the systemic mendacity of Church authorities, which also emerged as never before during this period. I mean the wholesale way in which it became clear that the apparent public bastions of possible truthfulness were little other than factional cheerleaders, champions of convenience, cowards, shameless masters of thuggery and cover-up. This, of course, may always have been the case, to greater or lesser degrees: the anthropological novelty is elsewhere.

What is new is that the advent of a non-traditional, interactive, Internet-based media means that alternative voices become available with astonishing rapidity – so that official lies can be 'called', however ineffectively, and people can see the shamelessness of liars as they live out their lies, but also that a welter of gossip and conspiracy theory can develop. In other words, what is dramatically altered is not necessarily the amount of truth that is available; however, the *illusion of authority* of certain forms of communication is entirely relativised, which means, undermined.

Now this, the sense that we may be heading back into being something much closer to an ancient city, riven by misinformation, gossip and factionalised mobs, but with enormous technological advances, cannot but be of huge significance for anyone who is interested in what is meant by the protagonism of the Holy Spirit. For part of that protagonism lies in giving us the ability to speak the words which come from the self-giving victim who is inaugurating a new way of being human, such that they can be heard by our sisters and brothers as coming from within themselves, in their own native languages. What is in question is the anthropological shape of authoritative truthfulness in the public sphere.

A number of significant voices – for instance, Alasdair MacIntyre[12], Pope Benedict[13], and most recently David Bentley Hart[14], have indicated the importance of some sort of rediscovery of monasticism as the key to keeping the flame of truthfulness alive – not necessarily a formal monastic movement in a physical desert, but maybe so.

---

12 At the end of *After Virtue* (London, Duckworth, 2007).
13 In his various meditations on Benedictine monasticism and Europe.
14 At the end of *Atheist Delusions* (New Haven, Yale University Press, 2009).

I wonder about this myself, both in the sense of asking myself whether they are right in the negativity of their evaluation, but also in the sense of trying to consider and face up to the same reality that they are describing. I wonder what shape will be taken by the visible signs of the protagonism of the Spirit that we are to birth in modern western cities, as we undergo the collapse of the illusion of authority, and learn how to create ecclesiality without entering into rivalry with the ecclesiastical carapace? I wonder what structures will be required for us to take the time and the energy and the patience to be able to imagine together, and bring into being, an imperishable good for the most vulnerable of our brothers and sisters? I wonder how *will* we live out that deferment of gratification, of recognition and approval, accompanied by the loss of reputation, prestige and power, which is the sign of the one who is being empowered to live in the midst of death without being run by it? And, with enormous difficulty, I try to move beyond wondering, praying that the Spirit will show us our way into the practical charity of befriending the vacuum.

❖❖❖❖❖❖❖❖❖❖

CHAPTER 16

Brokeheart Mountain:

reflections on monotheism, idolatry and the Kingdom

In August 2006, I had the pleasure of visiting the Holy Land as part of a small interfaith pilgrimage[1]. The plan was for a group of Jewish, Christian and Muslim, lesbian and gay shapers-of-opinion, well schooled in, and committed to, a recognisably orthodox version of our respective theologies, and with heads at least slightly above the parapet, to visit significant places for each of our traditions. We would read our sacred texts with each other *in situ* as we attempted to help each other discover what it might mean to be truly Jewish, Muslim or Christian and gay, and how we could support each other and others in similar situations. In the event, I am sad to report, we were unable to find a gay Muslim religious leader who could safely stick his or her head above the parapet for this purpose, so our pilgrimage became an exercise in Jewish-Christian sharing. It was for me, even so, a wonderfully enriching experience. The end of our pilgrimage coincided, deliberately, with World Pride, held that year as a rather small affair in Jerusalem, where we met up with some of our more liberal co-religionists, now indeed from all three backgrounds. And it was in the run up to World Pride in Jerusalem, that we discovered the true unity of our religions. For the Chief Rabbi, the Grand Mufti, the principal representatives of Orthodox, Protestant, and (owing to slow bureaucratic communications) last,

---

1   This chapter was born as a presentation for the annual COV&R conference, held in St Mary's University College, Twickenham, London, in July 2009, a contribution to a day of discussion with distinguished Muslim scholars concerning the 'fearful symmetries' between Christianity and Islam. COV&R is the international association of those interested in developing and applying the thought of René Girard, and more can be learned about its activities on www.uibk.ac.at/theol/cover.

but not least, Catholic religious authority, all joined together with varying degrees of fury and conviction to condemn and repudiate the presence of sodomites desecrating the Holy City, begging the secular authorities to keep us away.

As the Israeli press pointed out, it was the first time in anyone's memory that the notoriously factional and divided religious authorities of Jerusalem had managed to agree on anything. And it brings me to why I consider it very appropriate to be conducting our discussion today under the heading 'fearful symmetries'. The way in which our different religious leaderships manage to come to unity around this single issue, one which is either entirely marginal to, or not present at all in, our respective sacred texts, means that, to my mind, any claim which our groups make about how peaceful they are, how they only desire the good of humanity and how firmly committed they are to love of God and neighbour, should be taken not with a pinch, but with a bushel of salt. Frankly, the unity of religious leaders is more often a nightmare than a dream: a fearful symmetry indeed.

And, of course, it was the fact that we were in a secular state marked by the rule of law that offered us safety against such outbursts of religious unity. Gay Christians living in Christian-dominated countries, where the rule of law is tenuous like Jamaica or Uganda, are not at all safe from bands of the roving righteous. Any more than are gay Muslims in countries like Iraq, or Iran. Here is a very clear area where the relationship between religion and murder is not merely academic.

In September of 2006, a month after the events I have just described, Pope Benedict gave a speech in Regensburg. His gaffe and the intemperate reaction that ensued, temporarily occluded the sensible point he had sought to make. Nevertheless, the whole kerfuffle put the issue of the relation between faith and reason firmly on the agenda at the centre of discussions between Muslims and Christians. Several Muslim scholars responded to the Pope's remarks, indicating the importance of reason for them, and, since then, the Holy Father has returned to the theme on a number of occasions, most recently on his trip to the Holy Land earlier this year.

Since 2006, people like me have been listening out to see if we can hear from our religious authorities anything suggesting that what they mean by reason, and the way it interacts with faith, might have the slightest impact on their own attitudes, or the attitudes of their followers, towards the sodomites in their midst who have recently provided so endearing an occasion of passionate unity. In other words: all our authorities seem to agree that faith is reasonable, that reason illuminates faith, and that faith purifies reason. But, just as soon as anyone suggests that this might lead to any actual learning about something, and wonders why in the, small, unimportant, and no doubt 'icky' sphere of matters gay, it seems not to, then the same religious leaders either turn remarkably quiet, or weigh in to claim that this particular form of violent hatred, with its stereotypical accusations, is not violent and not hatred but is the direct fruit of a divine teaching, and so off the table as regards learning.

Put this another way: either the conversation about faith and reason we are supposed to be having is simply self-innocenting cant, the never-to-be-drawn ideological drapes of a pretty religious summer house; or it actually means something, in which case it must be able to be cashed out in a form that might be described as a faith-inspired anthropology of learning. And that faith-inspired anthropology of learning must be capable of being set out in a way that has historical incidence.

So, I thought that I might engage in a bit of equal opportunity hatefulness by insisting on lowering the tone of our discussion concerning monotheism, idolatry and the Kingdom of God to the level of engagement with the small, ultimately rather unimportant, apparently 'icky', but nevertheless persistent piece of the human puzzle that currently goes by the name of 'gay'.

And I would like to do this, hoping that we can avoid some of the passions that the subject arouses, by means of a hypothetical test case. By that I mean something that starts with the question 'What if?' In other words, I do not want to waste your time and attention today with a discussion of whether or not it is *true* that being gay or lesbian is some sort of defective state in a humanity that, by its nature, is intrinsically heterosexual, or whether it is not rather true that being gay or lesbian is simply a regular and non-pathological minority variant in the human condition. That is a discussion for elsewhere.

What I want to do instead is to pose the question: 'Let us imagine, hypothetically, that it *were* true that being gay or lesbian is a non-pathological minority variant in the human condition. How might this impact the discussion concerning the relationship between faith and reason in our respective religious groups?' In other words, I am proposing a test case: what would it look like for *our* group to undergo some sort of learning in this sphere *on its own terms*?

That phrase 'on its own terms' is the one that is important to me here. I am absolutely not interested in some general theory of secularisation, which disdains the particular ways of doing things of particular religious groups. What I am asking for are accounts of how particular religious groups come, over time, to discover things that are true about being human on this planet, such that this discovery of what is true can be seen to have been the outworking of their own inner resources and then becomes a stable and creative part of how that religious group envisions the world in which we live.

Let me say that I would not dare to raise this issue here if I were able to make a triumphalist Christian point: 'See, we can be self-critical and learn, unlike the Muslims, who are quite incapable of self-criticism.' It is precisely because in this sphere, my own religious group, the Catholic Church, which I love, and of whose central tenets I am an ardent exponent, has thus far proved incapable of applying to its own teaching what it says aloud to others, that I feel able to raise the matter. Can equal opportunity hatefulness become the grounds for equal opportunity self-critical learning?

So, if I may, I propose to sketch out a hypothetical argument concerning how, in the light of Girard's mimetic theory, it might be the case that the Catholic faith could find itself at home with the sort of faith-inspired anthropology of learning that I have mentioned. And, at various points, I will ask the open-ended question, to which I do not expect a quick answer: can you imagine, hypothetically, how Muslims might imagine an analogous process? Does the process of learning look entirely different? And, if it does look different, what do you mean, in practice, by the relationship between faith and reason? What is your faith-inspired anthropology of learning?

So to my sketch of a hypothetical argument to show how Catholics, for reasons which are internal to, and flow from, the sources of our faith, might hypothetically be able to learn something new about being human in this sphere. My argument has two parts: what gives us permission to think that we might have something to learn here?; and what might the shape of our undergoing that learning look like? Broadly speaking, these two parts correspond to an understanding of monotheism and Creation, on the one hand, and the aimed-for Kingdom of God, on the other. Or, in other words, they are attempts to look at 'where we come from' and 'where we are going'.

So, let me start with monotheism, creation and idolatry. I take it for granted that when we talk about God, we are not talking about a god, a large and powerful member of the genus 'gods', who just happens to be the only one. We are talking, in the wake of the great Hebrew breakthrough into monotheism in the post-exilic period, of God who is not one of the gods. Of God about whom it is truer to say that God is more like nothing at all than like anything that is, because God is not a member of the same universe as anything that is, not in rivalry with anything that is. God is not an object within our ken; we find ourselves as objects within God's ken. God is massively prior to us, and God's protagonism is hugely more powerful than any possible action or reaction which we might imagine. Or, in the phrase my late and belovèd novice master, Herbert McCabe, used to enjoy saying: God and the Universe does not make two.

The question then arises of the relationship between everything that is ,and God, who is utterly prior to it. Is that relationship something like a symptom, such that from things that are, including ourselves, we can glean something about the One who brings them into being and sustains them? And, if that is the case, do we have any criteria at all for what is a reflection of God's creative will and power, and what is a defection from it? And this, for me, is the central point in any discussion about monotheism and idolatry: what is the criterion by which we can learn the difference between idolatry and worship? The answer which the Catholic faith gives me is this: the reason why it is possible to be non-idolatrous is because God has given us God's own criterion for what it looks like to be non-idolatrous. And that criterion, given that God has no parts or divisions, and in every movement towards us is One, is also God. The criterion takes the form of a lived-out, fully human, life story, that of Jesus, whose meaning was the reverse of all the human criteria that are usually brought into play in such stories. God gave, as God's own criterion for God's own power, not the power of emperors, legislators or priests, but the ability to occupy the space of losing, curse, shame and death, without being run by them, in such a way that that space, and the whole anthropological structure of human existence that depends on it, is able to be relativised. Idolatry is seen to be an involvement in the human cultural reality of death from which God longs for us to be free.

Catholic teaching further tells me that God not only gave us God's own criterion for idolatry, which is God, but, as the light flowing from God's own criterion for idolatry, God gave us God's own interpretation of God's criterion for God, which we call Holy Spirit. God's interpretation of God's own criterion for God is also God, since God has no parts or divisions, and in every movement towards us is One. It is in this way, and this way only, that we can begin to engage in a process of non-idolatrous learning: that we are aware that we *do* have a criterion by which to learn, and we *do* have the possibility of interpreting the criterion, but neither the criterion nor the interpretation comes from us. In other words, it is not only the Creator who is utterly Other. The living criterion by which we can recognise the Creator, and the living interpretation through which we can worship the Creator, are both utterly other than, not dependent on, us. Nevertheless, we find that we can become symptoms of them in the same way as we are symptoms of the Creator, because they are the same protagonism as the Creator.

Now I want to say that this criterion is a very radical criterion. It suggests that, in the world as we know it, we are all very markedly idolatrous, and that our idolatry is principally linked to the way in which death and its fear clouds our imaginations, our minds, our judgments and our passions. It really does mean that there is no simple way to read off from the powers and glories of this world to the power and glory of God. Rather the reverse. It suggests that our access to the power and glory of God involves us in a very radical process of re-learning about everything that is, so that we can discover what it really is when no longer prisoner to our failed imaginations and to our violence which holds truth captive.

Now let us take our hypothetical test case: it has long been assumed that gay and lesbian people are simply some sort of defect of an intrinsically heterosexual humanity. This assumption has led to many different ways of dealing with the regular, but culturally varied, presence of gay people in different societies. But the mainstream ways in monotheistic religion seem to have been to regard it as either a vice, a pathology or some mixture of the two.

Here is the oddity: for as long as there was a certain sort of religious unity surrounding this issue, what we would now call culturally-specific versions of 'don't ask, don't tell' punctuated by occasional lynchings and burnings, there was no learning about what was actually going on in and for such people. And I should say that, as far as I am aware, there was, until the comparatively recent outbreak of fundamentalism in both the Christian and the Muslim worlds, a far greater tolerance towards this reality in the Muslim world than in the Christian one. However, it is in the modern West, as it has become possible for some people in some places not to hide this element of their being, since no longer afraid to suffer loss of life or livelihood, that it has become possible to ask non-moralistic questions about what makes people 'like that' tick, what pathologies, if any, can be properly attributed to them, what dangers, if any, they pose to the general population, what forms of viciousness, if any, characterise them, and so on.

In other words, the space of science is fairly literally, in this case at least, the space opened up by the suspending of a lynch mob. For, as long as the lynch mob can be persuaded not to stone, for that length of time we can start to see what is really going on in the lives of people who have traditionally been frightened to live openly, lest they become the victims of an outbreak of religious unity.

So, what I want to say very briefly is that here we have the beginnings of an understanding of how Catholics might learn something which flows from the central resources of our faith. The criterion we have for the relationship between our Creator and ourselves is a self-giving victim-unto-death, who occupies the space of death for us so that we may no longer attribute anything sacred to it, but instead be able to inhabit it ourselves in such a way that it loses toxicity; because of that, we are able to question any type of ganging up of all against one, of all against some obvious wrongdoer, and say: 'Stand back! Might it not after all be the living image of God, rather than a corrupting and seditious evildoer, that we are seeking to kill?'

This does not, of course, resolve the matter. And I want to make that very clear indeed. The mere fact that someone, or some group of people, is liable to being, or actually is, the object of mob violence, does not *ipso facto* mean that that person or group is either innocent, noble, sane or anything else. It does mean that humans who think they are in some way pleasing God by putting such people to death are mired in idolatry, and can never learn anything about themselves or other people while this is their solution to their group problems.

So here I am talking about the anthropological condition of possibility of our learning. And I want to claim that it is a perfectly reasonable development of Catholic Christian self-understanding to say that God's criteria for God, the life and self-giving up to death of Jesus, revealed as of God in his resurrection, acts, in this sphere, as in all others, as a brake against our unwillingness to learn, by suggesting that if we find ourselves gathering together in the name of God against some group of people, then the chances are we are being idolatrous, and that it is not until we subtract ourselves from such fake and easy forms of unity, that we will begin to be able to ask ourselves about causality in a non-idolatrous way.

It is because of this that I do not at all respect the religious authorities of my own Church when they avoid the question of whether their own characterisation of gay and lesbian people as objectively disordered is true, but instead seek to create religious unity with other like-minded religious leaders at the expense of the possibilities of freedom and flourishing of gay and lesbian people. I think, and this is but one instance among many, of the Catholic bishops in

California, who successfully made common cause with Mormon religious leaders, with whom it is not at all clear that we have a common understanding of the criteria for idolatry, to have gay and lesbian Californians stripped of their right to civil marriage.

Or again, I think of one Catholic archdiocese in the United States that was perfectly happy to take part in ecumenical gatherings alongside Christian denominations which deny such things as the Real Presence of Jesus in the Eucharist, that Mary is properly called the Mother of God, the existence of the sacramental priesthood and other first-order Catholic teachings. However, when the Metropolitan Community Church, whose members tend to have a rather Catholic-friendly understanding of basic Christianity and its liturgical life, but which is predominantly gay in its composition, was admitted to the group, the Archbishop ordered the ecumenical links to be broken. What good does it do to have the Vatican explain to Catholics that there are different orders of teaching, of different levels of importance for the life of the Church, when an archbishop's inability to contemplate honest disagreement concerning a low-order teaching can so easily trump a charitable ability to contemplate honest disagreement with much higher-order teachings? But that is chewing over the Christian cud.

My first set of questions to our Muslim sisters and brothers is this: supposing that we can even be having this discussion at all, do you understand there to be a criterion at the anthropological level, by which God enables us to understand anything about God?; how does that criterion avoid the charge that it is idolatrous?; how does that criterion work to create an anthropological condition of possibility for us to learn anything real about the world we live in?; and, how might this be applied to the possibility of our learning that gay and lesbian people are simply a regularly occurring, non-pathological variant of human being, rather than a defective form of an intrinsically heterosexual humanity?

Please note that I am not asking for an answer concerning the truth of the matter at hand. I am asking for a consideration of the hypothetical framework, within which a discussion about the truth of the matter at hand would be seen by you as being consonant with, flowing from, your own understanding of the resources made available to you by Islam. And I am doing so alongside a parallel offering of a sketch of a Christian response to the same question.

The second part of the argument that I want to develop is that of the end game, the Kingdom of heaven: what it is that we think God wants us to live for, to build, together, and how we do it. That the One God wants us to be one as God is One, is not in doubt. But the shape of that one-ness, and the criterion for it, are hugely in question. There is all the difference in the world between the sort of one-ness that is the product of shared hatred, over against an 'other' who is being annihilated, and the sort of oneness that is made available by someone humiliating themselves, offering themselves as a peace offering, whose gesture is then gently received by all present.

The reason I ask this here is because the question of the Kingdom, and the sort of unity that is envisaged by it, is intrinsically tied to the question of Creation and to the question of learning. In other words, there is an intrinsic relationship between the project of which we are symptoms, the Creation, and the project in which we are becoming active participants, the Kingdom. My question is: what is the shape of our being opened out from one to the other? Or: what kind of transformation of us does our recognition of God's criteria for our idolatry lead us to, and what kind of pathway or direction does God's interpretation of God's criteria open up for us?

The reason why this is important for the hypothetical case that I have put before you is as follows. Just because something *is* does not automatically mean that something is *good*. So, the fact that we find ourselves suspending our lynching of a particular group of people, owing to our idolatry being challenged by God's criterion of God-self towards us, does not automatically mean that the members of that group are simply good and innocent. It does mean that before they are anything else, they are like us, and that, therefore, in the space of the suspended lynching, we can begin to learn something about what we and they really are.

But whether something is good or not has to be seen by its fruit over time. This is part of what is meant by the Creation: what is *is*, in as far as it gives glory to God, gives witness to the power of which it is a symptom. It is perfectly possible to point to things and see them just as tending to nothing at all, being futile, vain, having no possibility of flourishing. We can all, under certain circumstances, tell the difference between self-destructive forms of human being, leading to nothing but misery and sadness, and other forms of human being which seem to light up something more than themselves, have a point, a purpose, a 'what for'.

And this is the question that seems to me to be central to a faith-inspired anthropology of learning in the sphere of matters gay: can we learn that the 'just is' is part of a 'what for', or are we left saying: 'well, we're not going to stone you to death, even though we know from our sacred texts that we should, but, on the other hand, you aren't really a full part of Creation, just a function of futility. Anything less than a heterosexual relational pattern is part of vanity and doesn't give glory to God.'

So how, hypothetically, might a Catholic learn that the 'just is' of being gay or lesbian is, indeed, objectively part of a 'what for'? And here, I am, of course, attempting to sketch out a Catholic version of a faith-inspired anthropology of learning. Part of the answer is: by spending time in the space of the suspended lynching. Our belief is that God's criterion for God is a forgiving human victim, and, thus, that those who recognise God breaking into our typical victim-creating circles, as the victim who forgives us, are able to learn not to be frightened of being in that place ourselves. Which means that we can lose our fear of being wrong, of being shamed, and of losing. And losing the fear of being wrong and of being shamed is an indispensible part of learning anything at all. The safer you feel about the consequences of getting something wrong, the freer you are to dare to learn about getting it right.

So, God's living criterion for God – the human victim, Jesus of Nazareth – is intrinsically linked to God's living interpretation of God's criterion for God – the power of forgiveness, which flows from Jesus and opens up Creation. Or, in other words, a regular pattern of desire has as its protagonist the victim in question, and flows towards any who will receive it, and this pattern of desire, which we call Holy Spirit, teaches us what is God's will for us, showing us what it is really to be Children of God.

Now, what is claimed, and I think that Girard's thought enables some absolutely vital precisions to be made in this sphere, is that, since we find ourselves having the pattern of desire that is run by rivalry, vengeance and fear of death undone in us, we are also able, over time, and despite many errors, to learn to distinguish between those patterns of desire which are part of the new building up which is 'for something', and which are not idolatrous, and those patterns of desire which are the remnants of patterns, from which the ability to undergo death in advance and dwell in it peacefully has freed us. Precisely because we do not need to justify ourselves, and we are not expected to be innocent, merely penitent, we can find ourselves wanting to respond in love to the love and forgiveness we have received.

This, in fact, has been my experience, as it has been the experience of many gay and lesbian people who have put themselves through what are known as 'ex-gay programmes', only to come out at the end as gay as ever. Over time, it becomes possible to detect what are the rivalistic, compulsive, self-destructive patterns of desire which do indeed run gay and lesbian people, as they run everybody else, and of which gay and lesbian people, no less than anybody else, need to repent, on the one hand, and, on the other hand, to detect what is the solid 'given' of sexual orientation, which is the condition of possibility of our being able to love as humans at all, and to repent of which would be a form of kicking the Creator in the teeth. It was enormously important to me personally when Girard showed how the same mechanism is responsible for all the pathologies of desire, and is relatively independent of the gender of the subject or the object of desire. He exposed the nonsense of claiming, for instance, that Dostoyevsky suffered from 'latent homosexuality', merely because, although the object of his sexual desire was clearly female, the significant and obsessive drivers of his relationships were male. And this made perfect sense to me as soon as I read it, since there was not the slightest tinge of the erotic in my experience of a phase of deep jealousy of a woman who had married a man I loved. Not for one moment did the experience make me a latent heterosexual!

This is a tiny little distinction concerning desire. The distinction between saying, on the one hand, 'all human desire is intrinsically corrupt, and so nothing can be learned from its vagaries about what humans are really meant to be', and saying, on the other hand, 'human desire is very seriously corrupt, yet as humans find themselves brought to life by God's self-interpretative desire, which is God, they can indeed find elements that are of the Creator and which may yet learn to tend to the Creator'. It is this distinction that, at least within a Catholic framework for a faith-inspired anthropology of learning, enables science to be born.

In this particular sphere, it enables us to answer the 'just is' question a little more fully: here we are talking not merely of something that 'just is', but of something which has, at its root, a 'what for', which has so far not been recognised or allowed to flourish. So the question is: can we dare to allow the attempts at flourishing, with a view to finding out, over time, what the 'what for' looks like when it is allowed to be?

Now the beauty of Church teaching concerning marriage is that it does firmly offer a sense of a very particular, and narrowly defined, form of sexual love over time, that is open to procreation, as being non-idolatrous, and as being capable of bearing some sign not only of the 'just is', but also of the 'what for'. Though it must be said that the principal stress of the teaching has been on the giving of each one to the other in love unto death, rather than the capacity for procreation. It is the baptismal living out of love unto death that makes a marriage sacramental. Jesus himself suggests the idolatry of being too concerned with procreation, when God is infinitely able to create[2].

So, the question becomes: is it conceivable, as we discover that heterosexuality is not the normative, but rather the majority, human condition, that we also discover that there are forms of relationship between gay and lesbian people that have a 'what for' that is proper to them? In other words, are there certain regular sorts of flourishing which we can see in this sphere which point to more than

---

2   Matt. 22:23-33.

themselves, which delate, give away, point up, something about God? And what would the criteria for such flourishing be?

Well, I do not want to go any further with this now, since all I wanted to do was set up the second part of the hypothetical Catholic framework for a faith-inspired anthropology of learning. This is a way of saying that, for a process of learning to be recognised as leading to something true about being humans, it is not enough to note the existence of something, or even to declare it 'OK' on merely empirical grounds. The element of the 'just is' has to be linked to some sort of 'what for' if we are to be faithful to belief in the Creator. And I have begun to set out some of the dimensions of how that link might be explored. If followed, it would lead to a situation where it would be perfectly obvious to people reading the texts of the Bible, which are currently used to attack gay people, that what are being condemned are idolatrous cultic rites, and that these have no more, and no less, to do with the fairly stable class of people which we call gay or lesbian than they do with everybody else.

So, my question for our Muslim sisters and brothers is this: what would be the critical process, consonant with Islam, and flowing from your own resources, by which you explore the link between the 'just is', and the 'what for', of Creation? In the, as I say, hypothetical case, that gay and lesbian people are not defects from an intrinsically heterosexual human condition, how would it become self-evident to any thinking Muslim that such people cannot, by the mere fact of being who they are, be considered liable to any of the loopholes, exceptions, to the rules of peace and love which all our sacred texts seem to leave open? It is those loopholes that give permission to kill.

Please excuse me if, by forcing an 'icky' topic on your ears, I have made it difficult to attend to what I hope is a discussion that is worth our while undertaking, regardless of which specific area of possible learning we explore. I do not, as I say, expect a quick answer to any of the questions I raise here. And I am well aware that the reactions which some of you could face by raising such questions yourselves might be a good deal more than 'icky'. My plea is: if we are to have serious conversations about the interplay of faith and reason in our lives, then please do not let us engage in ritual, self-congratulatory window-dressing. Please can we allow ourselves to be questioned by hard cases which demand from us that we set out a faith-inspired anthropology of learning that has incidence in our lives?

I began by telling you of my visit to a Holy Mountain, Mount Zion, and I hope to return one day, if not to the earthly, then to the Celestial Jerusalem. If any of us, Christians, Muslims or Jews, are able to make a pilgrimage together in which gay and lesbian people are to take part, fully ourselves, and fully in need of all the same graces as everybody else, it will only be because we will have undergone an arduous process of learning in which we will all have been stripped of different sorts of idolatry. A painful and disorienting process, for it is our hearts that will have become detached from forms of belonging to which they ought not to have been attached, so as to become aligned with something imperishable. On the way, we will have learned things about being human that none of us knew before, and what we know will be real. Our unity will no longer be that inspired by the fierce guardians of idolatrous righteousness. Our bonds will have become those of the broken-hearted.

❖❖❖❖❖❖❖❖❖❖

Luke 7:18b-35 (NRSV)

So John summoned two of his disciples and sent them to the Lord to ask, 'Are you the one who is to come, or are we to wait for another?' When the men had come to him, they said, 'John the Baptist has sent us to you to ask, "Are you the one who is to come, or are we to wait for another?"' Jesus had just then cured many people of diseases, plagues, and evil spirits, and had given sight to many who were blind. And he answered them, 'Go and tell John what you have seen and heard: the blind receive their sight, the lame walk, the lepers are cleansed, the deaf hear, the dead are raised, the poor have good news brought to them. And blessed is anyone who takes no offense at me.' When John's messengers had gone, Jesus began to speak to the crowds about John: 'What did you go out into the wilderness to look at? A reed shaken by the wind? What then did you go out to see? Someone dressed in soft robes? Look, those who put on fine clothing and live in luxury are in royal palaces. What then did you go out to see? A prophet? Yes, I tell you, and more than a prophet. This is the one about whom it is written, "See, I am sending my messenger ahead of you, who will prepare your way before you." I tell you, among those born of women no one is greater than John; yet the least in the kingdom of God is greater than he.' (And all the people who heard this, including the tax collectors, acknowledged the justice of God, because they had been baptized with John's baptism. But by refusing to be baptized by him, the Pharisees and the lawyers rejected God's purpose for themselves.) 'To what then will I compare the people of this generation, and what are they like? They are like children sitting in the marketplace and calling to one another, "We played the flute for you, and you did not dance; we wailed, and you did not weep." For

John the Baptist has come eating no bread and drinking no wine, and you say, "He has a demon"; the Son of Man has come eating and drinking, and you say, "Look, a glutton and a drunkard, a friend of tax collectors and sinners!" Nevertheless, Wisdom is vindicated by all her children.'

❖❖❖❖❖❖❖❖❖❖

Ecclesiastes (Qohelet) 2:18-3:4 (NRSV)

I hated all my toil in which I had toiled under the sun, seeing that I must leave it to those who come after me – and who knows whether they will be wise or foolish? Yet they will be master of all for which I toiled and used my wisdom under the sun. This also is vanity. So I turned and gave my heart up to despair concerning all the toil of my labors under the sun, because sometimes one who has toiled with wisdom and knowledge and skill must leave all to be enjoyed by another who did not toil for it. This also is vanity and a great evil. What do mortals get from all the toil and strain with which they toil under the sun? For all their days are full of pain, and their work is a vexation; even at night their minds do not rest. This also is vanity. There is nothing better for mortals than to eat and drink, and find enjoyment in their toil. This also, I saw, is from the hand of God; for apart from him (Hebrew has 'apart from me') who can eat or who can have enjoyment? For to the one who pleases him God gives wisdom and knowledge and joy; but to the sinner he gives the work of gathering and heaping, only to give to one who pleases God. This also is vanity and a chasing after wind.

For everything there is a season, and a time for every matter under heaven:

a time to be born, and a time to die; a time to plant, and a time to pluck up what is planted;

a time to kill, and a time to heal; a time to break down, and a time to build up;

a time to weep, and a time to laugh; a time to mourn, and a time to dance;

❖❖❖❖❖❖❖❖❖❖❖❖

Hebrews 5:5-11 (NRSV)

5 So also Christ did not glorify himself in becoming a high priest, but was appointed by the one who said to him, "'You are my Son, today I have begotten you'"; 6 as he says also in another place, "'You are a priest forever, according to the order of Melchizedek.'"

7 In the days of his flesh, Jesus offered up prayers and supplications, with loud cries and tears, to the one who was able to save him from death, and he was heard because of his reverent submission. 8 Although he was a Son, he learned obedience through what he suffered;

9 and having been made perfect, he became the source of eternal salvation for all who obey him, 10 having been designated by God a high priest according to the order of Melchizedek.

Philippians 2:5b-11 (NRSV)

...Christ Jesus 6 who, though he was in the form of God, did not regard equality with God as something to be exploited, 7 but emptied himself, taking the form of a slave, being born in human likeness.

And being found in human form,
8 he humbled himself and became obedient to the point of death-- even death on a cross.

9 Therefore God also highly exalted him and gave him the name that is above every name, 10 so that at the name of Jesus every knee should bend, in heaven and on earth and under the earth, 11 and every tongue should confess that Jesus Christ is Lord, to the glory of God the Father.

Philippians 2:5-11

5 τοῦτο φρονεῖτε ἐν ὑμῖν ὃ καὶ ἐν Χριστῷ Ἰησοῦ,
6 ὃς ἐν μορφῇ θεοῦ ὑπάρχων οὐχ ἁρπαγμὸν ἡγήσατο τὸ εἶναι ἴσα θεῷ,
7 ἀλλὰ ἑαυτὸν ἐκένωσεν μορφὴν δούλου λαβών, ἐν ὁμοιώματι ἀνθρώπων γενόμενος·

καὶ σχήματι εὑρεθεὶς ὡς ἄνθρωπος
8 ἐταπείνωσεν ἑαυτὸν γενόμενος ὑπήκοος μέχρι θανάτου, θανάτου δὲ σταυροῦ.

9 διὸ καὶ ὁ θεὸς αὐτὸν ὑπερύψωσεν καὶ ἐχαρίσατο αὐτῷ τὸ ὄνομα τὸ ὑπὲρ πᾶν ὄνομα,
10 ἵνα ἐν τῷ ὀνόματι Ἰησοῦ πᾶν γόνυ κάμψῃ ἐπουρανίων καὶ ἐπιγείων καὶ καταχθονίων
11 καὶ πᾶσα γλῶσσα ἐξομολογήσηται ὅτι κύριος Ἰησοῦς Χριστὸς εἰς δόξαν θεοῦ πατρός.

❖❖❖❖❖❖❖❖❖

John 5 (NRSV)

After this there was a festival of the Jews, and Jesus went up to Jerusalem. Now in Jerusalem by the Sheep Gate there is a pool, called in Hebrew Beth-zatha, which has five porticoes. In these lay many invalids – blind, lame, and paralyzed. One man was there who had been ill for thirty-eight years. When Jesus saw him lying there and knew that he had been there a long time, he said to him, 'Do you want to be made well?' The sick man answered him, 'Sir, I have no one to put me into the pool when the water is stirred up; and while I am making my way, someone else steps down ahead of me.' Jesus said to him, 'Stand up, take your mat and walk.' At once the man was made well, and he took up his mat and began to walk. Now that day was a sabbath. So the Jews said to the man who had been cured, 'It is the sabbath; it is not lawful for you to carry your mat.' But he answered them, 'The man who made me well said to me, 'Take up your mat and walk.' ' They asked him, 'Who is the man who said to you, 'Take it up and walk'?' Now the man who had been healed did not know who it was, for Jesus had disappeared in the crowd that was there. Later Jesus found him in the temple and said to him, 'See, you have been made well! Do not sin any more, so that nothing worse happens to you.' The man went away and told the Jews that it was Jesus who had made him well. Therefore the Jews started persecuting Jesus, because he was doing such things on the sabbath. But Jesus answered them, 'My Father is still working, and I also am working.' For this reason the Jews were seeking all the more to kill him, because he was not only breaking the sabbath, but was also calling God his own Father, thereby making himself equal to God. Jesus said to them, 'Very truly, I tell you, the Son can do nothing on his own, but only what he sees the Father doing; for whatever the Father does, the Son does likewise. The Father loves the Son and shows him all that he himself is doing; and he will show him greater works than these, so that you will be astonished. Indeed, just as the Father raises the dead and gives them life, so also the Son gives life to whomever he wishes. The Father judges no one but has given all judgment to the Son, so that all may honor the Son just as they honor the Father. Anyone who does not honor the Son does not honor the Father who sent him. Very truly, I tell you, anyone who hears my word and believes him who sent me has eternal life, and does not come under judgment, but has passed from death to life. 'Very truly, I tell you, the hour is coming, and is now here, when the dead will hear the voice of the Son of God, and those who hear will live. For just as the Father has life in himself, so he has granted the Son also to have life in himself; and he has given him authority to execute judgment, because he is the Son of Man. Do not be astonished at this; for the hour is coming when all who are in their graves will hear his voice and will come out – those who have done good, to the resurrection of life, and those who have done evil, to the resurrection of condemnation. 'I can do nothing on my own. As I hear, I judge; and my judgment is just, because I seek to do not my own will but the will of him who sent me. 'If I testify about myself, my testimony is not true. There is another who testifies on my behalf, and I know that his testimony to me is true. You sent messengers to John, and he testified to the truth. Not that I accept such human testimony, but I say these things so that you may be saved. He was a burning and shining lamp, and you were willing to rejoice for a while in his light. But I have a testimony greater than John's. The works that the Father has given me to complete, the very works that I am doing, testify on my behalf that the Father has sent me. And the Father who sent me has himself testified on my behalf. You have never heard his voice or seen his form, and you do not have his word abiding in you, because you do not believe him whom he has sent. 'You search the scriptures because you think that in them you have eternal life; and it is they that testify on my behalf. Yet you refuse to come to me to have life. I do not accept glory from human beings. But I know that you do not have the love of God in you. I have come in my Father's name, and you do not accept me; if another comes in his own name, you will accept him. How can you believe when you accept glory from one another and do not seek the glory that comes from the one who alone is God? Do not think that I will accuse you before the Father; your accuser is Moses, on whom you have set your hope. If you believed Moses, you would believe me, for he wrote about me. But if you do not believe what he wrote, how will you believe what I say?'

Index

Our Lady 4–5, 17–19, 23–7, 29–32, 136

Padilla, José 85–6
pain 186–207
Palestine 143–4
parables 140, 142, 144–50, 152, 156
Parma University 161
Passion 43, 238, 255
Passover 252, 254, 257
Patriarchs 150
Paul 40, 45–6, 56, 69, 81, 83–4, 106, 131, 135, 141, 149, 209–29
Paul VI, Pope 1
Péguy, Charles 208
Pentateuch 107
Pentecost 254
Pepinster, Catherine 75
persecution 209–11, 213–14, 226
Peter 7, 12–13, 50, 75, 88, 136, 194–7, 219, 258
Pharisees 41, 45, 69, 100, 102, 105, 143, 145, 174, 226, 235
Philippians 215–16, 218–27, 283
Pilate, Pontius 86
Pio, Padre – Now St Pio of Pietrelcina 2
pneumarchy 139
Popes 1–2, 7, 13, 16, 175, 192–7, 213, 261, 263, 266
post-Freudianism 26
post-modernism 47, 127, 212
presence 125–39
Prodigal Son 140, 142–4, 146
Proposition 8 186, 189

protagonism 125–39, 152, 263–4, 269, 275
Protestant Church 1–2, 4, 265
Psalms 219, 222, 230–32, 252

Al Qaeda 86
queer perspectives 1–16, 34–53
Qumran manuscripts 31

Rabbis 105, 214, 265
Rachel 141
Ratzinger, Josef 7, 192, 194, 197, 213, 261; *see also* Benedict XVI Pope
reciprocity 62–6, 93, 165–8
recognition 168
Red Sea 231, 257
Regensburg address 197, 266
Republicans 172
Requiem Mass 5
Resurrection 31, 108, 133, 141, 149, 221, 227
Reuters 192
Revelation 26, 39, 239
Rio de Janeiro 4
Rock of Israel 6
Rossini. Gioacchino 18–23
rovesciamento 109–14, 116–19, 121–2, 124

Sabbath 232–5
sacrifice 73–91, 148–56, 158, 217, 220–3, 228, 244, 251, 255
Sadducees 41
St Augustine 67, 74
St James 28
Salome 136